Yezhov

J. ARCH GETTY AND OLEG V. NAUMOV

With the assistance of Nadezhda V. Muraveva

# Yezhov

## The Rise of Stalin's "Iron Fist"

Yale University Press   New Haven and London

Set in Galliard Old Style type by
Integrated Publishing Solutions, Grand Rapids, Michigan.
Printed in the United States of America by
Vail-Ballou Press, Binghamton, New York.

Library of Congress Cataloging-in-Publication Data
Getty, J. Arch (John Arch), 1950–
Yezhov : the rise of Stalin's "Iron Fist" / J. Arch Getty and Oleg V. Naumov ; with
the assistance of Nadezhda V. Muraveva.
p.  cm.
Includes bibliographical references and index.
ISBN 978-0-300-09205-9 (cloth : alk. paper)  1. Ezhov, Nikolai Ivanovich,
1895–1940.  2. Soviet Union. Narodnyi komissariat vnutrennikh del—Officials
and employees—Biography.  3. Soviet Union—Politics and government—
1917–1936.  I. Naumov, Oleg V.  II. Title.
DK268.E93G48 2006
947.084'2092—dc22
[B]   2007044692

10  9  8  7  6  5  4  3  2  1

# Contents

Acknowledgments vii
Soviet Organizational Acronyms and Abbreviations ix
Notes on Terminology xi
A Note on Sources xv

INTRODUCTION
Constructing the Commissar xvii

ONE
Epilogue as Prologue: The Commissar at Work 1

TWO
The Making of a Bolshevik 14

THREE
In the Provinces 36

FOUR
The Party Personnel System 68

Contents

**FIVE**
Sorting Out the Comrades  96

**SIX**
Yezhov on the Job: "Cadres Decide Everything"  115

**SEVEN**
Yezhov and the Kirov Assassination  135

**EIGHT**
Enemies Large and Small  156

**NINE**
Angling for the Job  179

Conclusion  206
Notes  225
Index  273

*Illustrations follow page 134*

# Acknowledgments

Special thanks go to Nadezhda Vladimirovna Muraveva, without whose hard work this book would not have been possible. She and the entire professional staff of RGASPI deserve tremendous credit for facilitating not only this book but Russian archival research in general.

Oleg Naumov would like to thank his parents, Vladimir Pavlovich and Valentina Ivanovna, for their continuing support.

Arch Getty is grateful for the support of the University of California, Los Angeles, Academic Senate, the UCLA Division of Social Sciences, and the American Philosophical Society for their support of this work. Scholars who have influenced him through his scholarship and friendship are too numerous to mention, but such a list would have to include, in the West, Ken Bailes, Jeff Burds, Bill Chase, Bob Davies, Sheila Fitzpatrick, Graeme Gill, Igal Halfin, James Harris, Roberta Manning, Robert McNeal, Alec Nove, Lewis Siegelbaum, Lynne Viola, and Stephen Wheatcroft. He owes special thanks to Gabor T. Rittersporn, who so generously shares his deep knowledge of the 1930s and of Soviet culture of all kinds. In Russia he has benefited greatly from conversations with V. P. Danilov, O. V. Khlevniuk, V. A. Kozlov, V. P. Naumov,

A. P. Nenarokov, Nikita Petrov, A. K. Sokolov, L. V. Veintraub, and V. N. Zemskov. He received indescribable additional help from E. S. Drozdova, L. V. Poliakov, Teo Ruiz, and N. P. Yakovlev. Alice and Earl know who they are and what they did. Finally, he could not have completed this work without the support of his family, who put up with a lot to make this book possible.

None of those mentioned above are responsible for the views expressed in this book. They deserve credit for anything good in what follows. We alone are to blame for any errors.

The authors are grateful to Cambridge University Press for permission to quote from J. Arch Getty, "Stalin as Prime Minister: Power and the Politburo," in Sarah Davies and James Harris, *Stalin: A New History*, Cambridge University Press, 2005; and to Yale University Press for permission to quote from J. Arch Getty and Oleg V. Naumov, *The Road to Terror: Stalin and the Self-Destruction of the Bolsheviks, 1932-1939*, Yale University Press, 1999.

# Soviet Organizational Acronyms
# and Abbreviations

| | |
|---|---|
| CC | Central Committee. See also TsK |
| CCC | Central Control Commission. See TsKK |
| ChK (CHEKA) | Extraordinary Commission for Combating Counter-revolution and Sabotage (1918–22). Political police; predecessor of GPU, OGPU, NKVD, MGB, KGB |
| gorkom | City Committee of the VKP(b) |
| GPU | State Political Directorate attached to the Council of People's Commissars (SNK) of the USSR. Successor to CHEKA and GPU and predecessor of NKVD |
| GUGB | Main Administration for State Security of the NKVD of the USSR |
| IKKI | Executive Committee of the Communist International |
| kolkhoz | Collective farm |
| Komintern | Communist International (1919–43), an international revolutionary proletarian organization to which the Communist Parties of various countries belonged |

| | |
|---|---|
| Komsomol | All-Union Leninist Youth League (VLKSM), a party organization for young people in the USSR |
| KPK | Commission for Party Control attached to the Central Committee of the VKP(b) |
| kraikom | Regional Committee of the VKP(b) |
| MOPR | Central Committee of the International Organization for Assistance to Revolutionary Fighters |
| Narkomvnudel (NKVD) | People's Commissariat for Internal Affairs |
| Narodnyi Komissar (Narkom) | Head of a People's Commissariat; equivalent to minister |
| obkom | Provincial committee of the VKP(b) |
| OGPU | Unified State Political Directorate attached to the Council of People's Commissars (SNK) of the USSR. Successor to CHEKA and GPU and predecessor of NKVD |
| Orgburo TsK VKP(b) | Organizational Bureau of the CC of the VKP(b) |
| Orgraspred | Organizational-Distribution (Personnel) Department of the Central Committee |
| ORPO | Department of Leading Party Organs of the CC of the Russian Communist Party (Bolsheviks) |
| Politburo TsK VKP(b) | Political Bureau of the CC of the VKP(b) |
| Prezidium TsKK (or KPK) | Supreme Governing Organ of the Central [after 1934, Party] Control Commission of the VKP(b) |
| Raspredotdel | Personnel Distribution Department of the Central Committee |
| TsIK | Central Executive Committee of Soviets |
| TsK | Central Committee of the Party |
| TsKK | Central Control Commission of the VKP(b) |
| VChK | All-Russian Extraordinary Commission for Combating Counterrevolution and Sabotage (1918–22) |
| VKP(b) | All-Union Communist Party (Bolsheviks) |

# Notes on Terminology

In transliterating from Russian to English we use the Library of Congress system, except for proper names, for which we adopt the form familiar to Western readers (Trotsky, not Trotskii, etc.)

In the 1930s the Communist Party was known as the All-Union Communist Party (Bolsheviks) [Vsesoiuznaia Kommunisticheskaia Partiia (bol'shevikov)], or VKP(b) in its Russian acronym. In practice, its highest policy-making body was the Politburo, which in the 1930s consisted of roughly ten full (voting) members and five candidate (nonvoting) members. In the beginning of the period covered by this study, the Politburo met about once per week; by the end of the period it was meeting about once a month. Each meeting technically had dozens or even hundreds of items on the agenda, but increasingly these were decided without formal meetings, by polling the members. Politburo meetings produced protocols, which are outlines of the questions discussed, often with an indication of the decision reached and sometimes with attachments or appendixes. Other top party committees included the Secretariat and the Orgburo, both of which were largely concerned with personnel assignments.

The Central Committee of the VKP(b) (of which the Politburo, the Orgburo, and the Secretariat were formally subcommittees) consisted in the 1930s of about seventy full voting members and about seventy candidate members. A meeting of the Central Committee (CC) took place from two to four times a year and was known as a plenum. Minutes (stenograms) were taken at CC plena, and many of them are available in Russian archives.

Below the level of the CC, the party was divided into a hierarchy of regional party committees based on provinces, territories, districts, and places of work. These bodies also conducted meetings (plena) but the real work was usually done in an inner executive committee known as a buro.

Parallel with this hierarchy, and subordinated to the Central Committee, was another structure of party committees known as the Party Control Commission (KPK). The KPK was charged with various kinds of inspection and discipline in the party apparatus. Its mission was to investigate and punish cases of ideological deviance, corruption, and violation of party rules.

A parallel state apparatus was formally separate from the party but in reality subordinated to it. The ostensible government of the USSR was in fact closely controlled by the party and was used to implement and execute party decisions. The state structure was topped by a Congress of Soviets with hundreds of delegates; formal legislative power resided in a Central Executive Committee (TsIK) of Soviets, consisting of several dozen members. Day-to-day administration and confirmation of legislation at this level was conducted by the Presidium of the Central Executive Committee, whose chair served as nominal president of the USSR. Below the Central Executive Committee and formally subordinated to it was the government cabinet, known in this period as the Council of People's Commissars (Sovnarkom), which consisted of ministers ("commissars") representing various branches of the economy and state administration. Finally, below this central state structure was a hierarchy of elected provincial, city, and district soviets that might be thought of as organs of local administration.

The territorial structures and designations of the USSR can be confusing. The USSR was a union of republics, with each republic being the political organization of a nationality. The Russian Republic (RSFSR) and the Ukrainian Republic (USFSR) were the largest of a series of "states" that included Belorussians, Georgians, Armenians, Uzbeks, and the other constituent peoples of the USSR. The RSFSR was clearly the most powerful, and its administration overlapped in general with that of the USSR.

Each republic was divided into regional units, each of which was known as an oblast' (province) or a krai (territory). Thus at various times in the 1930s, the RSFSR consisted of between seventy-five and ninety provinces and territories. Although technically all republics were on an equal footing, in practice the status attached to a major province or territory of the RSFSR was equal to that of a non-Russian republic. The next subdivision (into which provinces and territories were divided) was known as a raion (district). Districts could be rural or urban, perhaps roughly equivalent to counties or boroughs. Cities had separate administrations that fell between district and provincial or territorial level.

Republics, provinces, territories, cities, and districts each had party committees, party control commissions, and state bodies. Their titles and acronyms and the translations used in this book are summarized below:

| Russian territory | English usage | Political organization | Abbreviation |
|---|---|---|---|
| oblast' | province | provincial (party) committee | obkom |
| | | provincial (party) control commission | oblkk |
| | | provincial (state) executive committee | oblispolkom |
| krai | territory | territorial (party) committee | kraikom |
| | | territorial (party) control commission | kraikk or kkk |
| | | territorial (state) executive committee | kraiispolkom |

(continued)

| Russian territory | English usage | Political organization | Abbreviation |
|---|---|---|---|
| gorod | city | city (party) committee | gorkom |
| | | city (party) control commission | gorkkk |
| | | city (state) executive committee | gorispolkom |
| raion | district | district (party) committee | raikom |
| | | district (party) control commission | raikk or rkk |
| | | district (state) executive committee | raiispolkom |

# A Note on Sources

The vast majority of documents used or cited here are from the Russian State Archive for Social-Political History (Rossiiskii gosudarstvennyi arkhiv sotsial'no-politicheskoi istorii, RGASPI), which is the former Central Party Archive of the Institute of Marxism-Leninism of the Central Committee of the Communist Party (TsPA IML pri TsK KPSS). Russian archival documents are cited and numbered by collection (*fond* or f.), inventory (*opis'* or op.), file (*delo* or d.), and page (*list* or l. or in plural, ll.): for example, RGASPI, f. 17, op. 165, d. 47, l. 3.

# Constructing the Commissar

Nikolai Ivanovich Yezhov was head of the Soviet political police (NKVD, or People's Commissariat of Internal Affairs) in the 1930s during the worst period of the Great Terror. As People's Commissar (minister) for Internal Affairs from September 1936 to November 1938, he was appointed by Joseph Stalin to carry out millions of arrests, imprisonments, deportations, and executions associated with the terror.

Even had he not been involved in such terrible events, his career trajectory would have made him worthy of historical notice. At the apogee of his power, he held so many key positions that, after Stalin, he was the most powerful man in the USSR. In addition to his NKVD post, he was a member of the Bolshevik Party's Central Committee and sat on its three powerful subcommittees—the Secretariat, the Orgburo, and the Politburo—as well as the inner security subcommittee of the Politburo. He was head of the Party Control Commission and a Presidium member of the Supreme Soviet and of the Communist International. His speeches arraigned, his investigations framed, and his staged trials brought down some of the most prominent members of the Lenin-era generation of "Old Bolsheviks."

During his meteoric career, poets wrote to and about him; schoolchildren sang songs about him; towns, schools, and districts were named for him. Dinamo Stadium in Kiev became Yezhov Stadium. His presence graced the most important ceremonial occasions. As the elderly Kazakh poet Dzhambul sang,

Reaching the age of one hundred, old Dzhambul
Heard the swelling sound on the steppes.
The million-voiced resounding word
Will fly from the people to the fighter Yezhov:
Thank you, Yezhov, that, raising the alarm,
You stood on guard for the country and the leader![1]

Millions may or may not have shouted their gratitude to him, but after two years at the very center of the Soviet limelight, Yezhov suddenly vanished from the public eye without a trace.[2] Even in the controlled and closed information system that was Stalinism, some reason was almost always offered to explain the sudden fall of a prominent figure. But unlike other key party leaders whom Stalin liquidated, Yezhov was never publicly accused of anything. After early 1939 he was simply never mentioned again publicly during Stalin's lifetime. Unlike L. D. Trotsky or N. I. Bukharin, his name was never dragged through the mud, and he was never labeled an enemy of the people. Millions of Soviet citizens who came of age after the 1930s had never heard of "Stalin's iron fist," although they certainly knew the name of his successor at the NKVD, Lavrenty Beria, who had arrested Yezhov and supervised his extermination. It was not until Nikita Khrushchev launched his de-Stalinization campaign in the 1950s that Yezhov's name was officially uttered. Even then, there were only fleeting mentions of him until the Gorbachev period. His career was meteoric: a striking and swift rise apparently from nowhere, followed by a short but brilliant flight and a quick burnout.

This is not a book about the Great Purges of the 1930s in the Soviet Union. Insofar as currently declassified Soviet archival material permits, that ground has been covered by numerous studies, both old and recent.[3] Instead, this study seeks to examine Yezhov's career leading up to the point at which he took over the NKVD in 1936. Where did Yezhov come from?

We share a methodology with other studies that focus on early life and career of important historical figures.[4] Unlike them, however, our approach is not psychohistorical. Our focus here is on the "times and life" of Yezhov, rather than vice versa. Our attention is drawn not only to him as a person, but to what his rise might tell us about the Soviet system. We will examine him not only as a personality but as a product of his times and in relation to the political and social matrixes in which he functioned. Because Yezhov's life touched so many locations crucial to Soviet history (the 1917 Revolution, the Civil War, provincial administration in non-Russian areas, personnel administration, agriculture, industry, and police matters), following that career will also allow us to make some conclusions about Soviet social and political history in general. To tell his story is to unfold the first two decades of Soviet history. Accordingly, our story of Yezhov's early career organizes itself around three related biographical questions, each of which poses a larger systemic historical question about the origins of Stalinism. Our questions thus come in pairs, a biographical one and a historical one.

First, was Yezhov just Stalin's pawn? What was the scope of power for politicians working under a dictator?

The standard interpretation of Yezhov's career is simple: he was nothing more than a dimwitted and obedient tool, nothing more than Stalin's obedient executioner mindlessly carrying out a terror under the close control of the master. The tool did its work and was discarded when no longer needed.[5] This version is implausible and ahistorical on its face. Here Yezhov is not a person but rather a faceless instrument. He has no background, no independent experiences, no options or opinions. He takes no decisions or actions and makes no career choices that influence anything or anybody. He has no real existence, no agency, and is a kind of tabula rasa on which Stalin wrote. This story looks backward from his two-year career as police chief and sees nothing.

We shall see that this view has little to do with the available evidence. In fact, Yezhov was an intelligent, hardworking and ideologically committed official with a shrewd sense of the politics of handling those above as well as those below him. We shall see that Yezhov was not a mindless cipher who suffered a mysterious personality change into a robot, and at the end of our story, we will see him actively manipulate even Stalin in order to get what he wanted: leadership of the Soviet secret police.

Of course, Stalin's lieutenants all carried out his policies. But as powerful politicians in their own right, they had considerable space for maneuver, patronage, intrigue against one another, in general conducting their own politics within the limits of Stalin's General Line. We shall see that the politics of implementation can be just as significant as those of policy formulation. No one at Yezhov's level was merely a tool.

Second, how did Yezhov climb the ladder? How did one rise and prosper in Stalinist administration?

The standard view is that Yezhov, a pleasant enough fellow in his youth, was spotted early on by Stalin, who identified him as an instrument for terror and sponsored his career for years. In fact, as we shall see, Yezhov pulled himself up the ladder by means of his own considerable abilities and by mastering the Stalinist "rules of the game." We will watch him directing the most crucial elements of Bolshevik administration: personnel selection and patronage.

This was a system of personalized politics.[6] The rules of the game in Stalin's time had to do with how one maneuvered in a matrix of personal relationships. The Stalinist political system relied on bureaucracy far less than on charismatic, personalized politics from top to bottom. Yezhov steadily rose through a system governed by these rules.

He became the party's leading expert in "cadres," or personnel selection. Political practice at various levels was a matter of using personal contacts, refereeing between personalities, and adjudicating disputes more than it was about policy formation or execution. In such a system, a hardworking official with career expertise in personnel selection and skill at negotiating disputes within a personalized system would become a very powerful person indeed. Yezhov had these qualities; they were the same ones that had helped Stalin rise to power.

Third, who could do these things; what did he believe? How did Stalinist Bolsheviks see the world in general?

It is tempting to think that Stalinist leaders were completely cynical politicians who could not possibly have believed in such widespread conspiracies of traitors, spies, and saboteurs; they could not have believed what they said.

In fact, Yezhov was not an amoral careerist, and he took ideology seriously. When he had time to read, he read Lenin. Belief involves complex processes of identity shaping and formation and the creation of personal subjective meaning. We shall see, for example, that as a radicalized worker in a time of revolution and civil war, Yezhov's early experiences and attitudes and those of his generation can explain much about conflict and brutality of the subsequent Stalin period. He believed what he said and believed in what he did.

Who was Nikolai Yezhov? Where did he come from? Was he, like Hannah Arendt's Adolf Eichmann, striking only for his banality, his ordinariness? Historians have been able to learn little about the origins of this enigmatic figure and his career, aside from a skeletal outline of the posts he held (and disregarding contemporaneous hagiography). The secondhand sources available to us, which are mostly memoirs of people who briefly knew him, are contradictory. Some call him a "malignant dwarf," like a "Moscow street urchin." Others, including the relatives of some people he arrested, thought him "charming," "courteous," "honest," and a "good party worker." Even the surviving photographs of him are contradictory; his image in newspaper photos sometimes suggests a man with a wide head, prominent ears, and mussed hair. Other photos show him with a handsome face and styled hair. During his period of prominence (and unlike many leaders of lesser stature), he never wrote collections of speeches or articles. A long book he wrote on the sins of Stalin's enemies was never published.

Despite some recent publications, he remains a historical phantom.

In the past few years, one scholarly biography and several popular books and articles on Yezhov have been published.[7] Although they are of varying quality, even the best of them concentrates on his tenure as head of the NKVD, 1936–38, virtually ignoring the 90 percent of his life that led up to it.[8] Based on a close reading of documentary materials, primarily from the Communist Party and Yezhov's own archives, this book is meant to trace his life and career leading up to that ominous NKVD appointment in 1936.

Because of the amount of contradictory speculation about Yezhov, it seems particularly important to bring the tools of careful source criticism to bear on the problem. Our close focus on archival materials, however, does not mean that we take them at face value, or that we shall exclude other sources, which will be incorporated as warranted. Because of the Bolsheviks' starkly utilitarian attitude toward truth (which was always defined as that which served the party's interests), it is always dangerous to read their documents uncritically, and nobody does. On the other hand, to assume that Stalinist archives are by their nature filled with lies is also wrong. Soviet archival documents were written for internal consumption and use, rather than for propaganda; they were the fuel that made the bureaucratic machine run. It would have been pointless and stupid for bureaucrats to lie to one another outrageously and constantly (and it was particularly dangerous to lie to Stalin), because they had jobs to do. Of course, like all archival documents, each was written by someone for a purpose; each had a specific vocabulary and discursive style. By carefully asking of them the same kinds of critical questions we ask of all primary sources, we can learn a great deal.

By contrast, we avoid reliance on literary accounts, which come in three genres: popular Soviet journalism since the late 1980s, memoirs, and "testimonies" about Yezhov beaten out of victims by police interrogators after his fall. Even if elements of them ring true, lacking independent confirmation we cannot know which parts to trust. Journalistic articles are undocumented collections of stories and rumors. Memoirs of those who knew Yezhov, few as they are, are important sources. Molotov's recollections, for example, although self-serving and recorded decades after the events they recount, are more important sources because he knew and worked with Yezhov. Memoirs of those who had no contact with him or who were far removed from the seat of power, whatever their other merits, are at best less important, at worst, unverifiable speculation. They may contain poignant and revealing material but cannot be taken as primary sources for our subject. The veracity of the dubious and fantastic testimonies of Yezhov's friends and lieutenants given under torture should speak for itself. Despite elementary rules of source criticism, such sources are commonly used even in scholarly works on Yezhov today. They deserve the most strict critical treatment because of their ideological and self-serving nature, and we are very chary of them.

Despite the availability of Yezhov's personal archive, on which much of this study is based, we have little to go on in trying to flesh out his personality.[9] His archive consists of 287 files, each containing from twenty to five hundred documents, with an average of about two hundred pages per file. It seems to have been formally cataloged only in May 1991 by the staff of the General Department of the Archive of the President of the USSR. At that time, the archive was organized into files (*dela*) which were sorted into sections (*razdely*) according to Yezhov's activities at various times. Some of the files are irregular, consisting of card files, book manuscripts, bundles of photographs, and in one case, a large leather briefcase. The archive does not cover all aspects of Yezhov's activities but rather falls into the category of a personal archive (*lichnyi fond*), strictly defined and accordingly "sanitized." As the archivists' introductory notes make clear, materials were removed from the archive and transferred elsewhere. These transfers include materials properly belonging in archives of other persons and, regrettably, important documents of an "operational character" belonging in the still-closed institutional archives of the agencies where Yezhov worked (KPK and NKVD, for example). The available archive, therefore, consists of the personal documents Yezhov decided to save, copies of working documents he wanted to keep personally, and copies of the correspondence he received. Many of the documents bear Yezhov's hand-written instruction to his assistants, "put in the personal archive."

Many of these materials suffer from a rather dry official character. Yezhov chose to save very few personal documents in his archive, and we have no diary and few personal letters. We have supplemented the sources in his archive with extensive use of party and state archival materials touching on his life. We searched and made extensive use of archives of the Central Committee's Politburo, the Orgburo, and the Secretariat, as well as those from the party's personnel department and local committees where he worked. We have therefore a good picture of his official life but precious few glimpses into his inner personality. Still, by studying his official correspondence (especially with Stalin and other top leaders), his initiatives, and his reactions to things in the course of his duties, we can get a good picture of him and of his times.

In Chapter 1 we set the stage for an examination of Yezhov's rise by looking at his subsequent peak and fall. The well-known story of his horrifying deeds poses the questions we shall consider about his rise.

In Chapter 2 we introduce Yezhov's life from childhood through the end of the Russian Civil War in 1921. Drafted in World War I into the army, he spent 1917 in the provinces as a Bolshevik factory organizer. His activities as a founder of Red Guards in the provinces and as a po-litical commissar in the Civil War further radicalized and hardened the young Bolshevik.

The subject of Chapter 3 is Yezhov's rise through a series of responsi-ble party positions in the non-Russian periphery: Tataria, Kirgizia, Kazakhstan. His experience with nationalities and his skill in committee work paralleled Stalin's own party trajectory, and we will see something of Bolshevik administration in smaller republics of the USSR.

In Chapter 4 we discuss the origins and formation of the party's per-sonnel assignment system, which was perhaps the most vital part of Bolshevik administration and in which Yezhov would plan an impor-tant, and ultimately leading role.

In Chapter 5 Yezhov comes to the capital, where he found work in that system. Again distinguishing himself as an efficient administrator,

Yezhov took charge of many key personnel assignment recommendations.

In Chapter 6 we find Yezhov hard at work in the mechanics of party personnel administration. In 1929, when Stalin took the monumental decision to collectivize agriculture, he chose Yezhov to oversee personnel appointments in the new USSR Commissariat of Agriculture. The following year Yezhov was moved back to a reorganized party personnel office, this time as chief of distribution and assignment of all party personnel.

Yezhov's investigation of the assassination of Politburo member Serge Kirov is at the center of Chapter 7, along with his subsequent administration of the investigation of the NKVD. At the same time, he began carefully to angle and maneuver for Genrikh Yagoda's job as chief of the NKVD.

In Chapter 8 we discuss Yezhov's administration of the 1935 purges that followed the Kirov assassination: a new screening of the party membership and an offensive against Avel Yenukidze, a high-ranking Bolshevik leader.

In Chapter 9 we see Yezhov conduct a series of adroit maneuvers to finally undermine NKVD chief Yagoda and take over the leadership of the NKVD.

ONE

# Epilogue as Prologue

### THE COMMISSAR AT WORK

On 25 September 1936 Nikolai Ivanovich Yezhov, a pleasant and friendly little man who danced well and entertained guests with a fine baritone singing voice, was appointed head of the Soviet secret police (NKVD). He was a forty-one-year-old former factory worker and the son of a worker, born in 1895, the year that Marconi invented radio, Gillette perfected the safety razor, and Roentgen demonstrated X-rays. Yezhov was younger than the Stalin generation of Old Bolsheviks that controlled the party—Joseph Stalin was sixteen years his senior—but roughly the same age as the younger cohort of Stalinist insiders. He was two years younger than L. M. Kaganovich, one year younger than Khrushchev, and one year older than A. A. Zhdanov. He was three years older than Chou En-Lai, two years younger than Mao Zedong, six years younger than Hitler, and eleven years older than Adolf Eichmann. He was four years older than his successor-to-be, L. P. Beria.

Yezhov was known as a quiet fellow, a modest, self-educated former worker whom friends called "Nicky the bookworm." His predecessor at NKVD, Genrikh Yagoda, was widely disliked and distrusted as a venal and corrupt cop (a "reptile," as one of Stalin's lieutenants called him), who blackmailed his subordinates into obedience and who fabricated cases against innocent victims.[1] Yezhov, on the other hand, had made his career in the Communist Party, not in the police. He had long been a personnel specialist there; he knew everyone and everyone liked him. It was widely assumed at the time that an honest party man with a good reputation would restore honest supervision to that nest of crooked cops, would refuse to fake cases, and would generally clean up the NKVD. N. I. Bukharin, a leading former anti-Stalin dissident who knew Yagoda's frame-ups, thought that Yezhov would not fabricate cases.[2] One of Stalin's lieutenants called Yezhov a "solid party worker," and another wrote to his friend, "Things will go well with Yezhov at the helm."[3] They did not.

As soon as he took over the NKVD, Yezhov put the persecution of former ideological dissidents into high gear. A month earlier he had helped organize the first of the three Moscow show trials, in which sixteen defendants, including G. E. Zinoviev, L. B. Kamenev, and other of Lenin's most well-known comrades had been forced to admit to treason.[4] They pleaded guilty, asked for no mercy, and were all shot. Prosecutor A. Ya. Vyshinsky's concluding speech captures the hysteria of the times:

Before us are criminals, dangerous, hardened, cruel and ruthless towards our people, towards our ideals, towards the leaders of our struggle, the leaders of the land of Soviets, the leaders of the toilers of the whole world! The enemy is cunning. A cunning enemy must not be spared. The whole people rose to its feet as soon as these ghastly crimes became known. The whole people is quivering with indignation and I, as the representative of the state prosecution, join my anger, the indignant voice of the state prosecutor, to the rumbling of the voices of millions! . . . I demand that dogs gone mad should be shot—every one of them![5]

Yezhov took each spent bullet from the execution, carefully wrapped it in paper, labeled it with the victim's name, and put it in his desk drawer.[6]

To prepare the party for the trial, Yezhov had written a dramatic letter to all party organizations, "Concerning the Terroristic Activity of the Trotskyist-Zinovievist Counterrevolutionary Bloc," dated 29 July 1936. He wrote,

> It can be considered an established fact that Zinoviev and Kamenev were not only the fomenters of terrorist activity against the leaders of our party and government but also the authors of . . . preparations for attempts on the lives of other leaders of our party and, first and foremost, on the life of Comrade Stalin.
>
> Now, when it has been proven that the Trotskyist-Zinovievist monsters unite in their struggle against Soviet power all of the most embittered and sworn enemies of the workers of our country—spies, provocateurs, saboteurs, White Guards, kulaks, and so on, when all distinctions between these elements, on the one hand, and the Trotskyists and Zinovievists, on the other hand, have been effaced—all party organizations, all party members must come to understand that the vigilance of Communists is necessary in every area and in every situation. The indelible mark of every Bolshevik in the current situation ought to be his ability to recognize and identify the enemies of the party, no matter how well they may have camouflaged their identity.[7]

As soon as the 1936 trial was completed, Yezhov began a dragnet of further arrests. Known associates of the trial's leading defendants who had long ago broken with the dissident leaders Trotsky, Zinoviev, and Bukharin were rounded up and subjected to harsh interrogations in the cellars of NKVD prisons. Yezhov bombarded Stalin with transcripts of their interrogations.[8] Through a combination of tactics that included threats to their families, appeals to their party loyalty, sleep deprivation, and physical torture, each was forced to admit to membership in some sinister underground conspiracy and to name other coconspirators. In turn, these others were rounded up and subjected to the same process. The circle of victims from former oppositionist circles expanded rapidly.

The first show trial had featured former leftist anti-Stalin figures Grigory Zinoviev and Lev Kamenev as defendants. (Left oppositionists had thought Stalin too conservative.) They were said to have allied with Lev Trotsky, who had been abroad in exile since 1929, to plot the assassination of Stalin and the overthrow of the government. The trail of NKVD interrogations of their former followers gradually led to arrests of former right-wing oppositionists in the fall of 1936. (Right oppositionists, led by Nikolai Bukharin, Aleksei Rykov, and Mikhail Tomsky, had thought Stalin too radical.) By the end of 1936 thousands of former dissidents were under arrest and confessing to all kinds of conspiracies. At the end of the year, Yezhov addressed the Central Committee and directly accused not only the Trotskyists but also followers of Bukharin, Rykov, and Tomsky of being part of the monstrous conspiracy:

> Many attempts were made to carry out terrorist acts of assassination. Comrades, it is well known to you that already at his investigation Zinoviev testified that the rightists Rykov, Tomsky, Bukharin, and Uglanov, at least so far as he knew about it, shared the views of the Trotskyist-Zinovievist bloc in their entirety and were informed of it. . . . Now this has been corroborated not only by the testimonies of Trotskyists and Zinovievists but also by the more concrete cases of the rightists recently arrested. . . . As for the work of the Cheka [NKVD], Comrades, I can only assure you that we shall pull up this Trotskyist-Zinovievist slime by the roots and physically annihilate them.[9]

Yezhov's move against Bukharin shocked the party. The popular Bukharin had been factual coleader of the party along with Stalin in the 1920s. Unlike Zinoviev, Kamenev, and Trotsky, who were considered odious and suspicious has-beens, Bukharin enjoyed a more positive reputation. Lenin had called him the "favorite of the party," and as late as 1936 Stalin called him by the familiar "you" (*ty*).[10] His opposition to Stalin at the end of the 1920s had not been as pointed and insulting as had that of the left. He had made his peace with Stalin quickly, and in the 1930s was still a prominent and even well-liked leader, a candidate member of the Central Committee, and the editor of the government newspaper *Izvestiia*. Now Yezhov was accusing him of treason. At the following meeting of the Central Committee in February-March 1937, Yezhov renewed his attacks on Bukharin and secured his arrest and interrogation for a future trial.

Meanwhile, Yezhov's police assault on the left continued, and in January 1937 the second show trial featured the former leftist leaders G. Piatakov, K. Radek, and fifteen others in the dock. As in the first trial, the defendants pleaded guilty, and most received death sentences. Referring to Piatakov, Yezhov said, "These swine must be strangled! We cannot deal with them calmly."[11] With the arrest of each former dissident, the circle of suspects widened, and Yezhov ordered the arrest of them all, both leftists and rightists.

With a Bolshevik voluntarism that did not worry about legal niceties, Yezhov recommended brutal punishments for those he arrested. He suggested shooting Piatakov and Radek without any trial. In the fall of 1936 he wrote to Stalin dividing those he had arrested into categories: "The first category, to shoot. . . . The second category, ten years in prison plus ten years in exile. . . . We should shoot a pretty large number. Personally I think that this must be done in order to finally finish with this filth. It is understood that no trials will be necessary. Everything can be done in a simplified process."[12]

Meanwhile, Yezhov had begun to build treason cases against Yagoda's former NKVD leadership. He did this gradually, because to go after all of Yagoda's men would leave the NKVD without experienced officials, and Yezhov needed them for the time being. But slowly he "turned" several of Yagoda's deputies to his cause and then arrested the others. Over the course of the next year, all of Yagoda's former lieutenants would be accused of treason and would join the growing numbers in NKVD jails. Yagoda himself was arrested in March 1937 and joined Bukharin, Rykov, and others in the dock of the third Moscow show trial the following year. Yezhov claimed that all the former NKVD leaders were German spies and is said to have demanded "purging,

purging, and more purging!" More than two thousand of them were arrested, and most of these were summarily shot.[13]

Yezhov drove his interrogators hard to get the maximum number of confessions from those arrested. He ordered his subordinates to prepare invented confessions for those arrested even before the interrogations. He often attended the brutal interrogations personally, exhorting his subordinates to "beat the necessary testimony out of them" and to force the accused to sign the prepared confessions. Later, he changed and edited those confessions to "improve" them. Once when the future Soviet leader Nikita Khrushchev visited Yezhov's office, the NKVD chief proudly showed Khrushchev blood spatters on his uniform that he had gotten while attending an interrogation.[14]

Beginning in the spring of 1937, Yezhov turned his attention to persecuting foreign Communists who had sought refuge in Moscow.[15] He ordered the roundup of virtually all former members of long-banned Russian socialist parties (Socialist Revolutionaries, Mensheviks, and others). He also ruthlessly purged the foreign members of the Communist International (Comintern). "The biggest spies are in the Comintern!" he declared, while devastating their foreign delegations resident in Moscow.[16]

At the June 1937 plenum of the Central Committee, Yezhov gave an amazing speech in which he announced the discovery of a grand conspiracy that united leftists, rightists, Trotskyists, members of former socialist parties, army officers, NKVD officers, and foreign Communists. This "center of centers," he said, had seized control of the army, military intelligence, the Comintern, and the Commissariats of Foreign Affairs, Transport, and Agriculture. He claimed that it had its representatives in every provincial party administration and was thoroughly saturated with Polish and German spies. The Soviet government was hanging by a thread![17]

In June 1937 his axe fell on the Soviet military high command. On 11 June the world was shocked by the Soviet press announcement that eight of the most senior officers of the Red Army had been arrested and indicted for treason and espionage on behalf of the Germans and Japanese. The list included the most well-known field commanders in the Soviet military: Marshal M. N. Tukhachevsky (Deputy Commissar of Defense) and Generals S. I. Kork (commandant of the Frunze Military Academy), I. E. Yakir (commander of the Kiev Military District), and I. P. Uborevich (commander of the Belorussian Military District), among others. Arrested the last week of May, the generals were brutally interrogated by the NKVD and had "confessed" by the beginning of June. On 12 June, at an expanded session of the Military Collegium of the Supreme Court, all were convicted, and they were shot the same day. In the nine days that followed, Yezhov arrested a thousand military officers. One week later, Yezhov received the Soviet Union's highest decoration, the Order of Lenin, "for his outstanding success in leading the organs of the NKVD in their implementation of governmental assignments." In 1937–38 more than 9,500 officers were arrested, and 14,500 were expelled from the party for suspicious personal connections to conspirators.[18]

The destruction of the party and state elite in the terror defies imagination. Yezhov issued orders "to confine all wives of condemned traitors," and even children over the age of fifteen years who were defined as "socially dangerous" were to be arrested.[19] Lev Kamenev's sixteen-year-old son was executed. Paranoia and xenophobia reached new heights. Yezhov's police arrested anyone who had worked for a foreign firm in tsarist times. Speakers of the international language Esperanto were rounded up. Bird watchers in Leningrad were arrested—could the birds carry cameras to photograph border regions? Stamp collectors with foreign correspondents were put under surveillance and arrested.

In the course of this hysterical hunt for "enemies of the people," Yezhov spared no one. His first boss after the revolution, A. T. Uglov, was shot. Lev Razgon, Yezhov's boss and patron in the 1920s in the party personnel office, was also shot, along with his wife, who had fed the sickly Yezhov in those days. Yezhov personally ordered the arrest and execution of many of his former close friends and colleagues. Ya. A. Yakovlev and Lev Mar'iasin had worked closely and socialized with Yezhov in the 1920s. Yezhov had the latter tortured with particular cruelty, even ordering him beaten after he had confessed. He ordered the arrest and execution of everyone from his own former doctor to his mistress.[20]

In July 1937 Yezhov turned his attention to purging outside the elite and directed the terror against ordinary citizens. On 30 July he composed the infamous NKVD order no. 447 "Concerning the punishment of former kulaks, criminals, and other anti-Soviet elements." This order targeted former kulaks (well-to-do peasants exiled in 1930–32), as well as "church officials and sectarians who had been formerly put down, significant cadres of anti-Soviet political parties . . . horse and cattle thieves, recidivist thieves, robbers, and others who had been serving their sentences and who had escaped and are now in hiding. . . . The organs of state security are faced with the task of mercilessly crushing this entire gang of anti-Soviet elements." As he had done in the past, he recommended harsh sentences by category and without trial:

a) To the first category belong all the most active of the above-mentioned elements. They are subject to immediate arrest and, after consideration of their case by the troikas, to be shot.

b) To the second category belong all the remaining less active but nonetheless hostile elements. They are subject to arrest and to confinement in concentration camps for a term ranging from eight to ten years. . . . The investigation shall be carried out in a swift and simplified manner.[21]

Yezhov prescribed "limits" of victims to be persecuted, broken down by province. In his initial order 75,000 were slated for summary execution and another 194,000 for confinement to camps. But by the time Yezhov was finished with this "kulak operation," 385,000 had been shot and 316,000 sent to camps.[22] Nearly all of them were ordinary citizens, not members of the party-state elite. Practically anyone could be caught up in these vague categories, and huge numbers of innocents perished. Yezhov is reported to have told his investigators, "beat, destroy, without sorting out!" When a lieutenant asked what to do with elderly people who were arrested, Yezhov ordered them shot. Yezhov is said to have told one of his assistants, "better too far than not enough," and "if during this operation an extra thousand people will be shot, that is not such a big deal."[23]

Following the "kulak operation" Yezhov launched a series of "national operations." His NKVD assistants, themselves later arrested, remember him telling them that "everyone should prepare for mass arrests of Poles, Germans . . . and anti-Soviet groups in the party and state apparatus."[24] But it was not only in the apparatus that Yezhov arrested foreigners. In a series of NKVD orders in the second half of 1937, Germans, Poles, Latvians, Estonians, Finns, Greeks, Afghanis, Bulgarians, and others resident in the USSR—and even citizens descended from these nationalities—were targeted for arrest as spies and traitors.[25] In the case of Poles, Yezhov sent out a hysterical circular letter positing the existence of a large-scale Polish Military Organization underground in the USSR that had supposedly "paralyzed" Soviet intelligence. He ordered the arrest of all former Polish prisoners of World War I who had elected to stay in the USSR, all Communist and other political refugees from Poland, all former members of the Polish Communist Party, and "the most active" anti-Soviet citizens of Polish extraction.[26] "The Poles should be completely destroyed!" Yezhov is reported to have shouted to an NKVD conference.[27] In a short time, more than three-quarters of those arrested (more than 111,000 people) had been shot in the "Polish Operation."[28]

Germans slated for arrest included Soviet citizens of German nationality, former German prisoners of war, German political émigrés, inhabitants of German districts, "consular contacts," former personnel of German firms, and others with "ties to Germany." Forty-two thousand were shot in the "German Operation."[29]

Yezhov ordered the NKVD to arrest immediately all Soviet citizens personally connected with diplomatic representatives and visiting either their working or living quarters. The national operations even devastated faraway regions. One hundred seventy thousand Koreans were deported from border regions. In Outer Mongolia, 11,000 were arrested and 6,000 of them were summarily shot. By the end of these "national operations," 247,000 people—almost all of them ordinary citizens—had been shot by lists.[30] In October, Yezhov decided that "as a result of the Polish, German, Korean, Kharbintsy, and other operations, it is clear that all countries are using refugees as spies." He complained that of 6,000 refugees stopped by border guards "only 244" spies have been found. He ordered the NKVD to arrest all refugees in the USSR. "Agents" were to be shot. The remainder, "suspected but not unmasked," were to be sent to prison camps.[31]

The terror that Yezhov administered hit hard among the elite. Ninety-eight of 139 members of the party's Central Committee were arrested, as were 1,100 of the 1,966 delegates to the most recent (1934) party congress. The Military Tribunal of the Supreme Court, which prosecuted most elite victims, passed death sentences on more than 40,000 people in 1937–38. But although the elite was hardest hit, most of the terror's victims were ordinary citizens. During Yezhov's tenure as NKVD Commissar, more than 1.5 million persons were arrested, and about 700,000 of them were shot, mostly without trial.[32]

In March 1938 Yezhov organized the third of the major Moscow show trials, that of Nikolai Bukharin and twenty other prominent officials. As in the other trials, the defendants were accused of fantastic crimes: organizing the assassinations of Soviet officials, for example, and the sabotage of the economy in the service of British, French, German, and/or Japanese espionage services. Yezhov is said to have promised Bukharin and others to spare their lives if they cooperated. But this time things did not go smoothly. Bukharin, while admitting overall responsibility for the crimes, systematically denied personal involvement or guilt, thereby putting the entire spectacle in doubt.

There are signs that by the middle of 1938 the winds were shifting against Yezhov. In April he was named Commissar of Water Transport, while retaining his leadership of the NKVD and the Party Control Commission. The appointment to Water Transport was not an illogical post for a chief of the secret police. The NKVD (and OGPU before it) had always been heavily involved in purging transport agencies and building canals with forced labor, and Yezhov brought a number of NKVD officials with him to Water Transport. On the face of it, the appointment seemed to be a promotion; he now headed three important agencies: NKVD, the Commissariat of Water Transport, and the Party Control Commission. Still, it could not have escaped notice that when Yezhov's predecessor Yagoda had been eased out of his police position, he was first appointed to a similar post.

In the summer of 1938 several signals pointed to a decline in Yezhov's status. In August, G. Liushkov, NKVD chief in the Far East Territory, fled across the Manchurian border and defected to Japan. A Yezhov intimate and assistant, Liushkov had participated in key police investigations from the Kirov assassination through the purge trials. His defection represented not only a serious security breach but a black mark against his chief.

At the end of August, Stalin brought L. P. Beria from Georgia to be Yezhov's deputy at NKVD. Beria was a career police official, but he was not part of Yezhov's central NKVD circle and represented an outsider inside Yezhov's administration. By the fall of 1938 Beria was signing NKVD documents on his own without Yezhov's approval and had begun his own investigation of a "conspiracy" within Yezhov's NKVD.

In October and November 1938 a special Politburo commission investigated NKVD "abuses" and produced a series of resolutions reining in the NKVD's power. The mass operations of the summer of 1937 were condemned, and henceforth no arrests could take place without the approval of the procuracy.[33] In effect, the NKVD was being blamed for the excesses of the past two years, which Stalin had, of course, authorized. Yezhov felt his power (and Stalin's confidence in him) slipping away. In self-defense, he began to assemble compromising materials on Beria and other Politburo members, including Stalin himself.[34] He began to drink heavily and to stay at home drunk with his cronies rather than going to work. Stalin complained that when Yezhov was needed, he couldn't be found.[35]

Toward the end of 1938, Yezhov's assistants began to be arrested. Beria encouraged them to testify against their boss, and Stalin was sent the records of their testimony. Yezhov's wife, accused of suspicious contacts, committed suicide. Finally, after a Politburo session in which Yezhov was attacked for protecting enemies, hiding files from Stalin, and neglecting Kremlin security, Yezhov resigned from the NKVD on 23 November 1938.[36] Based on the testimony of his former assistants, Yezhov was arrested on 10 April 1939.

Although we can never know Stalin's motivations in removing Yezhov, we might imagine several. First, and most obviously, Yezhov knew too much about the abuses of the terror and Stalin's role in it. More than that, however, Stalin may have perceived Yezhov as a security risk. When his assistant Liushkov fled to Japan, suspicion fell on Yezhov's circle in general.[37] Liushkov was sure to betray important secrets to Japan. Stalin always believed in the collective responsibility of groups; when one person fell, so did his associates, and the possibility could not be excluded that Liushkov's boss Yezhov had known in advance of his treason. Yezhov's chronic drinking with cronies also held out the possibility that he would babble secrets to those with no business to know them. Stalin may have decided that he could not take the chance that Yezhov's connections might find out too much.

Yezhov spent nearly a year in prison under interrogation. Now victim of the system of forced false confessions he had pioneered, Yezhov humbly admitted to a variety of imaginary crimes based on the fantasies of the investigators: plotting to assassinate Stalin, being a Polish and German spy, homosexuality, and abuse of position, among others. In the farcical rewrite of history that was Yezhov's "testimony," he became a Lithuanian. His father was transformed from a worker into a brothel operator, his mother became a bar hall dancer. The sadistic interrogators must have had a perverse amusement in inventing lurid details of Yezhov's supposed homosexual practices and beating others into admitting engaging in them with Yezhov.[38]

But at his perfunctory trial, he retracted his jailhouse confessions and lashed back. Nevertheless, he really believed in omnipresent conspiracies, spies, and in his righteous behavior:

It is better to die, it is better to leave this earth as an honorable man and to tell nothing but the truth at the trial. . . . During the twenty-five years of my party work I have fought honorably against enemies and have exterminated them. . . . I did not organize any conspiracy against the party and the government. On the contrary, I used everything at my disposal to expose conspiracies. . . .

Coming to the NKVD, I found myself at first alone. . . . After crushing the Polish spies, I immediately set out to purge the group of turncoats. . . . I purged fourteen thousand Chekists. But my great guilt lies in the fact that I purged so few of them. . . .

I request that Stalin be informed that I am a victim of circumstances and nothing more, yet here enemies I have overlooked may have also had a hand in this. Tell Stalin that I shall die with his name on my lips.[39]

We do not know whether he kept that vow, but he was executed by shooting immediately after his trial on 2 February 1940.

What kind of system could produce a Yezhov? What kind of person could do these things? What lifetime prepared him for his terrible deeds of these two years? What did he think he was doing?

# TWO

# The Making of a Bolshevik

No matter what happened at the factory, he was out front.

Nowadays [1936] we call this efficiency. . . .

What a lively and smart guy.

D R I Z U L

It was a hot and muggy St. Petersburg day and the seventeen-year-old boy slipped down the muddy path on his way to work. The factory where he worked was near the coastline of the Gulf of Finland, and even though the plant was near the center of the capital city of the Russian Empire, the way to work passed through stinking slums and marshy low ground that often resembled a fetid swamp. It was easier walking in winter, when the ground froze hard and the mosquitoes did not attack him, but then the damp and frigid howling wind off the gulf cut through his threadbare clothes and made him hurry to get inside the unheated but sheltered buildings of the factory. His father, himself a factory worker, had wanted his son to become a tailor, and as he made his way to the factory's gigantic, stuffy, and dirty shops, he must have wondered about his choice.

Still, Nikolai Yezhov was lucky. First of all, he was alive. Of all babies born to working-class parents, one in four died before their first birthday. Times were hard for workers, who typically spent half their income on food and another quarter on housing and clothing. The overall annual death rate for workers was twenty-three to twenty-six per thousand.[1] Living four persons per room on average, St. Petersburg workers paid the highest rents in the empire. In 1912 the governor general of St. Petersburg warned the tsar, "The most serious sanitary deficiencies continue to remain in the capital." The city lacked any underground system of sewage disposal; cesspools in backyards were the norm, and rubbish was piled on the streets.[2] Seven out of ten workers shared a room, but Nikolai still lived with his parents, and the extra income he brought home kept the family from starving or living in the miserable barracks that housed so many.

Second, Nikolai was lucky to be an urban born, literate Russian in a multiethnic peasant country dominated by Russians. Some 60 percent of the population of the capital were peasants who flocked to the city to take jobs in its rapidly expanding industries. They came in groups from particular villages or provinces, and once in the city they brought village friends and village ways with them. They tended to live together in collectives with others from the same place, baffled by city ways. To the city's longtime residents, they were a dark, rude, ignorant lot who took the most unskilled jobs for the lowest wages. Similarly, tens of thousands of non-Russians were constantly being recruited to work in the city's factories, among them Poles, Lithuanians, Latvians, Finns, and Jews (who were considered a separate nationality). Anti-Semitism and ethnic intolerance infected the Russian Empire and society from the bottom all the way up to the royal family. Not only was Nikolai a city Russian, he was apprenticed to become a skilled metalworker and therefore on the way to becoming a high-status proletarian of the "class-conscious" variety targeted by radical socialist labor organizers. As with many of his fellows, the proletarian class consciousness so prized by the Marxists did not prevent him from resenting and even detesting the peasants and non-Russians who worked alongside him.

Russians and non-Russians competed for jobs and often found themselves on opposite sides of union struggles; fistfights were common.[3]

Third, Yezhov worked at the "Red" Putilov Plant, the largest factory in the capital, employing some thirty thousand workers. He was proud to be a Putilov worker, to be a participant in the solidarity of Russian factory workers there. The factory's workers had played a major role in the radicalism of the 1905 revolution, and the new legal labor unions (among the concessions Tsar Nicholas II made to revolutionary pressure in that year) quickly took root in the giant plant. The workers there were well organized and prided themselves on their sick fund and strike fund. The anger they felt toward management, indeed toward any authority, led to a tight cohesion, and the young Nikolai felt that he was part of something great and just. And he was not unusually young: two-thirds of Putilov's workers had started work at age fifteen or sixteen, receiving the same bitter, class-conscious education as Nikolai.

There was little love lost between workers and management in most large Russian factories. The hierarchical lines of authority in the plants mirrored those in Russian society at large. As one historian has written, workers "were subjected to immeasurable exploitation, to the unrestrained arbitrary power of the factory administration, both large and small, inside the workplace, and to the savage law of the fist enforced by the tsarist police regime on the outside."[4] Another has noted, "The close propinquity in which rich and poor lived in the central quarters, as well as the greater social and physical distance between privileged and underprivileged in the outskirts, contributed to the crystallization of the class consciousness of at least a minority of skilled workers and to the inchoate, inarticulate, diffuse resentments of the unskilled."[5]

There was a clear class line in the factory. Managers and engineers thought of themselves as members of the intelligentsia, and their self-image caused them rarely to appear on the shop floor or talk to or consult with workers. Those in charge of the factory seemed unconcerned that workers worked ten-hour days in dark and poorly ventilated shops. They provided little or nothing in the way of safety rules or equipment, and Putilov averaged one accident resulting in a worker injury every two days. Foremen thought of themselves as part of management and bossed the workers around like medieval bailiffs with serfs. Capriciously administered petty fines were inflicted on the workers for even minor infractions, and there was rarely any attempt to reconcile or negotiate disagreements. Workers were angry and resentful and naturally united against the other side. In the words of the veteran worker Ivan Babushkin, "Old methods of struggle die hard; the workers couldn't think of a strike unless it entailed the beating up of a foreman."[6] Riots usually began with workers attacking their factory or mine and the residences and persons of their superiors.[7] As V. A. Giliarovsky quoted a Moscow proletarian,

And happy-go-lucky directors walk up and down the factory; they don't allow us to buy groceries in other stores: for example, if you want onions, send your son to a factory store to buy on the account of the next month's salary! Cheap and rotten! . . . In the city the factory owner is like a count; he benefits from fines [from workers] and from [selling to them] groceries—so he is winning everywhere. The production also gives him extra percentage; that is, he gets his money from everywhere. "We'll not lose a cent of our own, we'll cheat anyone out of their money. What could be better!"[8]

And as a popular poem had it,

The happiness of life dies.
The people suffer torture.
All day long, from morn to night,
It's "work!" It's "toil!"
The parasites, the bosses,
Beware of them, watch out!
No one appreciates our work,
Our labor's not for us:
He who lives and thrives from it
Is he who tortures us.[9]

Workers "challenged in a variety of ways the all-pervasive authority of factory managers, foremen and petty workshop proprietors." Younger workers were particularly concerned for their dignity and demanded polite address. "It represented a desire for respectful treatment in place of the arbitrary abuse of power by supervisory staff—the foul language, beatings, ill-treatment of women, fines, searches and medical inspection."[10] Because of the peculiar nature of Russian industrialization, their anger was not limited to the shop floor. Economic grievances easily blurred into political ones. Beginning in the 1890s the Russian government had embarked on a program of top-down, state controlled industrialization. Skipping the smaller, gradual stages of spontaneous industrial capitalism that had characterized industrial revolutions elsewhere, Russia plunged headlong into a rapid process that favored large-scale heavy industry from the start. Eager to attract European and American capitalists, the Russian government offered powerful incentives to those investing in or building factories in Russia, including tax breaks, low labor costs, and financial participation with the government itself, generally putting the power of the state at the disposal of management.

In labor-management disputes, the Russian state was never neutral, and more than once saber-wielding Cossacks attacked crowds of strikers. Small wonder, then, that Russian workers saw little difference between factory management and the government. Economic demands could quickly become political. Reformist sentiments never amounted to much in the Russian labor movement, and radical organizers who claimed that only revolt against the establishment could solve the workers' problems got a sympathetic hearing from the sullen and resentful workers in the factories.

Stormy Putilov, and factories like it, were the sites of young Nikolai Yezhov's first education. Born in 1895 into a working-class family, he had dropped out of school after only a year of primary education. In line with his father's ambitions for him, Nikolai seems to have been a tailor's apprentice for a short time. The work apparently did not appeal to him, and at age thirteen or fourteen he went to work in the factories.

He may have left Petersburg for a time; one source has him in Poland and Lithuania at this time, looking for work and working for a time in the Til'mans Factory in Kaunas (Kovno), Lithuania.[11]

Returning to St. Petersburg, Yezhov worked first at the Prelovsky Necktie Factory and then at Putilov. Twenty years later, the Socialist Realist writer Alexander Fadeev claimed that Yezhov was "a genuine son of this most-revolutionary-in-the-world proletariat . . . an active participant on the fighting barricades of Petersburg."[12] Yezhov himself more modestly recalled, "I was no different than any other of the masses, except that I read a lot. I was never a strikebreaker, I participated in strikes, demonstrations and so forth, suffered repression like many others." His friends called him "Nicky the bookworm."[13]

But even as a young teenager, Nikolai participated in radical activities in the factory, taking part in his first strike in 1912, at age seventeen.[14] This action may have been part of the reaction to the Russian government's massacre of striking workers in the Lena goldfields in April 1912, which caused a wave of protest strikes to sweep across the country. For the next twenty-eight months, until the beginning of World War I, Russia experienced a dramatic upsurge of worker radicalism, strike activity, and labor violence that recalled the revolutionary days of 1905. Delegates from the radical Bolshevik faction of the Marxist-oriented Russian Social Democratic Labor Party (RSDRP) replaced representatives of the more moderate Menshevik wing on union committees as workers voted for drastic solutions.[15] The Lena massacre had brought things into sharp relief for Yezhov and his fellows, to whom the struggle seemed black and white. The government was intransigent, the battle lines were drawn, and it had become a matter of violence and killing.

The lesson young Nikolai and his fellows took from this, and indeed the essence of his early education, was that the world was a stark and irreconcilable conflict between "us" and "them." This binary view of the world was not limited to the Russian working class before 1917, and indeed had deep roots in Russian plebeian culture. According to Russian Orthodox traditions (of which Russian socialists and even atheists were cultural products), there was always a black and white, correct and incorrect, true and false, us and them. "To an unusual degree, the sense of community in Russia was always in opposition to some other group . . . exhibiting a tendency toward a dual experience of the world in terms of 'we' versus 'they.'"[16] We shall see that this binary view of the world would show itself in the deep divisions in Russian society in 1917 and in a particular understanding of democracy during and after the revolutions of that year. Later, in the Soviet period when Yezhov and his generation came to power, it would manifest itself in an intolerance of dissent or any concept of a "loyal opposition," in a view that "enemies" were ubiquitous and ultimately unreformable, and in a conviction (expressed in Nikolai Yezhov's 1935 book manuscript "From Factionalism to Open Counterrevolution") that any dissidence inevitably led to treason. Although these attitudes are often associated uniquely with Stalin, they were in fact shared by a generation of Bolsheviks who came of political age along with Yezhov.

In 1915, as World War I went into its second year, Nikolai Yezhov was drafted into the infantry of the Russian Imperial Army. He was wounded at the front and given a six-month recovery leave. He returned to Petrograd, where he worked again in the Putilov plant, by his recollection, until the end of 1916.[17] At that time he was remobilized, this time into the noncombatant 3rd Reserve Regiment in the rear, first in Petrograd and Peterhof and then in Vitebsk.[18] The Russian government was reluctant to send radical troublemakers to duty at the front, and it is not clear whether his noncombatant status derived from his wounds, political unreliability, or simple good luck.[19] In Vitebsk he was assigned work as a metalworker in the 5th Artillery Works of the Northern Front, where he worked until the middle of 1917.

The overthrow of the tsar in February–March 1917 propelled the country into a frenzy of political activity. Exiled radicals returned from Siberia and from abroad, and political parties appeared or were reorganized into new forms. In the cities and towns of Russia, local soviets representing workers and soldiers competed with moderates and liberals and affiliated with the radical Petrograd Soviet or the more moderate Provisional Government in Petrograd, respectively.

The "us" vs. "them" element in Russian social psychology came to the fore in 1917. Several historians have noted that the deep divisions in Russian society between the poor bottom and everyone else were reflected in conflicting loyalties to the Soviet (us) and the Provisional Government (them).[20] One study of documentary texts produced in 1917 shows that "freedom and power both, as should be evident, were often understood in the light of a view of the social and political world as divided between enemies and friends, between others and oneself. . . . We find in these texts a dualistic vocabulary of enemies and traitors on the one side and friends, comrades, and brothers on the other." The "language of otherness" became the "language of class" in 1917.[21] Workers and peasants viewed those above them as an undifferentiated "them," using words like "Junkers" (military officers), "burzhui" (bourgeois), and "pomeshchik" (rural landowner) interchangeably.[22] From the other side of the social abyss, one officer wrote home in 1917 of the lower classes: "When we talk about the narod [the people], we mean the nation as a whole [*natsiia*], but when they talk about it they understand it to mean only the democratic lower classes [*demokraticheskie nizy*]."[23] Such views could bode no good for any inclusive understanding of democracy or equality.

In Vitebsk, as in the capital and elsewhere, political prisoners were freed and a city soviet sprang up parallel with the assumption of administration by representatives of the Provisional Government. The first soviets of 1917 were dominated by moderate leftist or liberal groups with names like Trudoviks, Mensheviks, Bundists, and Socialist Revolutionaries. These stood against a resurgence of tsarism or a takeover by rightist conservatives, and in watchful association with Petrograd's Provisional Government, where liberal Kadet influence was strong.[24] Radicals like Lenin's Bolsheviks or the anarchists had little presence or influence early in 1917, largely because the tsarist police's repression of them had been so thorough during the war.[25]

By all accounts, the twenty-two-year-old Nikolai Yezhov soon became a radical activist in the local Marxist group in Vitebsk. In most towns in 1917 there was little or no formal distinction in Marxist circles between "hard" Bolsheviks and "soft" Mensheviks, and they tended to work together in loose organizations. In Vitebsk the local group was called the RSDRP "Internationalists"—Marxist groups with a strong antiwar stance typically were called internationalists—and like many soldiers, Yezhov quickly joined it. Exiled Bolsheviks soon began returning to Vitebsk, where they found sympathizers among the workers of the 5th Artillery Works and the 4th Aviation Park. Within weeks, some members of the RSDRP Internationalists had renamed themselves "Bolsheviks," although it is not clear that they formed a separate organizational entity until autumn.

The date at which one joined the Bolsheviks would later become a kind of credential for party members, but it is difficult to fix for thousands of other new party members who "joined" in the confusion of 1917. In Vitebsk, as elsewhere, organizations were informal and overlapping. Yezhov would later date his Bolshevik Party membership from March or April 1917, but archival records show him on the rolls and still paying dues to the RSDRP Internationalists as late as August–September of that year. Elsewhere the files indicate his formal entry into the Bolshevik Party in October. Given the fluidity of organizations and their names during the year, there is no necessary contradiction among the dates.[26]

His Putilov past and affiliation with the radical Bolsheviks early in 1917 are not the only signs of Yezhov's radicalism.[27] During the stormy months of the revolutionary year, he devoted himself to politics. He organized Marxist cells and workers' committees in the factory where he worked and was frequently elected secretary of them. He helped organize street kiosks in the city to distribute revolutionary literature. He maintained communication with comrades arrested by the Provisional Government after the crackdown on the left in July.

Yezhov's activities during 1917 in Vitebsk seem to mirror Stalin's in the capital, although the two had never met. The impression is of men who worked behind the scenes, on committees doing organizational work and coordination. Both were self-taught commoners who had read widely but independently and naturally took to administration; both were probably heavily involved with paperwork in 1917. Neither was a good orator. A fellow worker in Vitebsk later remembered that in mass meetings and rallies, "Yezhov said little. He would say two or three words. He was a laborious orator, and this trait remained with him. He did not love speaking."[28] The same things were said of Stalin. The events of 1917 transformed Yezhov and many plebeian autodidacts like him from workers to politicians, from proletarians to organizers. It is perhaps symbolic of this tremendous social transformation that during the year, Yezhov stopped being listed as "metalworker" on various forms and started being listed as an "office clerk."[29]

But even though he was not a charismatic public "face," Yezhov was not without personality or ability to influence people. His fellows remembered not only his efficiency and tireless work but his enthusiasm and a lively sharp wit, which he directed against particularly unpopular foremen and military managers in the factory. He was, in the memory of a comrade, "everyone's favorite" among the workers and "one of those unique people who always stood at the head. No matter what happened at the factory, he was out front. Nowadays [1936] we call this efficiency. . . . What a lively and smart guy." The same contemporary waxed eloquent to the point of hagiography and remembers Yezhov as a passionate but methodical political worker. "I think he burned, just at the point of exploding, but at the same time logical and consistent." A colorful young man, he went around town in military uniform complete with bandoliers and belts, although his dashing image might have been somewhat reduced by his stature: full-grown, he stood a shade under five feet tall.[30]

Vitebsk was an important town at the time. Its artillery works, where Yezhov worked, was an important defense plant employing more than one thousand skilled workers. The city was the rear supply point for the Russian 12th Army and an important railroad junction. From Vitebsk rail lines went west to the front, and the city controlled the southern rail approach to the capital. As a place where soldiers, railroad, and factory workers were concentrated, it was also fertile ground for radical organizing. Leftist organizations grew in strength all year, and young Nikolai Yezhov took an active part in forming a Red Guard, or workers' militia detachment, in Vitebsk.

The political, economic, and social crises facing Russia intensified during 1917; the fall of the tsar had in itself done nothing to alleviate the collapse of the economy or the bloodshed at the front. The Provisional Government's reluctance to end the war, embark on land reform, or control prices had led by autumn to the loss of any mass support it may have enjoyed. Finally, in October, a Bolshevik-led coup in the capital overthrew the Provisional Government in Petrograd and placed power in the hands of the soviets, which by now were dominated by the Bolsheviks.

Local soviets also took power in provincial towns, but the process was often more complicated. In Vitebsk in October, the local Bolsheviks already dominated the factory committees and soviet and now used their influence to eject any competitors from political authority in the town. A Menshevik speaker at one of the factory meetings protested the Bolshevik coup in Petrograd; he was physically ejected from the meeting and thrown into the street. Several workers grabbed a broom and demonstratively swept away his footprints "so that none of this bastard's tracks remain."[31] Other stories from around the country recount similar popular violence against moderates.

Although Lenin and his Bolsheviks had taken power in the capital and in several key cities, their regime was hardly secure. It had been ratified by the national Congress of Soviets only after the moderate socialists had walked out in protest, leaving Lenin a voting majority. And it still remained to be seen what position the long-awaited Constituent Assembly would take on the Bolshevik regime. But the most immediate threat to the Bolshevik government was military. In the period after the October Revolution, there was no shortage of military units at the front and near the capital that were commanded by officers hostile to the Bolsheviks. The undisciplined and poorly equipped pro-Bolshevik garrison and Red Guards in Petrograd would have been no match for a trained and well-equipped unit entering the city. The Bolsheviks sent a barrage of telegrams to their comrades in provincial cities, ordering them to do everything to delay or stop hostile forces from approaching the capital. Nikolai Yezhov had been elected deputy, then leading political commissar, of the Vitebsk railroad station in October.[32] It became his job to help organize these blockades.

Already before October, Yezhov and his fellows had turned back a military force summoned by Provisional Government head A. F. Kerensky to the capital. At that time, the Vitebsk Red Guards had turned the soldiers back with propaganda and fraternization. A more serious challenge arose after October, when a force of several thousand hostile Polish Legionnaires (Polish soldiers attached to the former Russian Imperial Army) approached Vitebsk on the way to Petrograd. The local Red Guards numbered only about three thousand and understood that they would lose any open battle with the Poles, who refused to negotiate or talk with the Vitebsk Reds. The local Bolshevik leaders, Yezhov among them, decided on a combination of "playing to their human feelings" and trickery.

They selected a local Polish woman sympathetic to the Bolsheviks. She led a Red Guard delegation to the Polish camp waving a red flag and declaiming herself to the Polish soldiers as "your sister." It worked: the Poles admitted a half-dozen Vitebsk Bolshevik negotiators. As the discussions proceeded, the Poles could hear and see train after train arriving from Vitebsk. With each arrival, a mounted courier arrived at the talks and asked the Bolshevik commander, one Krylov, where the arriving echelon should deploy. Krylov gave directions each time and returned to the talks. After several such interruptions, Krylov then presented the Poles with an ultimatum: either surrender or we open fire. Convinced that the Vitebsk Bolsheviks must have marshaled several thousand troops in the area, the Poles dispersed. They should have been suspicious that the doors to the train wagons were always closed when in their view. Actually, the trains had been empty; there were no arriving echelons.[33]

Thus at the age of twenty-two, Nikolai Yezhov had played a significant role in defending the Bolshevik Revolution. Histories of 1917 stress the well-known revolutionary leaders in Petrograd or in Moscow who made the headlines and staffed the prominent positions in the new government. But it was provincial radicals like Yezhov who manned key points in the post-October days and provided vital breathing room for the new regime to consolidate itself. Because of Vitebsk's strategic location, Yezhov's position there was one of the most important of these.

Yezhov was one of many radical activists spontaneously thrown up in the chaotic historical upheaval of 1917. Not all of these were Bolsheviks, however, and few of those who played important roles in defense of the Bolsheviks were lifetime professional revolutionaries. Many of them faded into the historical background or were killed in the subsequent Civil War of 1918–21. Many who had been active revolutionaries in October now considered that with a socialist government in power, their revolutionary days were over.

At first, Yezhov seemed to be one of these. After an unsuccessful campaign for a seat in the Constituent Assembly, he returned to life as a worker. After a short time in Petrograd, he moved to Vysshy Volochek, the second-largest industrial town of Tver province, where he found work in the Volotin glassworks. His mother and sister were there, and for more than a year he worked in the factory. Although he was not a professional Bolshevik, he was a consistent rank-and-file member of factory workers' committees, trade unions, and Bolshevik Party cells until 1919, when he was drafted into the Red Army at the height of the Civil War.[34] The sources are silent about why, given the parlous straits in which the Bolshevik regime found itself, Yezhov had not volunteered for army service along with so many of his comrades. It is entirely possible that his short stature disqualified him from military service until the Bolsheviks became desperate and began large-scale conscription.

After being drafted in a "party mobilization" of 1919, Yezhov served for several months in the town of Zubtsov as a "specialist" in a Special Designation Battalion (*osobogo naznacheniia*). Yezhov's autobiographical sketch is silent about this battalion or his duties in it. Such battalions carried out a wide variety of special tasks, from guarding railroads to punitive operations. Many of them were involved in catching and shooting spies and deserters in cooperation with the secret police (CHEKA), or in preventing unauthorized Red Army retreats by stationing themselves in the rear and shooting those who fell back without orders. Given the generally unsavory reputation of such formations and the silence of those who served in them, it is safe to imagine that Yezhov was involved in missions having to do with intelligence or punitive force.[35]

If so, this preview of his future life did not last long. In August 1919 he was sent to Saratov province on the Volga to help reorganize sagging party organizations among military garrisons, and later that month, in the face of Red Army losses along the Volga, he was evacuated to Kazan, where he was assigned to the 2nd Radiotelegraph Base. He spent the remainder of the war in Kazan, and by his own account never saw combat.[36] Nevertheless, he held a fairly important position, serving first as political commissar of the radiotelegraph school, and from April 1921 as commissar of the entire base, making him effectively second in command. The 2nd Radiotelegraph Base was an important research and training institution for telephone and radio technicians and operators. Professor A. T. Uglov, who had installed Lenin's Moscow telephone system, worked there. During the Civil War, the base graduated nearly eight thousand specialists and was well known throughout the country.[37] During this time, Yezhov also worked as a propagandist for and member of the Tatar Party Committee, based in Kazan.

Once again, Nikolai Yezhov found himself in the midst of a powerful political struggle. The Russian Civil War swept back and forth across the country for three years, killing hundreds of thousands of people. As the pro-Bolshevik "Reds" and anti-Bolshevik "Whites" traded territory in bloody battles, the industrial and agricultural base of Russia was destroyed. In the midst of this, the influenza epidemic of 1918 and recurring typhus outbreaks may have killed more people than the fighting. As agricultural lands were laid waste, famine broke out and a large number of people starved. Hunger was particularly severe along the Volga, where Yezhov worked, and there were numerous verified reports of cannibalism, even in Kazan.

It was a fight to the death. It was also a time of betrayal. Defection, desertion, and sabotage plagued both sides. Few prisoners were taken, and executions of hostages and civilians were common. Those suspected of treason were routinely rounded up and killed by the Bolshevik secret police, the CHEKA, which originated and grew powerful during the Civil War. Foreign intervention on the side of the Whites led to a kind of siege mentality among the Bolsheviks, in which enemy spies and saboteurs could be everywhere: foreign, domestic, across the front, or even in our midst. The bitter, uncompromising struggle again reduced politics to the simple dichotomy "us" vs. "them." Workers and peasants had long understood the gulf between them on the one hand and the oppressors on the other. Even before the bloodshed started, these lines had hardened in 1917. Already during that revolutionary year we find documents about traitors, enemies, and betrayers and calls to "be merciless with enemies of the people." Even ideas of freedom and democracy in 1917 had been socially specific. "True freedom necessitated silencing the voices of those who opposed the struggles and demands of workers, soldiers, and peasants."[38]

Wars are always brutalizing experiences for those who actually fight them, but in this case the preexisting binary social attitudes both increased and focused the brutality. Shades of political difference and theoretical platforms were forgotten, and each side took the view that one was either for us or against us. And those against us, the enemy, were to be killed.

The writer Isaac Babel traveled with a Cossack cavalry group during the Civil War and has left us with vivid pictures of the brutality of the times. Even though he was a supporter of the Red cause, his class origins made it difficult to fit in with his plebeian comrades. When he arrived at his new Red Army unit, complete with Bolshevik credentials and recommendations, the commander told him: "With spectacles on your nose! Ha, you lousy little fellow, you! . . . Here you get hacked to pieces just for wearing glasses!" One Cossack told Babel, "Then I started kicking Nikitinsky, my master, I kicked him for an hour, maybe even more than an hour, and I really understood what life actually is. With one shot, let me tell you, you can only get rid of a person. A shot would have been a pardon for him. . . . But there are times when I don't spare myself and spend a good hour, maybe even more than an hour, kicking the enemy."[39]

Babel also witnessed a good bit of mindless violence himself. In one episode, red Cossacks were sorting out prisoners they had taken, trying to decide which were officers and which were soldiers. When captured by the Reds, the officers had shed their uniforms to avoid identification as class enemies. "'Our mothers don't knit drawers like that for us,' he told me slyly. [Then to the prisoners,] 'Your officers threw their uniforms here!' he yelled. 'We're going to have a little fitting now, and whoever the uniforms fit, I'm going to finish off.' He picked out a cap without a brim [a junior officer's cap] from the pile of rags and put it on a lanky man's head. 'It fits,' Golov whispered. He stepped up closer to the prisoner, looked him in the eyes, and plunged his saber into his gullet."[40]

It was a time of brutality in which an entire generation came of age. For those like Yezhov and his peers, the Civil War was their formative education. It taught them that politics (as well as life) was revolutionary and combative, rather than evolutionary and peaceful. It taught a relentless struggle to the death with "them," the class enemy whose Russian and foreign representatives were allied against the people. It taught them that political dispute and difference could best, or even only, be solved with violence and that compromise was treason. "Implacable" and "iron-willed" and "merciless" were to become positive attributes used to describe the "best Bolsheviks."

The profound and bitter struggle of the Civil War had a lingering effect on many levels. First, death and dying at the hands of the enemy produced deeply embedded memories and grudges. Decades later, service (however minor) on the White side was cause for expulsion from the party and arrest. Second, the war militarized the Bolsheviks for years to come. In the following decades, a simple military tunic and shaved head became the fashion for hard, uncompromising party members, and Bolshevik propaganda long used images about storming fortresses, even when referring to education, agriculture, or other peaceable policies. Third, the paranoia of siege mentality would long remain in the consciousness of Bolsheviks, who drew no distinction between what they regarded as ubiquitous internal and external enemies. Internal conflicts were internationalized (and vice versa) in Bolshevik thinking, leading to the attitude that the party was always at war even when the international scene was peaceful. The enemy never slept, whether in his domestic or foreign incarnations, and the struggle was constant. In the dire conditions of the Civil War, with people dying everywhere, the use of terror did not seem evil or outrageous, as it does to us. In short, we see in the Civil War the genesis of the political outlook and mentalities that would support Stalinism.[41]

So even though Nikolai Yezhov was behind the lines, he was never far from the violence, hatred, and suspicion that were everywhere. In this sense, no place in Russia was really a rear area because conflict, violence, disease, and hunger were everywhere. Even government and party officials, whose lower ranks Yezhov joined in Kazan, were close to the brutality wherever they worked. Yezhov and his fellows remembered being hungry and seeing dead people by the road. They were to remember the masses of starvation victims. Among the major activities and party jobs Yezhov's wife listed on her questionnaires in this period was organizational "struggle against hunger." Even the First Secretary of the Bolshevik Party, Yakov Sverdlov, apparently safe behind Kremlin walls, died of typhus. Nobody was safe in these years, and nobody was shielded from the terrible violence and suffering. It would be a mistake to imagine that Yezhov's service at the radio school was somehow removed from the war, hatred, and mass death.

It was in this terrible milieu that Nikolai Yezhov met Antonina Alekseevna Titova. Two years younger than Yezhov, Titova was Russian born and raised in the Tatar Volga region around Kazan. Her father was a poor tailor who had died of tuberculosis in 1917, leaving a wife and two hungry children. Surviving for a time by working a small piece of land she rented from a peasant, Titova's mother had recently moved to Kazan with her children. When she finished school and entered the local university in 1917, Titova had gravitated to a circle of local Bolshevik radicals, and she formally joined the party in 1918. She was active in educational-propaganda work for the Tatar party committee. She organized women's party circles along with her mother, who was also a party member, and wrote for local party newspapers. In the middle of 1919 she became an organizer for the local branch of the Chemical Workers' Union, and she became a prominent local party activist at about the time she met Nikolai Ivanovich Yezhov. The two apparently hit it off right away and were married almost immediately, probably in the summer of 1919. The following year, Antonina was promoted to head the Cultural Department of the Central Committee of the Chemical Workers' Union in Moscow. Her work took her back and forth between Moscow and Kazan, where she organized local union conferences and congresses and continued her agitation and propaganda work.[42]

With the end of the Civil War early in 1921, Nikolai was demobilized from the Red Army. At the time he mustered out in June, he moved seamlessly into civilian party work, and there was every reason to believe that his party career was on a fast track. He was soon named the party's chief of agitation and propaganda (*agitprop*) for the Tatar Republic party organization, member of the Kazan city executive committee (city administration), and member of the Tatar Republic executive committee (provincial administration).[43] These posts made him one of the top party and state leaders of the Tatar region and put him on the list of leading officials (*nomenklatura*) whose appointment had to be initiated or confirmed by the Central Committee in Moscow. Moreover, his service as a political commissar during the Civil War would prove to be an important credential, one shared by the likes of such prominent Bolsheviks as L. M. Kaganovich, G. K. Ordzhonikidze, S. M. Kirov, and Stalin himself. In fact, the vast majority of Stalinist Politburo and Central Committee members before World War II had seen Civil War service as political commissars.

Yezhov was thus a member of an elite club, and his career was only beginning. On 15 February 1922 the party's Orgburo appointed Nikolai Yezhov to the post of "Responsible Secretary" for the Mari regional party organization.[44] On the Volga above Kazan and below Nizhny Novgorod, Mari was not a particularly important province, but this was a big job for a young man. It would be difficult to find in other European countries many twenty-six-year-old provincial governors of working-class origin and with virtually no formal education. Such appointments were not uncommon in these years, and, as we shall see, they speak volumes about the early Bolshevik regime.

Nobody could have imagined that the boy trudging to work in the Putilov factory before 1914 could, in the space of a half-dozen years, become one of a small team running an entire province and climb into the circle of politicians running the entire country. His unimpressive stature and lack of formal education (he would always write ungrammatical and misspelled Russian) might appear to doom him to a life of poverty and obscurity. But the earthshaking turmoil of the Russian Revolution made paupers of the great and catapulted simple people into leadership positions.

Not everyone climbed the ladder, however. Revolution alone did not guarantee power and status. To begin with, one had to have the luck not to be killed or disabled, as so many millions were in the world war and internal strife. Those who survived and benefited from the overturn of society had to exhibit a bundle of qualities that included energy, activism, capacity for hard work, and loyalty. Although Nikolai Yezhov's work history in the party was just beginning and we have little information on his job performance at this stage, his work in the next period of his life would confirm that he had these attributes. With the end of the Civil War, he was placed into positions of power and trust by those above and below him.

Moreover, the same qualities that attracted certain people to the hard and uncompromising Bolshevik positions were reinforced during the terrible storm of 1914–21. Those who followed Lenin tended to be those who saw the world in black and white, friend and foe, proletarian and bourgeois, us and them. Consciously or unconsciously, they felt that history and human progress (even understood in terms of conditions for workers) advanced and improved through conflict; this they shared with Marx and Lenin. Bolsheviks, especially working-class Bolsheviks, dreamed of turning the tables, overthrowing the upper crust, and building a society of economic and social equality. Such dreams and beliefs had little to do with elaborate theories or the ideas of philosophers. They were elemental parts of plebeian mentality in pre-revolutionary Russia, and there is every reason to believe that Nikolai Yezhov shared them. Writing to a friend in 1922 of his comrades in Kazan, Yezhov was proud that "they put their hopes on me thinking I can uphold the class line."[45]

And this complex of attitudes and ways of understanding the world were only reinforced by the Civil War. Horrible as it seems to us, the savagery, brutality, and terror of that conflict were not inconsistent with the worldview of the Bolsheviks who fought through it. Brutality, after all, had always been part of the lives of poor Russians, so the Civil War was different only in degree and severity. Bolsheviks like Yezhov were hard men—even at a tender age—before the time of war and revolution, and that disaster only confirmed and reinforced the ways of their lives.

Although we have precious little information about him as a person, what we do have suggests something other than a monster, a murderer, a brutal soldier-commissar. From those of his fellows who shared his class and experience, we see numerous glimpses of a not unpleasant fellow. Those who remembered him from Putilov, Vitebsk, or Kazan recalled a warm and personable friend, someone with a lively wit and sense of humor. Nikolai Yezhov seems to have been a modest young man without pretense or affectation. He was the first to volunteer and the last to quit; his persistence and diligence would also surround his reputation in the future. And, perhaps oddly for someone as politically hard as he, contemporaries remembered his kindness and generosity. Years later, a fellow soldier and friend from Kazan days recalled riding in a train with Yezhov as he traveled from one assignment to another. Yevgeny Sudnitsyn recalled a friendly fellow whose subordinates called him by his first name, who shared his ration packet with hungry soldiers around him, and who loaned money to his traveling companions. Later, when times improved, Yezhov would refuse to accept repayment. Sudnitsyn never became great; he never left Kazan and ended his days as a simple worker in an obscure soviet office.[46] He would have seen no contradiction among a competent administrator, an "implacable" and hard Bolshevik, and a kind and generous young man. For such as Sudnitsyn and Yezhov, there was no conflict between brotherhood and solicitude toward "us," combined with hatred and terror for "them." Such were the people and their times.

When the Civil War ended early in 1921, the Bolsheviks faced truly daunting problems. The country was wrecked; industrial production had collapsed, and hunger stalked the population. A desperate attempt to win the loyalty, or at least neutrality, of the Russian peasantry had forced Lenin and his followers in 1921 to abandon confiscatory policies and immediate socialist dreams and implement a semi–market economy under the rubric of the "New Economic Policy," which would last until the end of the 1920s.

Although the White forces had been defeated on the battlefield, anti-Bolshevik political parties still existed, either legally or underground. Recent uprisings in various provinces and of the Bolsheviks' own supporters at the Kronstadt naval base signaled that violence could break out at any moment. Foreign military detachments had withdrawn by 1921, but the continuing hostility of most other countries, and a recent short war with Poland, also showed that further fighting with foreign invaders was always a possibility.

In order to remain in power, the Bolsheviks were ready to use whatever force was required. The CHEKA, although reorganized and variously renamed, lost none of its powers, and although it had been created in the wartime emergency, it continued to function as the "unsheathed sword of the revolution" in peacetime. Opposition political groups were hounded and arrested, newspapers were closed down, and elections to the soviets at all levels were controlled and rigged to exclude meaningful opposition to the regime. Factional groups within the Bolshevik Party critical of Lenin's majority were formally banned at the 10th Party Congress in early 1921.

One might think that the transition from revolutionaries to Red soldiers to government officials would have softened plebeian and Bolsheviks "us" vs. "them" attitudes, and to some extent it did. But the idea of government that the Bolsheviks instituted owed much not only to the Civil War violence but to basic notions of government that had already appeared in 1917. The entire 1917–21 span was a single period of class violence, without firm lines between Revolution and Civil War. Already in 1917, for workers "a just government would not mediate among interests, for the competing interest of the factory owner had no legitimacy. . . . Everything was interpreted in terms of a binary conception of class opposition . . . friend versus enemy; we versus they; loyal worker vs. saboteur; and the like. All problems were caused by ill-intentioned people, by enemies of the people. . . . Formal rights, procedures, and laws have no place in a world where what is good and right is already known."[47] Peacetime implied only a slight relaxation for the Bolsheviks, whose siege mentality and defensive drive for party unity continued for years.

# THREE

## In the Provinces

To tell the truth, I'm so fed up with all the paper shuffling
that it's time to go back to the factory. Lately I've missed
factory life; it's time for a rest and to completely say
good-bye to this whole situation.

N. I. YEZHOV

In addition to the problems of staying in power and resurrecting the
economy, the Bolsheviks faced a more basic challenge: proving that
they could govern the country. It was not enough to moderate economic policy and repress real or imagined opponents. In hundreds of
areas from finance to transport to communications, the new regime
found itself facing real difficulties. In the capital, many former tsarist-
era ministries still existed, and until the Bolsheviks could staff them
with their own people (a process that would take nearly a decade), they
had to work with the old administrators. Many of the old regime's bureaucrats had died or emigrated during the Civil War, and those who
remained in place were largely hostile or indifferent to the Bolshevik
regime. Lenin's party was able to staff the tops of the ministries with
Bolsheviks who were loyal, but their inexperience often made them

little more than watchdogs over the office staffs that really ran things. Strikes and slowdowns of office workers and administrators were common in the early 1920s, and even when the "former people" worked, the Bolsheviks suspected them of foot dragging, passive resistance, and general obstruction. Referring to the central bureaucracy as a "pile," Lenin said in 1922, "I doubt very much whether it can truthfully be said that the Communists are directing this pile. In truth, they are not doing the directing, they are being directed."[1]

But it was in the provinces that the administrative problem was most acute for the new regime. The huge Russian Empire had spanned a dozen time zones and encompassed more than a hundred languages and nationalities. A single railroad line connected the two ends of the country, and it was a perilous lifeline. During the Civil War, first the Czech Legion and then other hostile groups had been able to seize most of Siberia simply by controlling the thread of the Trans-Siberian Railroad, along which most of the population east of the Urals lived. Telephone connections with much of the country were still in the future, and muddy primitive roads made travel to many settlements a seasonal matter. In the south, in Central Asia, and in Siberia "bandit" gangs (political, criminal, or both) disrupted transportation and made communication difficult and administration perilous.

In the provinces the former tsarist administration had largely evaporated during 1917, as peasants seized the land and drove off the former tsar's representatives. Townspeople had elected soviets, which replaced urban administration, and neither peasants nor townspeople had paid much attention to the rudimentary commissioners of the short-lived Provisional Government. Whatever orderly government remained was destroyed during the Civil War when Reds and Whites traded territory and took turns imposing ad hoc, wartime emergency bureaucracies on the localities. Years of chaos had followed the time when government functioned in Russia. In short, the Bolsheviks faced the problem of governing the largest country on earth without technical means, experienced administrators, or a governing structure.

Although Lenin had stridently claimed in 1917 that ordinary workers and peasants could easily learn the skills of government, few people around the world believed that, and by the early 1920s even Lenin and his comrades were starting to have their doubts. Much of the loyal cadre of factory workers and soldiers had been killed or dispersed by the Civil War and had been replaced in the soviets, trade unions, and other organizations by people the Bolsheviks considered "petty bourgeois" latecomers, who had signed on to the regime only when it had won or who simply lacked the socialist consciousness the regime valued and needed. Without the leavening of their loyal 1917 plebeian supporters, the Bolsheviks worried that the mass democracy from below they had formerly championed could be turned against them, either consciously by hostile political forces or unconsciously because of the "primitive" mentalities of the masses.[2] Until his death in early 1924, Lenin spent much of his time reflecting on this problem, thinking about "cultural revolution" to raise the level of the population and devising schemes and organizations to run the country, or to watch over those who did.

Obviously the Communist Party offered a vehicle for administering the territories, and this was the strategy ultimately selected. Battle tested, loyal to Lenin, and relatively disciplined, the party was actually the only tool to hand. But the Bolsheviks feared that if the party took direct charge of the country's administration, it could become "contaminated" by petty bourgeois, administrative mentality and lose its class edge and content. So the pattern that emerged was one of parallel government. The formal government, charged with implementation, would comprise a hierarchical structure of soviets from village to national level and including ministries, renamed commissariats. Behind the government, however, and parallel to it, another network of party organizations would exercise supervision and control over the system. And, as soon became clear, it was the party chain of command that mattered. Unlike the state structures, which contained a high proportion of nonparty people, the party was (at least in theory) a disciplined machine for transmission of orders and policies from top to bottom. According to the party's rules, obedience to superior party bodies was obligatory for party committees and their members, and in 1921 the point was driven home when Lenin sponsored a "ban on factions," which made programmatic splinter groups illegal in the party.[3]

It would be a mistake, however, to overstate the efficiency, discipline, or administrative capabilities of the party in these years. For many reasons, the party was not really a well-honed tool easily converted to political administration. First, the business of the party for most of its existence had been revolution. Its experienced members were skilled in organizing strikes and revolts, editing newspapers, evading the police, and working underground. They had never had to run anything. Only during the three years of the Civil War had they been forced to direct and administer, but at that time administration had been largely an ad hoc affair. The tides of war often forced party members to flee their posts. Communications were poor and such structure as existed often consisted of special emissaries (commissars) sent from Moscow to the localities for special purposes. Bolshevik administration during the Civil War was more about shooting, shouting, threatening, and waving revolvers than it was about any chain of command or reporting structure. If the goal in the 1920s was the creation of government, the experience of the Civil War would appear to have been a poor teacher.

Second, the distribution of party members in 1921 had more to do with accident and exigency than with the needs of an administrative network. When the fighting stopped early in 1921, Bolsheviks were stationed in haphazard locations around the country, corresponding to their chance locations in 1917–20, based on the concentrations of workers they were organizing, their assignments for special purposes, or the places where they happened to be demobilized from the Red Army. Thus in 1921, Nikolai Yezhov found himself in Kazan, in Tatar country, simply because that had been his wartime location and place of his demobilization.

Moreover, when Bolsheviks did move, they tended to locate themselves in the cities, where conditions were better and where their working-class supporters were concentrated. The Politburo member G. Zinoviev complained in 1923 that the party was concentrated in the cities and had barely begun to penetrate the countryside. In the early 1920s most villages (where most of the population still lived) contained no Communist Party members, and depending on the province, there was only one party member per ten to thirty villages. Only about 7 percent of the membership of village soviets were party members.[4]

Third, since 1917 the party had swollen into a mass organization. At first glance, this might seem an advantage, insofar as it could permit better coverage of a large area with party members. From a membership of about 24,000 in 1917, the party grew to 390,000 by March 1918 to 732,000 in March 1921.[5] The majority of the new recruits had less administrative experience than the Old Bolsheviks (party members before 1917) and were of uncertain political reliability, containing in large measure persons of all classes who were merely joining the winning side. Throughout the party's history, there would be such swellings of the membership as the leadership tried to recruit more party soldiers, preferably from the proletariat. In the Bolsheviks' understanding, behavior and political outlook were class determined, and social origins represented an important credential for the party. These mass intakes of new members were usually followed by a membership screening (*chistka,* or purge) aimed at expelling the uncommitted, the criminal, the incompetent, the "class-alien," and often the political deviant. In the screening of 1919 half the party had been expelled.[6] In 1921 a quarter of the new members were kicked out.[7]

But new party soldiers did not necessarily mean more or better party officers. Party leaders constantly complained about the political illiteracy of even provincial party secretaries, to say nothing of the membership as a whole. Training courses and stints at the Communist Academy or the like in Moscow were constantly prescribed for serving party secretaries. (Yezhov attended such courses later in the decade.) The inexperience of provincial party leaders translated into a crying shortage of "cadres," or personnel, for party leadership assignments, and much of the party's early history of personnel assignment was governed by this supply-and-demand fact of life. As a response to the shortage of politically experienced administrators, the party in March 1922 ordered that secretaries of *gubkoms* (provincial party organizations) must have been party members before the October 1917 Revolution; for secretaries of district (*uezd*) party committees the requirement was a mere three years in the party. The following year, however, the Central Committee was forced to admit that the rule could not be sustained even in Moscow province, due to a shortage of qualified party members.[8] The records of the party's Orgburo throughout the decade show the scant supply of qualified party leaders for assignment and, as we shall see, their appointments were at the center of intense bargaining and competition, as provincial party committees jealously protected their proven party personnel and demanded more from Moscow, which did the best it could to meet the demand.

On 10 February 1922 the Central Committee emissary (*instruktor*) N. A. Kubiak reported to the party's Orgburo on his recent inspection trip to the Mari Oblast' (province). Things were a mess there. Kubiak described ethnic conflicts between Russians and Mari, political cliques expelling one another from the party, personality squabbles and spats.[9] Five days later, the Secretariat of the CC, with V. M. Molotov presiding, accepted a staff proposal to send Nikolai Yezhov from Kazan to Mari, recommending him to the Mari Bolsheviks as their new provincial party secretary.[10] We do not know whether Yezhov's previous work in Kazan had been so good as to attract the attention of Moscow party personnel specialists, or whether desperation led them to select what appeared to be a competent candidate conveniently at hand. At any rate, the following month Nikolai and Antonina set off for Krasnokokshaisk (formerly Tsarevokokshaisk, today Iokshar-Ola), the capital of the Mari region.

His designation as "responsible secretary" illustrates one aspect of the centralization of the national party structure in this period and the growth in influence of party over state organizations. Gradually, by the mid-1920s, the party leadership insisted that one person be held responsible for a territorial party organization. Before this, during the Civil War and before, party organizations tended to be run by committee. But the resulting fragmentation, confusion, and even disobedience to Moscow's policies led the leadership to require that one person, the responsible secretary, be in charge and be responsible to Moscow.[11]

Although party leadership of a province was a major promotion for Yezhov, Mari was hardly a prestigious appointment. With a population of about 367,000, it had a party organization of only 398 members and 154 candidate members: a membership smaller than in a single large Russian factory and representing a tenth of one percent of the province's population. There were only forty-nine party cells in the entire province, and thirty-six of them were rural. The population was overwhelmingly peasant. There were only two substantial factories (both glassworks) in the entire province, employing some five hundred workers altogether, and only 3 percent of the working population belonged to trade unions. Given that Bolsheviks found their bases of support in urban areas, factories, and trade unions, running a party organization in Mari was not an enviable task.

Yezhov also walked into a human disaster in Mari. In the spring of 1922 the oblast' had not recovered from the disaster of the Civil War. About the time Yezhov arrived, the secret police were reporting to Moscow on famine and disease in Mari. Using the word "starvation," the police reported on 6 March that "hunger has assumed enormous proportions" there.[12] By 4 April the police reported that 97 percent of the population regularly suffered from hunger and that a typhus epidemic had broken out. The starvation did not abate until October. Recent forest fires had devastated the timber industry, producing what one party report called "a colossal loss of state resources." A lack of resources for clearing and restoring the burned territory meant that the losses would be practically permanent. Timber was a large employer in a forested region like Mari, and the provincial party organization had no resources for coping with and reassigning the unemployed.[13] By August severe shortages of raw materials also led to the closing of several factories in the province.[14]

Moreover, there were severe ethnic conflicts. The Mari, an Asian people related to the Tatars, outnumbered Russians two to one among the population; their educational and "cultural levels" were said to be low. Kubiak had seen the problem for himself, and his CC report noted that "the nationality question produced great friction" in the province, even within the Bolshevik Party organization.[15] Yezhov would soon discover this firsthand.

The duties of territorial party secretaries were many and varied. As Moscow's principal representatives out in the countryside, they came ultimately to be responsible for all areas of political and economic life. In addition to their traditional activities in the areas of "party work" (agitation, propaganda, press, journals, workers' organizations, rallies, and so forth) they came to supervise the work of trade unions and economic organizations as well. Thus although there were state procurement agencies separate from the party, the local party secretary ultimately answered for collection of the agricultural tax-in-kind. Even though various nonparty agencies were supposed to manage their own personnel appointments, the shortage of administrative talent for both party and nonparty posts meant that the local party secretary came to control these functions as well. Finally, the party secretary served the role of mediator in the myriad turf and personal conflicts that plagued the new, inexperienced, and frequently overlapping government agencies. In March 1922 CC Secretary Molotov had complained that local party organizations were forced to spend 70 percent of their time on questions other than their primary jobs of party work.[16] We shall see that party leadership involved refereeing and settling disputes as much as it did policy formation or implementation.

Overwork and a shortage of help were not the only problems territorial party secretaries faced. Depending on the area, they could find themselves literally in hostile territory. Non-Russian populations were sometimes antagonistic toward the mostly Russian Bolshevik administrations, and even where they were not, their cultural traditions often ran counter to Bolshevik understandings. For example, family and clan ties often cut across the class lines the Bolsheviks wanted to find. Similarly, the Bolsheviks' relatively modern ideas about women's rights frequently conflicted with ancient patrimonial societies in the Caucasus and Central Asia. The Moscow party leadership paid a good deal of attention to these sensitive ethnic and cultural frictions and worried about escalating conflicts. More than once, complicated ethnic alliances between and among Russian and native groups paralyzed local politics, and Moscow's Russian representatives were sometimes forced out by national hostility. As we shall see, Moscow's response to local friction in nationality areas was frequently to recall all of its feuding representatives and to send an entirely new team.[17]

So Nikolai Yezhov's appointment as responsible secretary in the Mari region was a mixed blessing: it was a promotion to an important position but one that threw him into the chaos of local ethnic politics in the early 1920s. He would serve there a little less than a year. On the one hand, it was here that he learned the routines of party leadership and demonstrated his abilities to his superiors in Moscow. On the other hand, though, he became so embroiled in vicious struggles between cliques in the local leadership and so entangled in the delicate "national question" that his subsequent autobiographies and official biographical blurbs would fail to mention his time in Mari at all.

One of the most important duties of territorial party secretaries was the writing of reports to Moscow. During and after the Civil War, Moscow had only intermittent contact with many of the party organizations in the country. In early 1919 party leaders had complained at party congresses that Moscow had little knowledge of who its cadres were in the provinces; the locals refused to complete questionnaires or provide other information to the center. By the end of that year one-quarter of the district party committees (*ukomy*) were still not sending regular reports on their activities; 5 percent of party committees never sent any information at all.[18]

Yezhov quickly mastered the form and format of report writing. Using the prescribed categories of information that interested Moscow (state and morale of the party committee, agitational work, economic life of the area, morale of the population, and so on), he produced crisp, well-written reports that showed him a quick study in the mores of party life.[19] His reports were neatly typed, well written, factual, and to the point. In fact, they seem too good to have been his alone, and he may have had help in correcting his texts from his newspaper editor wife.[20] Just as important, they show that Yezhov was learning the reporting style of the party's representatives. Party reports were expected to supply the established categories of information. But perhaps more important, they were texts that allowed their writers to demonstrate their adherence to specific aspects of party culture. A specific genre of document, the party report (like its relative, the "informational letter") was expected to embody particular stylistic conventions that helped to construct and reinforce the self-representation that party leaders had of themselves and which their superiors expected.

A Bolshevik Party secretary was supposed to be self-effacing, impersonal, and detached in his reports, emphasizing party virtues of hard work, discipline, selflessness, and party unity. Even though he was the single author of the report, he never used the first person; if it was necessary to refer to himself, he did so in the third person. Bragging or complaining was inappropriate, as were personal attacks on others in the committee (although the latter proscription was as often violated as observed). Because of the tradition of self-sacrifice, whining about the personal problems and difficulties of the author were also inappropriate. Personal pleading for reassignment was out of place, as was begging for more resources (although the latter was often done in an "objective" way to "help" the party committee). Overall, the tone was to be honest, frank, and hard-hitting about both accomplishments and failures.

Success in a given area of party activity was usually attributed to endless hard work, discipline, and the "help" given by the Central Committee, whether such had actually been given or not. Failures were explained by disunity, shortage of personnel, pressure of work in other areas, and lack of discipline. The "objective conditions" impeding successful party work (economic or cultural backwardness of the region, hostility of the population, shortages of everything) were often enumerated in descriptive parts of the report, but were rarely adduced to explain away failure. The idea was that a well-organized party committee could overcome any objective difficulty with discipline, careful planning, and the support of the Central Committee, and blaming failures on the impossibility of the environment and the tasks to be done was considered bad form.

Naturally, though, the writers of these reports were real people worried about their reputations and careers. They therefore found ways to emphasize success and background failure in an apparently objective, honest, and neutral textual style. Already by the 1920s party reports and reporting speeches had adopted the "*odnako*" ("although") discursive style that would characterize party discourse until the end of its existence. In the case of general success in a given area, for example, the accomplishments were first enumerated. This was followed by some variant of "but it is necessary to note that" or "however, serious problems and shortcomings remain" or "we also do not wish to hide our shortcomings," followed by a list of things not done or badly done. In the case of failure, a reverse grammar was followed: "The party committee has failed to . . . " or some problem "has resisted our efforts," followed by the predictable "however" and a section itemizing plans and promises for correction.

Yezhov quickly mastered the "although" style: "In the area of agitation and propaganda work, there has been a noticeable improvement in local newspapers, although their content is far from satisfactory."[21] He was also able to use these reports to maneuver. Although it was not proper to blame failures on one's comrades by name, it was possible in the reports to deflect blame from oneself by pointing to the collective shortcomings in the work of various nonparty organizations. In so doing, a skilled party secretary could denounce local rivals under the pose of objectivity.

Thus in 1922, collection of the tax-in-kind had been disorganized and poorly planned, thereby stirring up the population's resentment. Although the party organization of the province, headed by its responsible secretary, was ultimately answerable to Moscow for tax collection and a peaceful population, Yezhov shifted the blame to the state procurement representatives who did the actual collection. After taking responsibility for the difficulties, he pointed out that he had been the one to call attention to the failures of the provincial tax collectors, who were after all technically part of the state apparatus, not the party. He had requested that Moscow replace key members of the local tax apparatus; things

would run smoothly now.[22] Laying the blame for failures on subordinates was something less than ideal etiquette for a party secretary, but it
became common practice, and those like Yezhov who were good at it
managed to avoid or minimize blame. At the same time, however, he
took measures to improve the situation by lobbying for permission to
retain more of the tax for local use in feeding the population. He wrote
to a friend, "Today I'm going to the tax people to talk about us leaving
a part of tax-in-kind to ourselves."[23]

The fuss over tax collection was, however, symptomatic of a more serious problem in the Mari party organization. Throughout the early
1920s many provincial party committees were rent by factional struggles. Most of the time these had less to do with the well-known differences among oppositional groups like the Democratic Centralists or
Workers' Opposition[24] than with the effort by personal cliques for influence and control over the local party organization.[25] Given the shortage of qualified party personnel and the scant party membership among
the populace, it was natural for the local Bolsheviks to band together in
teams around an authoritative leader. In the absence of strong and
stable institutions, such groups rapidly developed into cliques and
eventually into the patron-client groups that came to characterize party
organization throughout the period.[26] In the early years the vagueness
or absence of concrete instructions from Moscow, combined with
echoes of factional disputes in the center, led to disagreements and
squabbles (*skloki*) among local party leaders about how to proceed, providing additional impetus to the formation of personal circles around
local leaders.

Almost from the moment of his arrival in Mari in the spring of 1922,
Yezhov became embroiled in such a personal "squabble," as the Central
Committee called them. His counterpart in the state apparatus was I. P.
Petrov, chairman of the Mari Soviet Executive Committee (*ispolkom*),
and it seems that the two of them fought constantly. The documents we
have do not tell us of the personal or political issues involved, if any, although Petrov later complained of Yezhov's "Russian chauvinism" in
his relations with the Mari locals. Yezhov's supporters returned the

favor by accusing Petrov of an "incorrect understanding of the party's nationality policy," and noted that even the Mari members of the provincial party committee had accused Petrov of "Mari chauvinism."[27] Such charges are hard to evaluate. Moscow's vague nationality policy could easily expose leaders to such accusations in their dealings with non-Russians. Moreover, any factional split between groups of Russians in a non-Russian area almost inevitably resulted in one group accusing the other of chauvinism of one kind or another. A Moscow-based party referee noted in a report that there was probably guilt on both sides.[28]

Petrov and Yezhov each wrote to Moscow complaining about the other. Shortly after his arrival in Mari, Yezhov wrote that on the instructions of the CC in Moscow, he had formed a Marxist study circle for "about fifteen young comrades" to combat the "almost complete indifference" of local party members to political events in Moscow. But almost immediately, Petrov's friends began to whisper that this was a "Yezhov group." Yezhov complained that party morale was seriously sagging: "the differences [*raskhozhdeniia*] among the activist comrades has become clearly evident [*sic*]. There is talk about the organization of two groups, a 'Yezhovist' and a 'Petrovist.'"[29]

Two months later, in August, Yezhov wrote again to the Central Committee complaining about Petrov and his followers. He noted that the provincial tax collectors, who were subordinate to Petrov, were "issuing their own directives" and ignoring the party committee, producing a "total breakdown" in tax collections. Yezhov had arranged for the arrest of two senior tax collectors and their replacement with new officials from Moscow. In the same report, obliquely observing party etiquette that valued party discipline and proscribed personal attacks as beneath the dignity of a serious "businesslike" Communist, Yezhov said that Petrov had made himself so unpopular that he nearly had failed to be elected to the provincial party or soviet committees. Despite the fact that Petrov "had struggled against my [political] line since I arrived here," Yezhov wrote that only honorable, comradely, and persistent efforts by the (Yezhov-led) party group had saved everyone from embarrassment and secured Petrov's election.[30]

Petrov replied in kind with his own letters to Moscow officials. He had demanded the appointment of a Mari (instead of Yezhov) as party secretary, rather colorfully writing that "either Mari Oblast' will exist or else she will fall under the influence of Russian chauvinism, be tormented, and then die."[31] He wrote of the "degeneration and demoralization" of the Mari party under Yezhov, and asked the Central Committee to send an observer to the August 1922 Mari party conference to see for himself. This, he wrote in his usual hyperbole, was "necessary to save the party organization."[32]

This showdown conference in August 1922, with Central Committee Instructor Avdeev present, went badly for Petrov and marked the beginning of his fall, although he later remarked that "the beginning of the collapse started with Yezhov's arrival" in the spring.[33] In any event, Avdeev reported back to Moscow that of the two, Petrov bore more guilt for the dispute and consequent paralysis of the Mari organization. Even though Petrov was reelected to the leading party committee with Yezhov's "help," shortly after the conference the Buro of the Provincial Party Committee (doubtless with Central Committee support based on Avdeev's recommendation) voted to fire Petrov from his ispolkom chairmanship and place him "at the disposal of the Central Committee" for another assignment. The buro accused him of factionalism, causing a split in the obkom, discrediting party members, "uncommunist behavior," "compromising friendships" with dubious elements, and a relapse into his "old alcoholism." Soon after, the expanded leading party group, the obkom plenum, confirmed Petrov's firing on a 9–1 vote.[34] Later, Yezhov's supporters in the Mari Control Commission piled on additional charges, accusing Petrov of trying to "spark revolts" among the Mari and of writing to his supporters in Mari that they should get "ours" into power there. The provincial Control Commission recommended expelling him from the party, and there was talk of arresting him, although this seems never to have happened.[35]

The Mari provincial party committee and Control Commission had lined up against Petrov, but when the matter reached Moscow, those friendly to Petrov on the Orgburo formed a committee that recommended keeping him in Mari. Yezhov was in Moscow at the time and was ultimately successful in persuading the Orgburo to confirm the Mari decision to remove Petrov. But it was not easy, and Yezhov had to take an active hand in lobbying Moscow officials to remove his opponent. The final resolution from the CC showed signs of a compromise favorable to Yezhov and his group. Petrov was indeed to be fired, but the Yezhov group was cited for "insufficient involvement of Mari nationals" in leading party work. As Yezhov wrote to his friend Petr Ivanov back in Mari:

And now, I came to the CC from Kislovodsk, and—horror—I found out that, OK, you had removed Petrov and the Control Commission approved the removal, but when the question was discussed in Orgburo [Moscow], they formed a committee, and the committee thought that Petrov should be sent back to Mar-oblast' [Mari oblast'] to have him work further in the same direction. You understand what my position was: "I didn't know anything," but had to insist and press my line. Nevertheless, after long meetings, etc. (I myself talked to each and every member of the committee), I was able to solve the question about Petrov positively, i.e., confirm the verdict of the OK [to remove him]. The decision was approximately the following: taking into account his former line/policy, and his hysterical statements, etc., he should be removed. Second, taking into consideration the insufficient involvement of the Mari nationals in the work, the oblastkom should pay attention to it. That's it. They wanted to insert something else, but it was too late.[36]

It is a sign of the shortage of administrative cadres that a character such as Petrov was eventually given a new post in Vologda.

Yezhov's victory over Petrov could be seen as another triumph of Great Russian chauvinism. After all, Petrov had championed the cause of Mari over Russian Communists, and the Central Committee had sided against him. But aside from clear indications of Mari-Russian friction, we know very few of the details of ethnic relations in the province.

It was often the case that Moscow's policies on such things as tax collection, agricultural policy, or redrawing district boundaries could stir up various ethnic frictions even though they had been adopted without nationality in mind. In several cases, proposed changes in provincial or district (*raion*) borders had the unintended effect of disadvantaging one or another ethnic group. The same land policies emanating from Moscow could hurt Mari in the Mari region and Russians in Kazakhstan, leading to charges of Mari or Kazakh chauvinism vs. Russian chauvinism. In other words, ethnic issues cut across many lines of policy in various places, and one is hard-pressed to see a consistent long-term policy of russification or nativization in this period.[37]

Moreover, Petrov's defeat seems to have as much to do with his own unpopularity and Yezhov's rapidly improving bureaucratic skills than it did with ethnic issues. Petrov was a difficult character: a loud and insulting alcoholic given to tantrums and hurling insults at his coworkers. One Moscow report described him as "so energetic as to be disturbing" and "chronically dissatisfied with everybody." On one occasion when he was offended, he refused to go to work at the provincial executive committee for two weeks.[38] By contrast, Yezhov seems to have had little difficulty winning over a majority of the local Communists, including those Mari who thought Petrov had gone too far.

His victory over Petrov left Yezhov in sole control of Mari region, but the sweetness was certainly tempered by the fact that he did not want to remain there forever. Like most party workers sent to the provinces, he dreamed of returning to the center or at least to an industrial area where he felt at home and where he could build a career. At about the time Petrov was being removed, Yezhov confided his feelings to an old friend in an informal (and characteristically ungrammatical) personal letter. Without revealing any of the details of his sordid political fight with Petrov, he wrote to his friend Berzina that he was terribly busy and lived "like a cockroach on a hot skillet." He went on:

I tell you that you can't find holes like this anywhere in the whole RSFSR—it's the original godforsaken place—really, Krasnokokshaisk, you can't imagine. Well, the hell with it. I tell you that you can say whatever you want about the low level of culture we have to deal with, but here ____. Well, the hell with it, it's my lot in life. To tell the truth, I'm so fed up with all the paper shuffling that it's time to go back to the factory. Lately I've missed factory life; it's time for a rest and to completely say good-bye to this whole situation.[39]

Nevertheless, Yezhov had assembled a group of comrades and friends around him in Mari. While in Moscow awaiting the outcome of the Petrov decision, he had written to a friend back in Mari about "our guys": "Now, if I by any chance can't come back, I'd like to have some memories from the guys from Krasnokokshaisk, Kosmodemiansk, of course from our guys. I think if it turns out that I'm leaving, you should take a photo of you all and send it to me. That's all for now. Anyways, my friend, there are very good guys there, though young."[40]

It seemed that Yezhov had won in Mari.[41] But at the precise moment of his apparent victory, he too was recalled from Mari. Again we lack details, but we do know that an Orgburo decision in early November extended Yezhov's annual "vacation" for another month at full salary, and we know that he never returned to his post in Mari. By January a new responsible secretary had taken over.[42] On the one hand, Yezhov's removal seemed a demotion, coming as it did at the moment of his victory over Petrov. On the other, he seems to have wanted and perhaps even lobbied to be taken out of Mari. He wrote his friend Ivanov about the Moscow party personnel administration, "Now about myself, here goes. I'm only telling you and mind you don't tell anybody yet. They agree to remove me from there. Everybody agreed except the Org-Instrukt Department, but there is already full agreement with Syrtsov and with Kuibyshev. Here's how it will be: I will go on vacation for a month, and in the meantime the Obkom of Marilanda will find me a replacement and I'll be transferred."[43]

Two elements of party policy were at work here. First, Moscow was sensitive about ethnic conflicts getting out of control. So when a conflict threatened peaceful relations between nationalities, it was often the Central Committee's decision to remove any suggestion of Russian chauvinism and to recall officials who might be identified with the tendency. The party's presence and control in non-Russian areas was thin and weak, and matters were difficult enough for the Bolsheviks without leaving any whiff of discrimination when it could be avoided. Since Yezhov's triumph might be seen as an insult to or oppression of the Mari, it was safest to remove him from the picture.

Second, the Yezhov-Petrov squabble was only one among many taking place in party committees in both Russian and non-Russian areas that were handled by transferring both combatants from the scene of the fight. The constant fighting, personal sniping, and appeals to Moscow were tiresome and inefficient; they tended to paralyze party work in the entire region. But they were common in this period. Yezhov had been sent to Mari by the Central Committee as responsible party secretary. One might think that he would immediately take charge and be obeyed, but this was not the case. Personal networks were so entrenched in local party organizations that newcomers, even if they came as chiefs with Moscow mandates, were not always able to take charge. When A. I. Mikoian was sent to Nizhnyi Novgorod, it took him nearly a year to establish his authority and overcome local "clan" resistance. In Mari, Yezhov established himself as unquestioned chief only with great difficulty, and the archives are full of similar cases in which leaders established from Moscow were either recalled or ejected by the locals.[44]

Since 1918 Moscow party leaders had complained about these personal squabbles. In 1919 G. Zinoviev told the CC that regular transfer of cadres from place to place was a good way to resolve local conflicts.[45] From 1919 to 1921 Central Committee Secretary for Personnel N. Krestinsky, regularly discussed such "squabbles" (*skloki*) at open party congresses. He noted that the CC was frequently obliged to transfer leading comrades from place to place ("to no less responsible positions") in order to break up cliques, although unlike Zinoviev he saw the transfers as a last resort after other means had failed. The pages of the CC's journal *Izvestiia TsK* are filled with discussions of these feuds, and Krestinsky specifically mentioned the most serious in Kazan, Saratov, Voronezh, and Briansk.[46]

For example, in Kostroma "certain comrades who love to push 'their opinions' everywhere cannot cooperate and by their activities divide comrades into 'your' and 'our' groups of partisans." In Astrakhan squabbles divided Communists into "old Astrakhaners" whose "localism" was based on alleged "special conditions in Astrakhan" vs. "newcomers from outside." The result paralyzed the party organization. In Arkhangelsk, Comrade Kulikov created around him "a tight group of offensive drunks" to run the party organization.[47] A celebrated battle between the party's Siberian Regional Buro and the Omsk party organization over prerogatives to appoint personnel involved local press battles, mutual party expulsions, and mass threats to resign from the party. Eventually, the Central Committee had to dissolve the Omsk organization, expel many of its leading party officials, and order a "re-registration" of party members in the area.[48]

At party congresses in 1921 and 1922, CC Secretary V. Molotov discussed some of the reasons for these conflicts, which included struggles between strong personalities and their clients, young and older party members, urban and rural cadres, local and recently arrived leading cadres (as with Yezhov in Mari), and returning Red Army Communists and the established leaderships, as well as disputes over nationality policy or simply between rival strong personalities with their followings. As Stalin told a party congress, "all these heterogeneous elements which go up to make the provincial committees bring with them different attitudes, traditions, and tastes, and on this basis brawls and feuds erupt." Real issues of principle were almost never involved.[49] Molotov agreed with his predecessor Krestinsky on the use of personnel reassignment as a last resort to stop the feuds, and he itemized the methods the Central Committee used before turning to reassignment: highlighting the conflict in the party press, sending secret CC letters to the party organization, and dispatching CC representatives (*instruktory*) to the scene to try to make peace. Only when these tactics failed was it appropriate to reassign leading cadres elsewhere, and even then there were several approaches: removal of a few key players, recall of one of the feuding groups, or, in extreme cases, recall of both feuding groups, to be replaced by entirely new party staffs.[50] This drastic "plague on both your houses" solution seems to have been especially prevalent when ethnic or national conflicts were part of the dispute.

Despite its local bitterness, the Mari dispute did not receive coverage at party congresses. Other feuds were much worse. But the CC's handling of the matter followed the procedure outlined by Molotov. The CC had sent at least two "party letters" to the Mari party organization, and there had been at least two visits by CC Instructors Kubiak and Avdeev. Finally, when all else failed in a conflict that threatened to have ethnic overtones, the leaders of both the Petrov and Yezhov factions were removed. A Central Committee reporter on the Mari feud noted, "I am inclined to think that Petrov is mainly at fault. [But] maybe it will be necessary to take measures not only against him."[51] Shortly thereafter, Yezhov joined Petrov as a recalled official. (Matters did not improve in Mari. In the following years, Yezhov's replacement I. I. Ivanov also became involved in personal squabbles, charges and counter-charges of criminal activity.)[52]

An anonymous performance report on Yezhov's work in Mari was critical, noting that even though he showed no signs of careerism or squabbling, he had a tendency to "one-man decision making and stubbornness bordering on bad temper and irascibility." The report added that his early "blunders" in Mari were "objectively understandable" because his lack of formal Marxist education and preparation left him without "the possibility to orient himself in especially complicated leadership situations." Yezhov was aware of his theoretical limitations. He used his vacation time to read Lenin, writing to a friend, "I'm also reading, finally got to do it, read already 2 volumes of Lenin, I'm studying the line of Vladimir Il'ich."[53] The same performance report, though it praised Yezhov's initiative, energy, connection with the masses, and ability to carry out practical work, suggested that he might best be used in a working-class province as a party leader of second or third rank.[54]

Nevertheless, Yezhov received generally positive work evaluations on his work in Mari. A report about him dated September 1922 noted that his proletarian origins gave him great authority among nonparty workers. He was said to be a good organizer who worked independently, showed initiative, and brought matters to conclusion. He was self-reliant and energetic, without careerist ambitions or any tendency toward bureaucratism.[55]

Even though the secret police reported at the time of Yezhov's departure that the state of the Mari party organization was "satisfactory," Yezhov's debut as a responsible party leader was something less than a complete success, and his official biographies in subsequent years would not mention it.[56] He seems to have moved back and forth between Kazan and Moscow, first on paid vacation and then "at the disposal of the Central Committee," until 1 March 1923. But his experience in Mari apparently did not outweigh either the shortage of good administrators or his demonstrated skill as an up-and-coming party worker. In discussions in the Central Committee in November 1922, Yezhov was first offered party secretary posts in Orel, Briansk, Northern Dvinsk, and the Urals. He wrote to a friend, "The choice is mine, but I haven't thought about it yet."[57]

His friends from Kazan wanted him to return to work with them. But despite his rough time in Mari, he still felt a party duty not to abandon the Mari party organization and his "guys" there. As he wrote to his friend Petr Ivanov,

Now about me. I hardly arrived Kazan when the guys from the Obkom came to me in a car and took me along to a conference that was taking place here at the time, and immediately, not letting me come to my senses, they wanted to get me into the Bureau of the OK. I hardly could persuade them not to do it, pointing at the absurdity of doing it to a person who still had another job. But it was not the end of it, they even didn't want to let me go from Kazan, didn't want to let me go to Moscow and come back, and I think (with confidence now) they wanted to make me stay by all means they had. You of course will ask my opinion. Here's what I think, frankly: of course, it is possible to change "Marlandia" [the Mari region] for Tataria, and it's even profitable, but there is a "but" here that makes one think twice, and first of all—it's about the state of the Mari organization, I, being a party guy, can't watch calmly the agony of the organization in Marlandia. And the second reason is all these promises I had given about coming back, etc. Of course it's nonsense, a promise, especially such as I gave, of course it's possible to break such promises, it's nonsense, but it can badly influence the "guys" [in Mari] especially, the locals, and it will make them view any newcomer as a barnstormer. And the third reason is the quarrels here in the Kazan organization. There'll be a lot of work, but it's not important, of course, if unity in Marlandia could be preserved if I leave, then, I repeat, it would be possible to change "Red Kokshogu" for Kazan.

I'll not write about the reasons that make the local guys press me to stay here [Kazan], and it's not worth writing, but they are in a very difficult position, and they put their hopes on me thinking I can uphold the class line.[58]

His friends from his former post in Kazan and Vitebsk lobbied for him to be sent there, but in late February, he was offered his choice of party secretary positions in Penza, Astrakhan, Semipalatinsk, or Pskov.[59] Yezhov and the Central Committee finally agreed on Semipalatinsk, and in early March 1923 the Orgburo assigned him to the post of party secretary of the Semipalatinsk provincial committee in central Asian Kirgizia. He was simultaneously awarded a three months' salary bonus at the level of responsible party worker.[60]

As with his appointment to Mari a year before, Yezhov must have viewed the Semipalatinsk assignment with mixed feelings. On the one hand, it was a major step upward for his career. Covering an area more than twenty times the size of Mari province, Semipalatinsk had a party organization ten times as large as the Mari organization: six thousand members organized into three hundred party cells, sixty-one of which were urban.[61] This was no backwoods Mari; Semipalatinsk was a major province, and with nearly a thousand proletarians in its party organization, it was a Bolshevik stronghold in Muslim Central Asia. He wrote to Ivanov, "The work is interesting, the organization is large (six thousand people), [there are foreign economic] concessions, Altai mountains, etc."[62]

But the assignment was also fraught with peril. As in Mari, the situation in Central Asia involved national frictions between ethnic groups. Kirgiz and other non-Russians outnumbered the Russian population by about three to two, which was roughly the proportion of non-Russians to Russians in Mari.[63] Russian and Kirgiz party members eventually would fracture and factionalize against each other in complicated ways. As in Mari, the native population was generally uneducated and of dubious loyalty to the Bolshevik cause. The thousand proletarian members of the Semipalatinsk party were a drop in the bucket, considering that the province's population was more than a million. At exactly this time, the Central Committee reported to the 12th Party Congress that the "political level" in Kirgizia was low. So weak was the Bolshevik presence in such places that the party had difficulty finding party secretaries with the requisite experience or even the required term of years in the party.[64] Here, as in other non-Russian territories, there were relatively few proletarians, and the "native intelligentsia," often traditional and hostile to Bolshevism, had great influence.[65]

Kirgizia was in crisis. Secret police reports described terrible problems. Mounted bandit gangs of up to two hundred members stalked the territory, stealing livestock and robbing and beating the population. In one instance, a Turkmen gang made off with three hundred cattle and forty "prisoners" they intended to hold for ransom. Frequent harvest failures led to hunger, anger and panic among the population, which turned to "food substitutes." There were outbreaks of malaria, and the state was able to provide practically no medical assistance.[66]

The peasant population, mostly Kirgiz, was in a constant state of protest—sometimes nearing revolt—about high taxes and related disputes about land allocation and valuation. Both party and secret police reports noted that drunken tax collectors beat the taxes out of Kirgiz peasants. Beatings and fistfights were common responses to tax collection, and tax evasion was chronic.[67] According to one report, tax collection had been completed on time but only at great "social cost." In one case, a peasant froze to death when tax collectors locked him in a barn for eight days for tax evasion. The party recommended arresting several of these renegade tax officials and sending them to drumhead military tribunals for misconduct. Moreover, the report went on, former soldiers of General Kolchak's anti-Bolshevik White Army had joined the party organization and as tax collectors used "beastly methods" against the population.[68]

And the party organization was in disarray. A letter from the Semipalatinsk provincial party secretary to the Central Committee written in February 1923 bemoaned the state of the party there and may well have occasioned Yezhov's dispatch to the province less than three weeks later.[69] At the same time, a summary of the situation in Semipalatinsk prepared at this time for the 12th Party Congress was no more optimistic about the party organization itself: "The condition of the party organization is grave, even aside from the squabbles and factions. There is a strong increase in drunkenness, property accumulation, weak discipline, and even guerilla aberrations and methods" among party members.[70] Very little political education, agitation, or other "party work" was taking place among the Kirgiz, with the exception of some organization of Kirgiz women in the city. The provincial party committee had virtually no connection with the localities, and had no instructors to visit them. The rural agricultural cooperatives—traditionally among the few well-organized rural organizations—were dominated by hostile Socialist Revolutionaries and well-to-do peasants (kulaks); they contained virtually no Kirgiz members.[71]

Police reports also described massive corruption in the party and state apparatus, but typically blamed the problem on "kulak elements" who had penetrated the apparatus. Bribery, drunkenness, and general "laziness" were common. In one place, a supply chief was siphoning grain off the harvest collections and selling it at half price for personal profit. In another district, the local prosecutor punished peasants who complained about high taxes by extorting two thousand rubles and two hundred puds of opium from them.[72]

Yezhov had his work cut out for him, and sometime in March 1923 he and Antonina made their way to Kirgizia. Antonina, who had worked as chief of agitation and propaganda for the Mari obkom, now found a position as head of the Press Department of the Semipalatinsk party gubkom.[73] Typically, there was confusion surrounding her new appointment. In March 1923 the Central Committee assignment apparatus Uchraspred sent an urgent telegram to Mari demanding to know "immediately" why Antonina Titova had been "removed" from the Mari Agitprop department and where she was currently working. In fact, Uchraspred itself had formally transferred her to Semipalatinsk.[74]

Throwing himself into the work with his customary energy, Nikolai Yezhov quickly sized up the party situation in Semipalatinsk and produced a lengthy report to the Central Committee in June. In the party report style that he had mastered so well (perhaps with some help from Antonina), his text was full of apparently frank and objective detail. It also incorporated the by-now standard "although" style: Yezhov frankly admitted "shortcomings" and problems while foregrounding pending improvements. In so doing, he implied that he was responsible for a turnaround without saying so in as many words, which would have seemed self-promoting and incongruous with Bolshevik traditions of modesty and impersonal speech.

Former White Army soldiers, Yezhov wrote, had "penetrated" the provincial land office "although" SRs and Mensheviks had practically no influence in the province. Although there had been an increase in support for the Bolsheviks from some poor peasants, kulaks had a "hostile attitude" toward the Bolsheviks; they had penetrated the cooperatives and were trying to turn the poor peasants against "Soviet power" by, among other things, running candidates for local Soviet elections. There had been a disturbing growth in religion, including a rise in support for "sectarians" and Baptists (which Yezhov misspelled) even among returning Red Army soldiers, although party agitational work was better and improving every month. There had also been a growth of Kirgiz clan-based hostility toward the regime, and traditional clan leaderships were still hostile to the party. However, this was always the case around the time of Soviet elections and in any case in some places clan loyalties were fortunately giving way to class hostility of the poor against the traditional leaders.[75]

Soon after his arrival, Yezhov faced an uprising in the countryside. His hagiographer Alexander Fadeev tells us that the unrest was caused by an "incorrect understanding" of the private property relations of the New Economic Policy. Given what we know about discontent among Kirgiz peasants, this probably refers to a land dispute. Fadeev also tells us that at great personal risk the brave Yezhov traveled alone to the rebellious self-proclaimed "Bukhtarma Republic" and put down the revolt single-handedly, although photos from the time suggest that he had considerable assistance.[76]

Despite the difficulties, Yezhov's work had so impressed his superiors, both locally and in Moscow, that after a year in Semipalatinsk, he was promoted in May 1924 to head the Organizational Department (ORPO) of the entire Kirgiz obkom. This made him responsible for all personnel assignments in Kirgizia. Several months later (by December 1924) he had become a full secretary of the Kirgiz Obkom, and in October 1925 he was made deputy responsible secretary of the Kazakhstan Territorial Party Committee and chief of its personnel (ORPO) department.[77]

He demonstrated a certain deftness in dealing with subordinate organizations and mediating between them and Moscow. In October 1924 the First Secretary of the Akmolinsk Provincial Party Committee was recalled to Moscow. As their superior party organization, the Kirgiz Obkom suggested to the Akmolinsk comrades that they ask the Central Committee in Moscow to recommend a replacement from outside. The Akmolinsk party committee instead proposed the candidacy of their own comrade, one Chirkov, to the Kirgiz Obkom. At first it seemed that the local party leaders were trying to protect their own prerogatives against Moscow's centralization and wanted to promote one of their own number rather than accept an outside Moscow candidate. But the situation turned out to be more tactically complicated than that. In fact, the opposite was true.

Yezhov discovered that the Akmolinsk recommendation of Chirkov came on a vote of five in favor, four opposed, one abstaining, with all the Russians voting against Chirkov and all the Kirgiz members in favor. Yezhov wrote to Akmolinsk, "The obkom does not think it possible that it can confirm the candidacy of a secretary who did not receive a unanimous vote, or even a majority, and that reflected disagreement between the Kirgiz and Russian parts of the leadership." The Kirgiz Obkom then reported the strife in Akmolinsk to Moscow and again proposed to Akmolinsk that it seek a nomination from the Central Committee.

This time, the truth came out. As it happened, Yezhov learned, the Akmolinsk comrades had deliberately and artificially staged a split vote to suggest serious dissension in its ranks, "not as any principled disapproval of Chirkov, but rather in the hope that they could get an extra worker from the Central Committee." Knowing that Moscow was short of skilled cadres for Central Asia, the Akmolinsk comrades were afraid that if they asked the Central Committee, Moscow would simply pick among the leaders already in Akmolinsk. Knowing also that Moscow was quick to send new party workers to places troubled by ethnic conflict, the Akmolinsk comrades faked a local conflict, hoping that the maneuver of a split vote would stampede the CC into sending them another pair of hands. Far from resisting Moscow's centralizing power of appointment, the Akmolinsk party committee was counting on it to send them help. As was often the case in these years, the shortage of administrative talent in the party was far more important than protection of turf.[78]

The Akmolinsk maneuver did not work. Caught in the act, Akmolinsk quickly voted again, this time unanimously for Chirkov. Yezhov and the Kirgiz obkom approved and the matter ended. In his final letter to Akmolinsk, Yezhov chided the provincial communists for their trickery and for making both Akmolinsk and the Kirgiz obkom look bad. But he also made clear that the storm was over:

One has to wonder what to make of [your] plenum meetings, which in the discussion of a new gubkom secretary managed to produce a 5–4–1 vote and somehow expected the obkom to approve. Do you really think it is proper to vote for or against a party secretary in order to get an extra worker from the Central Committee? Do you really think it is all right that after two telegrams from us recommending that you ask the CC, and after we had notified the CC of all this, that we and the CC suddenly and unexpectedly find out that you had then suddenly voted unanimously for Chirkov and that your [real] motive, to receive a new worker from the CC, was unknown to us until it fell on our heads at the last minute? The obkom hopes that now . . . it has become clear [to you] the position you put the obkom in with your peculiar vote. . . . The obkom regrets that, despite the obvious mistakes of the Akmolinsk gubkom, it was necessary for us to return to this problem which now we can regard as ancient history. We suggest that by means of this comradely letter we will consider the matter closed.[79]

As an administrator, Yezhov had made the best of a bad situation. To his superiors in Moscow, he was a leader who had bothered to get the facts, to get to the bottom of a strange situation and sort it out (in the process saving Moscow the expense of another cadre). To his subordinates, he had shown that he could not be fooled so easily. But Yezhov also knew that he had to work smoothly with such committees in the future, and although he scolded the Akmolinsk party committee, he could have been far more severe. His rebuke of them was firm and on the record, but it was also moderate and measured.

Although Yezhov handled these bureaucratic tiffs well, there were some problems that seemed intractable, and they had to do with his old nemesis: the nationality question. In Kirgizia and in the Kirgiz part of Kazakhstan, ethnic tensions ran high. Secret police reports of 1923–25 on the mood of the population constantly mentioned Russian-Kirgiz conflict. Some of these conflicts were no doubt exacerbated by brutal and high-handed Russian tax collectors, but other issues—including land disputes—also raised the temperature. Fistfights broke out between Russians and Kirgiz over land rights, and occasionally the fights turned into armed conflicts. Some Kirgiz settlements wanted to deport all Russians from Kazakhstan, and one settlement drove out the Communists altogether. At a meeting in one settlement, a speaker said, "If things continue this way we will have to revolt." In other places, there was talk of forming an "autonomous Cossack republic," as well as bizarre rumors that Trotsky would soon arrive with a Russian military detachment to arrest non-Russian Kirgiz officials.[80]

Clan politics played an important role in Kirgizia. Some Kirgiz settlements insisted, for example, on administration of justice by local beys from their own clans.[81] But it was not only a matter of Russians vs. Kirgiz. As usual, members of the Russian party contingent had differing views about how to handle the Kirgiz. And among the Kirgiz, splits ran in several directions: between intelligentsia and worker, Bolshevik and anti-Bolshevik, eastern and western. Kirgiz clans fought each other, and sometimes one clan allied itself with Soviet officials against their Kirgiz rivals. In other places, clans struggled among themselves to control local soviet institutions.[82]

Socially, among the Kirgiz there was a split between the intelligentsia, many of whom had been members of the Alash-Orda movement, and the poor Kirgiz, who were more likely to be Bolshevik supporters.[83] A Kirgiz party secretary wrote to the Central Committee in 1924 about the split in his own party committee. He noted that there were also "eastern" and "western" groups of Kirgiz, with the westerners maintaining too close a tie with the Alash-Orda intelligentsia. The western group had the opposite fault; they were too hostile to the nonparty intelligentsia.[84]

Among the Kirgiz Bolsheviks, at least two factions contended with each other and with different groups of Russian Bolsheviks. Thus a Kirgiz party member named Dzhangildin wrote to Stalin in April 1925 about the alliance between some Russian party leaders and the Alash-Orda intelligentsia. Identifying himself as a poor Kirgiz, Dzhangildin identified party secretaries Naneishvili and Yezhov as leaders of a faction that "had nothing in common" with the proletariat and associated not only with Alash-Orda but with "bey elements" that represented the traditional elites in Kirgizia. They were helped, Dzhangildin wrote, by Communists like the "petty bourgeois" Kirgiz Khodzhanov, who was a "Turkestan Kirgiz" rather than a proper proletarian eastern Kirgiz. He accused Yezhov and Naneishvili of operating behind the back of Central Committee instructor Tolokontsev, telling the party committee in Tolokontsev's absence that they did not need him to decide things.

Dzhangildin went on to complain that Naneishvili and Yezhov had no understanding of Kirgiz society, with its loyalties of clan, lineage, and orda (a territorial designation that originally referred to a Mongol camp). He pointed out that Yezhov's Kirgiz allies, the Khodzhanov group and their "petty bourgeois" Alash-Orda friends, understood the Russians' ignorance of the real groupings in Kirgiz society and used that ignorance to their own advantage against other Kirgiz. Dzhangildin suggested that Stalin send a new party secretary to Kirgizia from Moscow, and helpfully offered to provide a list of reliable Kirgiz proletarians to staff a new territorial party committee. He included in his letter a traditional component of such petitions and complaints: a lengthy statement on his own revolutionary services.[85]

Ethnic conflict in Kirgizia seems to have been as severe as it had been in Mari, and once again Nikolai Yezhov had been accused of Russian chauvinism. Indeed he seems to have been censured formally by the party for it a year earlier, in mid-1924.[86] We have already noted that given the high emotions and complicated politics in such regions, it is difficult to evaluate such accusations, and Yezhov's Kirgiz experience shows that they can mask a more complicated reality that may well have been mixed up as much with personal rivalries as with ethnic conflict.

Central Committee secretaries were also receiving statements and complaints from other Kirgiz, and more than once Moscow fired off letters to the Kirgiz party organization demanding that they stop disagreements and skloki and work together, especially in the top provincial leadership.[87] The same Khodzhanov who had been the target of Dzhangildin's anger sent his own letter to Stalin in March 1925. His complaint was a more general one against Russians' chauvinistic relations with the Kirgiz people. After outlining some of the personal conflicts in the Kirgiz party committee, he launched into a bitter denunciation of Russians' haughty attitude toward their Kirgiz comrades in party organizations. Russians ordered Kirgiz around, saying "I want . . . " or "I forbid . . . " or "I am commissioned by the Central Committee . . . " Accordingly, there was a good deal of suspicion between the two groups, and the Kirgiz had formed their own mutual protection group within the territorial party committee. First Secretary Naneishvili apparently tried to referee and mediate between the two nationalities, but Khodzhanov wrote that when Naneishvili was absent, the Russians on the kraikom ignored Khodzhanov, who was second secretary of the kraikom.[88]

Two weeks earlier, Khodzhanov had asked the Kirgiz kraikom to relieve him of his duties as second secretary. He pointed out that he had no clearly assigned duties in the position; his subtext was that he had become mere ethnic window dressing for a Russian-dominated committee. The kraikom had refused but had resolved to draw up a specific division of responsibilities among the secretaries.[89]

Yezhov was third secretary of the Kirgiz organization, subordinate to First Secretary Naneishvili and responsible for personnel assignments throughout the province. We have seen his efficiency and bureaucratic skill in action, and by 1925 he seems to have taken upon himself most of the work of running the entire province. Khodzhanov ended his letter to Stalin with a recommendation in a "P.S.": "Comrade Naneishvili, even though he is a longtime member of the party, has a mental limitation that is intolerable in someone in his position: he is incapable of directing anyone or anything. Yezhov can. Consequently, it would be good to appoint Comrade Yezhov as First Secretary of the kraikom, so that he not only does everything but would be immediately responsible for it."[90]

Khodzhanov's postscript again confirms Yezhov's tremendous energy and ability in party administration: he was running the province from the position of third secretary. The note also shows how complicated the charges of "chauvinism" can be. Dzhangildin had accused Yezhov of ig-

norance of Kirgiz society and of running roughshod over Kirgiz sensibilities. But Khodzhanov, who also complained about Russian chauvinism
in general, had recommended the Russian Yezhov for the top position.

In the rough and tumble world of ethnic politics on the periphery,
there were no safe approaches. One could be solicitous and indulgent,
catering to the sensibilities of non-Russians, but such conduct could
earn one accusations of going overboard with anti-Russian chauvinism,
as it had for Yezhov's rival Petrov back in Mari. Or Russians could ig-
nore local traditions and draw upon themselves the opposite accusation
of chauvinism. One could even try to steer a middle road, working hard
to be fair and impartial, and still run afoul of the charge because of divisions between Russians and divisions between non-Russians.

We know virtually nothing about Nikolai Yezhov's attitudes toward
or relations with either the Mari or the Kirgiz Communists with whom
he worked. We do not know whether he was biased or impartial. We do
know that he and Naneishvili had made common cause with one group
of Kirgiz. Such an alliance, with some native group or another, was a
practical necessity for Bolshevik administrators who needed the help of
influential groups of local people. But this infuriated other local factions, with the result that some Kirgiz wanted to promote Yezhov and
others accused him of chauvinism. It was probably impossible to carry
out party work in these territories of mixed ethnicity without being accused of some kind of chauvinism at one time or another.

Kirgizia was far from Moscow, far from the capital with its culture,
influence and power. Those like Yezhov who found themselves on the
periphery did everything they could to move closer to the center. The
constant ethnic one-upmanship and backbiting made assignments on
the nationality periphery seem like an even crueler exile. Yet the more
Yezhov demonstrated his loyalty, faith in Bolshevik principles, capacity
for hard work, and administrative skill, the more valuable he became as
a provincial leader able to work well in difficult situations. Given the
shortage of available talent for such assignments, Yezhov's work history
and self-promotion actually made it less likely that he would be brought
to Moscow. He was too valuable where he was.

FOUR

## The Party Personnel System

*And so, comrades, if we want successfully to get over the shortage*
*of people and to provide our country with sufficient cadres capable*
*of advancing technique and setting it going, we must first of all*
*learn to value people, to value cadres, to value every worker*
*capable of benefiting our common cause.*

JOSEPH STALIN

The history of the party in the 1920s is usually understood in connection with Stalin's rise to power, which was facilitated by his control of the levers of personnel assignment. Usually, when we think about the Stalinist personnel system, we think about it as a tool Stalin used to gain power through patronage, by promoting those loyal to him and removing those who challenged him. According to the theory of "circular flow of power," party secretaries at all levels were appointed by Stalin and returned the favor by supporting him against his rivals.[1] Yezhov, like nearly all territorial party leaders, was a Stalin supporter. Moreover, he was later to have a key role in the persecution and physical annihilation of anti-Stalin dissidents, or "oppositionists," as they were called. At this point, then, it is important to survey the history of anti-Stalin oppositions in the 1920s and how that story relates to the party's early personnel system. In so doing, we shall see how Stalin commanded the loyalty of party apparatus workers like Yezhov.

The New Economic Policy (NEP), adopted in 1921, allowed free markets in agriculture and in small and medium industry. (The Bolsheviks retained nationalized heavy industry in their own hands.) Lenin saw this concession to a limited capitalism in the form of market mechanisms as a necessary measure to appease the peasants and to allow market forces to help rebuild the shattered economy. NEP always enjoyed mixed popularity among the Bolsheviks. Rightist Bolsheviks, who clustered around the economic theoretician and *Pravda* editor Nikolai Bukharin (and eventually the trade union leader Mikhail Tomsky and the Council of Commissars chairman Aleksei Rykov), saw NEP as a long-term strategy by which the party could maintain its alliance (*smychka*) with an increasingly prosperous peasantry. Funds for industrialization would be generated by rational taxation and the general growth of the economy. Leftist Bolsheviks, on the other hand, favored "squeezing" resources from the peasantry at a faster rate. Led by the Communist International and Leningrad party head Grigory Zinoviev, the Moscow party chief Lev Kamenev, and the brilliant Lev Trotsky, the leftists were impatient with what they considered coddling of the peasantry and pressed for a more militant and aggressive industrial policy.

Aware that disagreements could lead to splinter groups and split the party, Lenin was worried about maintaining iron discipline. At the very moment of victory in 1921 the Bolsheviks passed a resolution banning the formation of factions within their own party. Lenin's ideas of party organization, known as "democratic centralism," held that party policies should be adopted democratically, but that once a decision was taken it was the duty of all party members publicly to defend and support that decision whether or not they personally agreed with it. Rather loosely observed in the party before and during 1917, these norms received strong reinforcement in the desperate emergency of the Civil War, and party leaders of all kinds had little trouble institutionalizing them as a "ban on fractions" at the Tenth Party Congress in early 1921. The Bolsheviks' insecurity and apprehension told them that maintaining party discipline and unity was the key to survival and was more important than the right to bicker and disagree.

Overlaying and sharpening economic disagreements was a classic personal struggle for succession that followed Lenin's death in 1924. The struggle for power among the Olympian Bolshevik leaders was complicated but can be summarized quickly. Beginning in 1923, Trotsky launched a trenchant criticism of Stalin's "regime of professional secretaries," claiming that they had become ossified bureaucrats cut off from their proletarian followers. Trotsky also argued that the survival of the Bolshevik regime depended on support from successful workers' revolutions in Europe, and he accused Stalin and other leaders of losing interest in spreading the revolution. To the other Politburo leaders, Trotsky seemed the most powerful and the most dangerous. By common recognition he was, after Lenin, the most brilliant theoretician in the party. More important, he was the leader of the victorious Red Army and regarded as personally ambitious and a potential Napoleon of the Russian Revolution.

Bukharin, Zinoviev, Kamenev, and Stalin closed ranks to isolate Trotsky, accusing him of trying to split the party because of his personal ambition to lead it. They argued that Trotsky was only using "party democracy" as a phony political issue: during the Civil War he had never been for anything less than iron discipline. Now, they charged, his criticism weakened party unity. Faced with the unity of the other Politburo members, the party's near-religious devotion to party unity and discipline, and Stalin's influence among the party apparatus, Trotsky could not win. He was stripped of his military post in 1924 and gradually marginalized in the top leadership.[2]

The following year, Zinoviev and Kamenev split off from the party majority by launching their own critique of NEP from the leftist point of view. This New Opposition said that the NEP policy of conceding constantly increasing grain prices to the peasantry was depriving the state of capital for industrialization, bankrupting industry, confronting the proletariat with high bread prices, and indefinitely postponing the march to socialism. In 1926 Trotsky joined Zinoviev and Kamenev in the United Opposition. To the Leningrad and Moscow votes controlled by Zinoviev and Kamenev, Trotsky brought the remnants of his supporters.

Stalin and Bukharin denounced the United Opposition as another attempt to split the party by challenging the existing policy and violating the centralism part of democratic centralism. Bukharin's impressive pragmatic and theoretical defense of "Lenin's" NEP, combined with Stalin's low-key pragmatic approach, made a formidable combination. The votes from the party secretarial apparatus, loyal to Stalin and disinclined to provoke a dangerous turn in party policy, won the day, and the United Opposition went down to defeat in 1927.[3] Zinoviev and Kamenev were stripped of their most powerful positions. Trotsky was expelled from the party and exiled to Central Asia. Two years later, in 1929, he was deported from the country.

Stalin, as General Secretary of the Party, had influence among the growing full-time corps of professional party secretaries and administrators. Toward the end of the Civil War the Central Committee had formed three subcommittees to carry out the party's work between sittings of the full body: the Political Bureau (Politburo), the Organizational Bureau (Orgburo), and the Secretariat. Stalin alone sat on all three subcommittees.[4] Although he did not always attend meetings of the Orgburo or Secretariat, Molotov did. As we shall see, up to 90 percent of all personnel assignments were based on recommendations by Orgburo staff, rather than by Stalin, Molotov, or one of the top leaders. The top leaders, sitting on either the Secretariat or the Orgburo, were there to vet the recommendations they received, and they nearly always rubber-stamped staff appointment proposals, often in batches and by polling the members rather than by actually meeting. Certainly the CC staff responded to Stalin's and Molotov's instructions and political tastes, but the image of Stalin personally and politically deciding each appointment is not accurate.[5]

In the usual understanding of party politics in the 1920s, Stalin's ambition is the driving force, and the history of the party becomes synonymous with his rise to power. There is much truth in this view, and Stalin's rise to unchallenged personal power in the party is impossible to understand outside of his control of the personnel process. Yet this understanding is incomplete in important ways. It cannot explain key aspects of that evolution, including the broad consensus in the party—even among oppositionists—in favor of strong discipline, centralization of personnel assignment, and a firm "organizational line." Indeed, much of the impetus for centralizing personnel assignment and the creation of a full-time party apparatus came originally from anti-Stalin oppositionists. Nor can Stalin's ambition alone explain why as his power grew in the 1920s, the number of centrally controlled personnel appointments actually *declined* year to year. The Stalin-centered story overemphasizes his personal direction of the apparatus, its efficiency, and even the centrality of the struggle with the opposition. We are thus often inclined to see workers in the party apparatus as mere puppets, without any independent views, interests, or control over their fates and careers.

For example, by equating the rise of centralized personnel practices with Stalin's person, we have assumed that Yezhov's rise through that bureaucracy must have been due to Stalin's personal patronage, and Yezhov is often characterized as someone Stalin spotted early and whose career he nurtured, even though there is no evidence to support this view.

Looking at the party's personnel process from the beginning forward, rather than backward from Stalin's victory, produces a rather different picture. By examining the environment in which the system took shape, we are able to highlight historical and structural factors other than Stalin's personality that pushed the process forward. Stalin was, of course, an ambitious politician who used this process for his own ends. But the process of centralized and undemocratic personnel assignment predated his rise to power and evolved from objective dynamics that often had little to do with him. Even without an ambitious politician aiming for dictatorship, even without an internecine struggle for

Lenin's mantle, the process would have proceeded much the same because it was a logical response to the interaction of party traditions and goals in a difficult environment. In fact, Stalin did not invent or impose the patron-client system; it was inherent in the situation.[6]

Ironically, it was oppositionist criticism (of the chaos in personnel) and proposals that first led to the systematization and professionalization of these functions and to the creation of a secretarial apparatus that Stalin would later use against them. In 1919 the oppositionists V. V. Ossinsky and Timofei Sapronov led the call for a "strong" Secretariat with the ability to distribute personnel and for the creation of a group of fulltime professional party workers; Ossinsky complained that a real "Secretariat does not exist." The future oppositionist G. Zinoviev seconded their call and argued for the CC's right to shift personnel around as needed to break up cliques and ensure obedience.[7] Lev Trotsky told the 9th Party Congress that the party needed a strong "organizational center" with the ability to appoint provincial party secretaries, regardless of the electoral principle.[8]

Although some oppositionists quickly changed their minds about the benefits of a "strong" bureaucratic personnel system (especially when it was used against them), others remained ambivalent. In April 1923 the Trotskyist Ye. Preobrazhensky warned against the tendency to appoint rather than elect provincial party secretaries, but conceded that the Central Committee needed such authority.[9] As late as 1925, when he came into open opposition to the Stalin machine as head of a dissident Leningrad delegation at the 14th Party Congress, Zinoviev took pains to criticize only Stalin's "political line," not his personnel policies (the "organizational line").[10] Early oppositionist calls for a tighter party machine and their continued ambiguity on the question made it easy for supporters of the Stalin majority to heckle them for hypocrisy when they complained about Stalin taking "organizational measures" against them. Thus V. M. Molotov, I. P. Rumiantsev, and others chided Lev Kamenev in 1925 for being in favor of iron discipline and a hard "organizational line" only when he was in the majority.[11] Martymian Riutin, who was to be shot in 1937 for writing a sharp condemnation of Stalin's rule in 1932, must have rued his 1923 statement that it was natural to have a stable leading group: "A party that discredits its leaders is unavoidably weakened. Parties are always led by chiefs [*vozhdy*]."[12]

Nikolai Yezhov probably agreed. He watched much of this struggle from far off Kirgizia, where, as we have seen, he was stationed until 1926. Like his fellow regional party secretaries, Yezhov probably had a narrow understanding of the inner dynamics of the party fights, first between Stalin and Trotsky and then between Stalin and Zinoviev. Much of their information came through official party channels that Stalin loyalists controlled, and Yezhov and his fellows almost certainly had a one-sided picture of the issues and dynamics behind the political struggles in Moscow. They also interpreted the struggle both personally and in their own terms as provincial secretaries.

The struggles and debates among the top contenders for Lenin's succession were always presented in terms of principled positions. The speeches in which hopefuls presented their candidacies to the party masses were invariably about agricultural and industrial options, foreign policy, and other grand strategies, and were always couched in and buttressed by theoretical references to the writings of Marx and Lenin.

But the truth is that all of them changed their principled positions constantly. Stalin's flip-flops are well known. An opponent of using bourgeois specialists in the Civil War, he defended them in the early 1920s, then attacked them again in 1928, then defended them again in the early 1930s. A staunch defender of the mixed-economy gradualism of NEP for most of the 1920s, he suddenly lurched to the left at the end of the decade and occupied a position not far from Trotsky's, which he had bitterly attacked just months before. Zinoviev and Kamenev, who had strongly supported a conciliatory policy toward peasants in 1924, attacked Stalin and Bukharin for that very thing in 1925–27. Trotsky, the ultimate disciplinarian of the Civil War, who had argued that party members should unquestioningly go where they were sent, had suddenly become a champion of inner-party democracy by 1923. Zinoviev, who had loudly and brashly attacked Trotsky's ideas on party life and the economy, was by 1925 saying that Trotsky was right.

To a great extent, therefore, the struggle of the party titans in the 1920s was a struggle of personalities, each of whom deployed personal political machines and defended or criticized policies as needed.[13] Most mid- and lower-level party members tended to attach themselves permanently to one or another of the top leaders, following him through his ideological and policy twists and turns. There were more or less consistent personal loyalties: regardless of the current ideological position of one of the top leaders, party members identified themselves as "Trotskyists," "Stalinists," or "Zinovievists." Loyalty and patronage were major parts of this struggle. Everything was personal. Motivations for attaching oneself to a major leader varied. It is easy to imagine personal ambition leading one to become one of the "-ists" in the expectation that one's career would rise with that of the patron. But it would also not be surprising to find midlevel party officials making calculations according to their specific work interests.

Yezhov, like his fellow regional party secretaries, owed his appointment to the Central Committee secretarial apparatus that Stalin dominated. Even though they probably had never met him, party secretaries in the provinces surely thought of him as the "boss" of the party chain of command of which they were part. His leadership of the apparatus that gave them their jobs was a crucial element in their loyalty to him. But bosses do not always automatically command the support and loyalty of their subordinates. Explaining their support of him purely as loyalty to a patron does not give us the whole picture. If Stalin had lost and Trotsky or Zinoviev had won, secretaries like Yezhov could easily have cut a deal with a new boss. Given the crying shortage of administrative talent and the reluctance of many Bolsheviks to take provincial posts, regional secretaries need not have feared wholesale purging or replacement in case of a Stalin defeat. They were valuable people with cards to play. To fully explain their support for Stalin, we need to look further into the precise situation in which these secretaries found themselves and the ways in which they understood their individual and corporate interests. To put the question another way, why was Stalin more appealing to them than Trotsky, Zinoviev, or any of the oppositionists?

First, many of the criticisms raised by the oppositionist challengers had little relevance to the day-to-day work and concerns of party workers in the provinces. Trotsky's and Zinoviev's critiques of Stalin's policy on the Chinese and German revolutions, their hairsplitting about theories of permanent revolution or "primitive socialist accumulation"—such issues seemed wholly irrelevant to them. Indeed, to those like Yezhov trying to govern with few loyal party supporters in a sea of hostile social and religious forces, it must have seemed bizarre, even annoying, to make so much of events in far-off places when matters were so dire right here at home, where violent bandits could still ride down on Soviet settlements and ambush party members. The oppositionists' concerns must have made Stalin's critics seem hopelessly out of touch.

Second, for those party workers who followed the twists and turns of the struggle for power in Moscow, it was easy to see the oppositionist leaders as opportunists and hypocrites on the question of party discipline. In their times, each of the oppositionist movements, from the Democratic Centralists to the Workers' Opposition to the Trotskyists to the Zinoviev-Kamenev group, had called for centralization and strict punitive personnel measures against the others for violating party discipline. Many remembered that it had been the oppositionist Democratic Centralists who had called for the creation of a powerful CC apparatus with a strong secretary at the helm. Now, though, when they had gone over to opposition, they had become champions of leniency, a soft interpretation of party discipline, the right to criticize, and the right to be immune from punitive "organizational measures" in the area of personnel. Because he always found himself in the majority, Stalin at least had a consistent record on party discipline.

Third, party workers trying to hold their committees together in the face of chronic and perennial local personal spats and conflicts placed a premium on unity and pulling together to do the job. The oppositionist groups had been the ones to challenge the status quo by launching their various critiques of the Stalinist majority. Right or wrong, they were dissidents and were rocking the boat. The principled critiques by local oppositionists not only were implicit challenges to the unity and patronage control shaped by the local secretary but were also disruptive sallies that weakened the local party effort by threatening to split it. Whatever the merits of the oppositionist critiques, anything that endangered the unity of local party cells was unwelcome to those in charge.

Too many of them remembered how the unpleasant personal squabbles (*skloki*) of the early 1920s had paralyzed the party in the provinces, and the oppositionists' challenge looked like just another divisive squabble. It was easy to think of them as squabblers (*sklokisty*). As we have seen, Yezhov had become involved in these personal battles and groupings, which in the 1920s were chronic in the party system. Sometimes these personal factional fights could paralyze the entire party organization. We can easily imagine that young party officials like Yezhov saw the challenge of the opposition in these terms, as a personalized *sklok*. Absent regular institutions and rules, personal links were not just adjuncts of ideology or bureaucracy, they were the very essence, the "sinews" of the system.[14]

The most general and decisive reason for the party secretaries' support for Stalin had to do with their basic aversion to risk. Many of them, Nikolai Yezhov included, found themselves in precarious positions. Party saturation in many provinces—the numerical strength of party membership—was dangerously low, and while the party's representatives could count on the backing of the police and army if necessary, they still felt themselves isolated from much of the population, which was not proletarian, and often not Russian. They never felt ultimately secure. In this besieged situation, they were responsible for carrying out an ever-increasing list of tasks from education to political indoctrination to party recruitment to agricultural policy to tax collection. They were overwhelmed and understaffed and often thought of themselves operating in hostile territory. The last thing they needed or wanted was a new personalized factional spat that could weaken not only their personal leadership but party work in general.

From their insecure position, any challenge to the precarious status quo must have seemed risky and dangerous. The party had swollen since the Civil War with the addition of millions of raw, untested members without revolutionary background and experience. Opening the party to full party democracy and control from below, as Trotsky argued in 1924, threatened not only their positions as local leaders but also the stability of the party and its traditions. What did the callow, ignorant youths and self-seeking newcomers who had recently joined the winning side know about the party or its goals? Cracking down on the economic liberties and position of peasants, who were the majority of the population—as Zinoviev and Kamenev suggested in 1925—seemed risky and even suicidal to the party's representatives in the countryside.

The party chain of command leading from them up to Stalin's CC secretarial apparatus was their lifeline. Without it, they would drown in a sea of local frictions, hostile social groups, and anti-Bolshevik sentiments based on everything from religion to nationality. The lifeline seemed thin and shaky, often held together by a single telegraph or telephone line over great distances. In the 1920s these local leaders were not interested in autonomy from Moscow or fearful of encroaching centralization. Quite the contrary: the line to Moscow was the source of support, reinforcements, resources, and, if necessary, defense. As we saw in Yezhov's handling of matters in Akmolinsk, local party committees wanted people sent to them from Moscow, and a variety of sources shows that before, during, and after the struggles with the opposition, they were desperate for Moscow's help and guidance on matters ranging from propaganda to personnel. Anything that shook things up jeopardized that lifeline. Busy as they were trying to implement Soviet policies (and sometimes just to keep their party committees together), they had no interest in shakeups, challenges, or disruptions. They were just too risky, and Stalin seemed the stable choice. His ability to portray himself as the injured party and to wail about the precarious nature of the Bolsheviks in general in the face of hostile encirclement and internal opposition just served to reinforce the risk aversion that provincial party leaders felt anyway. These party leaders were not simply Stalin's stooges. They had their own problems and interests, and even if Stalin had not been the one to give them their jobs, they probably would have supported him or anyone else who promised a stable party structure. And as good (or at least willing) provincial administrators at a time when such people were hard to find, their support was crucial. They were not merely clients or stooges of this or that Moscow grandee.

Stalin was an attractive leader for many other reasons. Unlike the other top leaders, he was not an intellectual or theoretician. He spoke a simple and unpretentious language suited to a party increasingly made up of workers and peasants. His style contrasted sharply with that of his Politburo comrades, whose complicated theories and pretentious demeanor won them few friends among the plebeian rank and file. He also had an uncanny way of projecting what appeared to be moderate solutions to complicated problems. Unlike his colleagues who seemed shrill in their warnings of fatal crises, Stalin frequently put himself forward as the calm man of the golden mean, with moderate, compromise solutions.

Nikolai Yezhov had first attended a party congress, the 14th, in December 1925 as a nonvoting provincial delegate from Kirgizia. Although he did not speak there and we have no record of his impressions, we can imagine that as a hardworking provincial party worker beset with problems including local hostility, he was horrified at what he saw and heard. At the 14th Congress, Zinoviev and Kamenev led a unified oppositionist Leningrad delegation in an attack on Stalin and his leadership. Zinoviev broke with the traditional united Politburo report and gave what he called a coreport that was sharply critical of Stalin's Politburo majority.

His attack was seconded by several well-known members of a Leningrad delegation that, while calling for party democracy, had rigged elections there to ensure that only oppositionists represented the city. A series of rather self-righteous (and, given identical practices against the opposition in the rest of the country, hypocritical) reports produced by the CC documented Zinoviev's Leningrad machine's crude use of patronage and electoral "repression" of pro-Moscow candidates. Antiopposition petitions were ignored, meetings were broken up, voting was faked.[15]

Other speakers at the Congress pointed out that the oppositionists had been all for discipline when they were in the majority and now suddenly were for open criticism.[16] Not even pleading from Lenin's widow, Nadezhda Konstantinovna Krupskaya, for sympathy toward the Leningraders could overcome the indignation felt by most delegates at what they regarded as Zinoviev's attempt to divide and split the party for reasons of personal ambition. The delegates laughed at her and at Kamenev's plea not to apply personnel sanctions against those who used their right to voice their opinions at party congresses.

We can safely assume that Yezhov was among the party workers who hooted and jeered Kamenev's call to replace the CC leadership and Zinoviev's suggestion to abandon the 1921 ban on factions. Party secretaries like Yezhov wanted a stable central leadership prepared to support local party committees and protect them from disruption and, if need be, their own populations. Oppositionist critiques and now their open sally against the party, which party organizers like Yezhov must have regarded as unseemly and out of line, were simply too risky.

There is no doubt that Stalin used his control over personnel to maintain his position and to weaken his critics. But so did Zinoviev, Trotsky, and all the other top competitors. Patronage was not just a feature of the system, it was the system itself. Stalin's actions against his rivals in the 1920s were nothing like the lethal force he would apply in the 1930s and tended to be measured and incremental. Throughout most of the decade, such "organizational measures" were aimed not so much at firing or demoting oppositionists but at breaking up concentrations of them. As we have seen, when a struggle between two factions (whether based on personal cliques or on political argument) paralyzed a party committee, the CC stepped in and either sent an emissary or removed one or both factions. The same techniques were used to break up oppositional concentrations in party committees, whose dissident members were dispersed to new positions. Celebrated cases in the Urals and Ukraine at the beginning of the 1920s followed this pattern, as party committees that had gone wholly over to the opposition had their members dispersed to new positions. This was the case following the

14th Congress, when Zinoviev's dissident Leningraders were "exiled" from the city to new (but not necessarily lower-ranking) positions elsewhere.

When this happened, Stalin and his supporters always had plausible justifications that sounded more practical than political. How could the party tolerate oppositionists rigging elections in Ukraine in 1920 to return a favorable majority?[17] How, Molotov had asked in 1922, could the CC tolerate oppositionist control in Samara, where party members who disagreed with the local oppositionist leadership were put in jail?[18] Local party activists desperately needed reliable personnel and did not particularly want to carry on ideological debates with local dissidents. They wanted to maintain local order and protect their own power bases, and Moscow's interventions served their interests. It was indeed sometimes the case that local party factions "chased out" ideological dissidents, demanding their recall to Moscow.[19] The fact that oppositionists also used patronage power and had themselves earlier demanded stern central measures against local party troublemakers did not enhance their case or lend sympathy to their complaints. And because of the shortage of talented and hardworking party administrators (remember Yezhov's multiple job offers in 1923), transferred oppositionists were usually offered equivalent positions elsewhere; the disruption of their circles did not seem excessively punitive.[20] In fact, the use of central personnel measures against troublemakers and dissidents enjoyed broad support in the party and was a matter of group consensus as much as it was Stalin's personal tactic. Everyone understood how the system of personalized politics worked.

Recalcitrant or determined oppositionists received harsher treatment. Some were expelled from the party for a time, but upon their statements of adherence to party policy they were readmitted: by the dawn of the 1930s virtually all leading and even minor oppositionists of the 1920s were in the party working in responsible positions. Particularly "dangerous" oppositionists, most of them Trotskyists, who were regarded as having broken state laws (over and above party rules) were imprisoned. This category of intransigent oppositionists included those who tried to organize secret political cells or illegal underground newspapers, or those who tried to lobby in the military.

It is perhaps surprising at first glance that in the files of Orgraspred there are almost no documents pertaining to punitive personnel appointments of opposition members. In the voluminous records relating to personnel, there is no paper trail indicating that oppositional membership was used as a criterion for appointment, nonappointment, or removal. On the other hand, responsible workers in Orgraspred did their best to keep track of oppositional backgrounds as part of their growing card files, and it is highly probable that when Orgraspred representatives presented personnel recommendations to the Orgburo or Secretariat, they orally mentioned such facts in a candidate's background.[21] At the very least, then, Orgraspred was keeping track of oppositional membership, and it is hard to imagine that this information did not influence appointments.

In any case, high politics and struggles between Stalin and his opponents were not the major determinant of the party's increasingly centralized personnel system in the 1920s. Much of the situation was dictated by geography, supply and demand of party workers, and the political situation. After 1917 the Bolshevik Party had to adapt itself from making revolution to governing a huge territory in which the previous administration either had fled, had been destroyed by civil war, or was hostile to its new Communist masters. Although the party had grown tremendously during the Revolution and Civil War (from about twenty-four thousand members at the beginning of 1917 to more than seven hundred thousand in 1921, when the Civil War ended), many of the recruits were undependable and uncommitted types who had simply joined the winning side. Even counting everybody in the party, moreover, the total was a drop in the bucket of the vast Soviet population. The peasant bulk of that population had won its centuries-long battle for the land and could be counted on to take a dim view of any nationalization schemes the socialist Bolsheviks might propose. Similarly, the mass of urban and rural traders were not likely allies.

The Bolsheviks, despite their enforced monopoly on the press, political organizing, and violence, found themselves a small minority floating in a hostile sea of peasants. As late at 1927, when Yezhov joined the CC apparatus, only one-half of one percent of the rural population were Communists. The party itself, in terms of its composition, was a blunt instrument, an unwieldy mass. The hundreds of thousands who had joined since 1917 did not share the prerevolutionary underground tradition of commitment, discipline, and singleness of purpose. They frequently ignored the Central Committee's orders. By mid-1924 only 25 percent of secretaries of district party committees (*ukom*) had been in the party before 1917; the figure for those running provinces (*gubkom* presidiums) was only 49 percent.[22] One in forty party members was illiterate, and one in four had fewer than four years of schooling. Some new party members had to ask what the Politburo was.[23]

Nevertheless, the Bolsheviks brought some assets to their attempts to build a working administration. As was the case with other European political parties of the day, policy had always been made in the center and promulgated through a network of committees. This shared party culture of political centralization would help to build a working administration, as would the Leninist tradition of "democratic centralism," in which central party decisions were obligatory and binding on all members. Although often observed only in the breach during 1917 and the Civil War, party discipline (if enforced) could be a powerful lever in creating a network of obedient administrators.

Lenin had laid the groundwork for such a network and had surrounded himself with talented and loyal lieutenants. Yet the personalized Leninist nature of the party—it was scarcely possible to imagine the party without him or to separate "Bolshevism" from "Leninism"—also had a negative side. When the founder and unchallenged leader died in early 1924, it was not clear what would follow his long-standing one-man leadership. Moreover, these same talented lieutenants were themselves ambitious men, guaranteeing a messy and disruptive succession struggle.

Throughout the 1920s it is fair to say that the party had only a primitive organizational structure. A Central Committee, dominated by Lenin and his closest associates, made policy and did its best to direct the Revolution and Civil War. In principle, CC orders were carried out by the network of territorial party committees, but as we have seen with Yezhov in Mari and Kirgizia, the system hardly worked as a well-oiled machine, and the Central Committee had a difficult time ensuring fulfillment of its decisions, especially in faraway locales. Until his death in 1919, Yakov Sverdlov acted as informal party secretary, making personnel assignments and allocations based on his personal connections and knowledge of a vast number of the party faithful. He worked largely according to personal contacts, sometimes receiving and assigning twenty-five party workers per day. As V. V. Ossinsky told the 8th Party Congress, "Sverdlov kept in his head information on all party workers in Russia and where to find them. At any moment he could tell you where each one was, and he could move them around. Now he is dead and nobody knows where any of the party workers are."[24]

After the death of the irreplaceable Sverdlov, everyone in the central party leadership agreed on the need for systemization of the party's personnel system. First, it was necessary to build and maintain communication links with the far-flung party organizations, such efforts being called the "organizational" (*organizatsionnaia*) or "informational" (*informatsionnaia*) task. This was to be done by insisting that local party committees regularly send reports of their decisions to the Central Committee and by dispatching emissaries (*instruktory*) to the committees to relay central decisions and verify fulfillment of them. Second, it was necessary to rationally and intelligently assign party cadres to places where they were needed according to their talents, experience, and reliability. Local party leaders, desperately short of help, were vitally interested in augmenting this "assignment" (*raspredelitel'naia*) task. Third, in order to distribute personnel rationally, the Central Committee had to gather information about who was in the party and create personnel files; this was the "registration" (*uchetnaia*) function.

In order to achieve "the systematic reallocation of party workers for . . . most productive use," the 1919 party congress created three subcommittees of the Central Committee.[25] The newly created 1919 Polit-buro (five members and three candidate members) was to decide the larger strategic and political issues; an Orgburo (eleven members) was to oversee personnel tasks and related functions; and a Secretariat (two members) was to supervise the Central Committee's growing adminis-trative and clerical apparatus (eighty workers in 1919).

That apparatus consisted of numerous departments charged with propaganda, the press, accounting, statistics, work among women, and, most important, personnel. Originally, personnel was handled by newly created Organizational (*Orgotdel*) and Registration-Assignment (*Uchraspred*) departments, with subdepartments for other functions with descriptive abbreviations and acronyms, such as *Orginstrukt*. These departments worked closely together on the registration, com-munication, and assignment tasks, and in 1926 they would be merged into a single *Orgraspred* department of the CC Secretariat.[26] Despite the structural changes initiated in 1919 and the general agreement in all po-litical quarters of the party that systemization, professionalization, and obedience were needed, the personnel assignment capabilities of the Central Committee remained weak and disorganized for years. Under-staffed and overwhelmed by its tasks, the assignment system was in chaos, relying on personal connections, accidentally spotting talent, and mass mobilizations rather than on any system.

In the first years, during the Civil War, it was necessary to draft ("mobilize") masses of party workers for large tasks. Every year until 1923, Uchraspred mobilized between twenty thousand and forty thou-sand Communists for various assignments. (As we have seen, Yezhov was mobilized in 1919 under such conditions.) Obviously there was no opportunity to know the characteristics of these party workers; the CC simply ordered local committees to provide party members by quota, and there was little time to attend to qualifications or experience. From 1919 through 1922, CC Secretaries N. Krestinsky and V. Molotov regu-larly lamented the wild "atmosphere" in the Secretariat and complained that the personnel allocation system worked on "impulse" and "shock work" more than on any system.[27]

Even after the end of the Civil War, the Secretariat and its personnel apparatus were overwhelmed by the quantity of work. A flood of paperwork and correspondence—120,000 letters and reports and 22,500 assignments in 1922 alone—simply choked the CC bureaucracy. Up to sixty party comrades per day showed up at Uchraspred offices looking for assignments; they were quickly dispatched without much ado, to whichever party committee needed someone the most.[28] Boris Bazhanov, who worked in the Orgburo apparatus in these years, remembers that for purposes of secrecy the staff of the Secretariat and the Orgburo were kept small, making it virtually impossible to deal with the "ocean of paperwork" that flooded in. Workers in the apparatus routinely worked twelve to fourteen hours per day, seven days a week. A request from the Politburo or Orgburo for some paper would produce many hours of frantic chaos through the offices as workers threw piles of papers from one place to another.[29] It was not until the mid-1920s that a filing system (*kartotek*) was introduced, a move celebrated at the end of 1925 when D. Kursky proudly announced that the Politburo and the Orgburo could now locate and review the decisions they had already made.[30]

A smoothly functioning personnel allocation system was impossible without some kind of record-keeping system for party members. Yet despite constant attempts to compile such a system, the task was never completed satisfactorily in the 1920s. A succession of CC secretaries and Uchraspred chiefs (Zinoviev, Krestinsky, Molotov, Kaganovich, and others) complained constantly about the failure of local organizations to provide information on their members, and about the inability of their own departments to build a file system. V. P. Nogin, a CC member who headed the Accounting Department, told the 11th Congress in March 1922 that despite the "endless questionnaires" the CC had solicited, he had looked into his own personnel file in Uchraspred and found only a letter from someone looking for him![31] Throughout the decade there was a constant stream of questionnaires, surveys, party censuses, and other campaigns to build a base of information on party members. The need to restart these campaigns every couple of years speaks for itself.

At various points in the early 1920s, the Central Committee apparatus produced for internal use reference lists of the party leadership groups in the provinces. Characteristically, at the end of 1923 the official list showed that the identities of comrades heading the government (chairman of the executive committee of the soviet) were unknown in Astrakhan, Yekaterinburg, Irkutsk, Kharbin, and Grozny. Identities of trade union chiefs, upon whom the Bolsheviks relied for mass support, were unknown in Briansk, Dagestan, Odessa, and Kharbin. The Communists running agitation and propaganda in Ivanovo, Tula, Tver, the Urals, Siberia, and Yekaterinoslav were a mystery to Moscow. The Moscow personnel department's own personnel assignment contacts (chiefs of organizational departments in party committees) were unknown in Vladimir and Novgorod.

Only by the end of the 1920s did Orgraspred even manage the beginnings of a personnel filing system, and even as late as 1935 Yezhov (by then the head of the CC personnel apparatus) complained that "in the apparat of the Central Committee we are presently beginning only now to find out the composition of the leading party workers in the regions and districts."[32] One can imagine the primitive nature of central records a decade earlier.

In an effort to surmount these disorders and difficulties, the party worked hard in the 1920s to regularize and systematize personnel selection. Repeated drives for biographical information laid the foundation for a cadres file, first in Uchraspred, then in Orgraspred. Mass mobilizations of party cadres gradually gave way to individual assignments, although as late as 1922 the party was mobilizing more than ten thousand cadres per year without individual vetting.[33] To cope with the work, as we have seen, filing and reference systems were introduced in the mid-twenties. Moreover, even though the staff of the Secretariat expanded from 80 in 1919 to 767 at the end of 1925, the job turnover rate in the Secretariat staff itself was nearly 100 percent per year![34]

Further rationalization came in June 1923 with the establishment of the "nomenklatura" system. The nomenklatura of a given institution was a list of the positions that institution had the right to confirm. In the 1923 system, of about five thousand positions to be confirmed by the Politburo, thirty-five hundred (Nomenklatura no. 1) in the party and state could be proposed and confirmed only by the Politburo, the Orgburo, or the Secretariat. An additional list of fifteen hundred jobs (Nomenklatura no. 2) could be filled by other bodies but were subject to confirmation and approval by these top three committees. The formation of the nomenklatura system was a major step in the creation of a privileged elite, identified by their presence on these CC lists, as well as an arrogation of political power by the Stalin-controlled Politburo, Orgburo, and Secretariat in order to build up a cadre of clients to defeat the opposition.

At the same time, though, the sources show that the nomenklatura system was really intended as a way to systematize existing ad hoc practice and even to decrease the appointment burden on the Central Committee apparatus. Months before its establishment, in March 1922, V. P. Nogin told a party congress that the Orgburo and the Secretariat were facing around one hundred issues per day. CC Secretary Molotov, who was becoming Stalin's right-hand man, complained that the apparatus—Stalin's apparatus—was burdened by far too many personnel appointments. The 22,500 personnel proposals passing through the apparatus in the previous year and the average sixty walk-in applicants per day were far too many to be handled properly. Molotov said that high-level confirmation of most of them was "unnecessary" and proposed sharply reducing the CC's appointment responsibilities to the leading responsible workers.[35] As we have seen, the original nomenklatura lists reserved for CC appointment or approval amounted to about 5,000 positions. This corresponded with existing practice: in the year before establishing the system, the CC had vetted 5,167 posts, and in the previous year 4,738.[36] The new nomenklatura system thus codified existing practice and scale for appointment of responsible workers.

Yet the goal was to reduce it. This may seem strange in light of our belief that Stalin sought to expand his power, but in 1926, a revision of the CC nomenklatura reduced the number of posts requiring direct CC appointment from 3,500 to 1,870 (with an additional 1,590 to be approved by commissions). Even so, the burden remained large, and it was to take several years to achieve the reductions Molotov wanted. At the end of 1926, 87.5 percent of Orgraspred's appointments were still outside the prescribed nomenklatura, although 1927 would bring the desired significant reductions.[37] Certainly, the creation of the appointive nomenklatura was the death knell to the short-lived revolutionary practice of electing local party leaders.[38] But since it merely codified existing practice with a view toward reducing the number of central personnel assignments, it was more an efficiency measure than an earthshaking political change.

The central nomenklatura system was designed to retain authority over the very top positions in the country ("the basic commanding heights," as Kursky put it) while reducing the workload of the secretarial apparatus.[39] Thus in 1929 in an average province, the posts requiring CC appointment or approval included the top party officials, chairman of the cooperative board, the top newspaper editors and trade union officials, and the provincial chiefs of the secret police, the procuracy, the courts, and higher educational institutions: eighty-eight in all.[40] All remaining mid- and lower-level positions were appointed by local officials without confirmation by the Central Committee.

Even with increased efficiencies of the 1920s, the jurisdictional lines between and among the Politburo, the Orgburo, and the Secretariat remained deliberately vague. Even a quick survey of the protocols of meetings of these three bodies shows the overlap in questions decided by the various bodies. Many positions were listed on several different central and/or local nomenklatura lists. Such items as the dates of upcoming party congresses, publication of new journals, communications and articles from oppositionists, and appointments at all levels could find their way to the agendas of any of the three top bodies.[41] Although this made for a certain confusion, the fuzzy jurisdictions were intentional. Twice Lenin himself had responded to criticism on this score by claiming that flexibility at the top was important.[42]

Lenin's idea of institutional flexibility at the top helps capture the way the system really worked. The interlocking three top bodies consisted of the top party notables, and their personal authority was more important than the multiple seats they held. By 1925 all five CC secretaries were also Orgburo members, and three of them were also on the Politburo. Three Orgburo members were also on the Secretariat and three on the Politburo. Protocols of meetings of the Orgburo and the Secretariat are kept in the same archives, and standard practice was that once or twice a week one or the other body met to do the same work. If several members were available, it was called an Orgburo meeting. If only two—or even a single—member could attend, it was written up as a meeting of the Secretariat; the agenda was the same. Although in theory the Secretariat was the most junior of the three bodies, CC spokesmen noted that the personal authority of a CC secretary chairing a Secretariat meeting meant that the body could tackle important questions.[43] Despite attempts to systematize and rationalize personnel appointment, this was a system of powerful persons acting as referees and confirming judges, not one of fixed and rule-bound institutions.

Personnel appointments, usually generated by staff, were therefore most often only casually vetted by one or more of the top notables, depending first on who was available to do it, and second on the importance of the post. As we have seen, a meeting of one of the top three bodies could carry hundreds of agenda items, and time permitted discussion of no more than ten to twenty of them. This meant that dozens, even hundreds of agenda items were approved by polling the members (*oprosom*) before or after the meeting. Already by 1923, 90–95 percent of the personnel questions coming before the Orgburo/Secretariat were quickly settled based on staff (*Uchraspred* or *Orgotdel*) proposals. The structure at the top of the party therefore, was really a kind of personal oligarchy. The quantity of work involved in assigning personnel far outweighed the ability of top leaders to cope with it. Nearly all of it was delegated to the CC staff.

The oligarchs at the top of the party, Stalinist and oppositionist alike, were veterans of the prerevolutionary underground and were Lenin's comrades in arms. They felt themselves awash in the sea of new party recruits and as a generational cohort must have felt matters slipping from their control. They had to delegate much decision making to staff but were unwilling to completely relinquish their elite supervision, so they had to settle for a system of vetting and approving prepared decisions. The sense of oligarchy and elite supervision is demonstrated by these "flexible" arrangements at the top: any of the three top bodies could ratify personnel appointments, and even if only a single member of their number was available to do it, it was done as a meeting of the Secretariat.[44] According to party rules, decisions of the Secretariat could be appealed to the Orgburo, and the latter's decisions could be appealed to the Politburo. But the flexible personalized oligarchy created by Lenin and his generation of party leaders meant in practice that this hardly ever happened. Powerful persons worked it out informally.[45]

Most of the Central Committee's work related to personnel, and most personnel decisions originated in Orgraspred proposals. A group of seven "assignment commissions" in Orgraspred worked out proposed appointments in consultation with the party organizations concerned.[46] By 1925 Orgraspred was working out the agendas and work plans for the Orgburo. Conferences of Orgraspred assistants (*pomoshniki*) worked out the important appointments for the Nomenklatura no. 1 ahead of time for the Politburo, the Orgburo, and the Secretariat. When provincial party secretaries arrived in Moscow to deliver reports to the Orgburo, they gave them first to Orgraspred, where they were critiqued and edited.[47]

Orgraspred was "enormously powerful."[48] It was responsible for making rational personnel assignments not only to party committees but to major economic and industrial institutions. It therefore became a kind of research think tank, holding conferences on such issues as agricultural techniques, various kinds of metal production, rural cooperatives, and the like. Responsible officials in Orgraspred developed specialties. For example, in Orgraspred's 1928 roster of assignments, Deputy Chief Zh. I. Meerzon was responsible for following the work of local party organizations, monitoring "self-criticism" in party committees, investigating questions of party growth and nationality, and organizing mass work among new party members. Deputy Chief

N. Zimin had authority over cadre assignments for the Commissariats of Foreign Affairs and Education and for the press, as well as working out the Orgburo's appointments of workers in science. Young assistant G. M. Malenkov oversaw the Stalingrad party organization, questions of labor discipline, and studies of a proposed seven-hour working day. Additionally, each of about twenty-five instruktory was responsible for a group of provinces, as well as other specialties.[49]

As the diversity and number of these duties suggest, Orgraspred was always busy studying a wide variety of questions and was seriously understaffed and overworked. Responsible workers of Orgraspred like Meerzom, Zimin, Malenkov, and others were responsible for two to six broad areas of personnel assignment each. Moreover, the more than five thousand possible posts that Orgraspred was responsible for—dozens or even hundreds per meeting of the Orgburo/Secretariat—were handled by a fairly small staff of workers. In the late 1920s Orgraspred's total staff roster was in the seventies, with twenty to thirty of these classified as "technical": typists, receptionists, archivists, and so forth. That left only forty or fifty responsible officials (fifty-three in 1928). Of these, several were involved in other organizational areas (*orgrabota*, or contact and communications with party committees, for example), leaving in 1928 only forty-one assignment (*raspredelrabota*) officials to make the actual personnel recommendations. Five of these positions were unfilled in 1928.[50] Assuming something like a normal distribution of personnel slots across the group, each official would therefore have been responsible for expertise on a bit more than 140 different cadre positions.

Within this group of responsible workers, the work environment seems to have been fairly egalitarian. The chief (*zaveduyushchii*) of Orgraspred (Ivan Moskvin), his nine deputy chiefs, and the twenty-two responsible instructors each made the same salary (225 rubles per month); the nine assistant chiefs for personnel assignments made 200–210 rubles. There seems to have been little difference among their specializations or assignments (*osnovnaia rabota*, or basic work) in terms of importance, regardless of their ranks.[51]

Despite the central importance of their jobs, Orgraspred's responsible workers did not themselves hold high party rank. Only the chief, Moskvin, was a member of the Central Committee, and there were periods in the 1920s and 1930s when Orgraspred chiefs did not hold CC rank. Of the forty or so responsible officials under him, only a handful—sometimes not even including his deputies—received invitations as nonvoting delegates to party congresses. Thus most of the party workers making the most important personnel choices were not visible or important leaders in their own right.

Nevertheless, Orgraspred's importance in the Stalinist system was manifested in at least two other ways. As we have seen, the department made most of the decisions on personnel appointment. Certainly the handful of most senior appointments (Central Committee members, territorial party first secretaries, ministers, and senior police officials) were carefully considered in the Politburo, with or without staff input. But the vast majority of the thousands of important nomenklatura and other appointments originated in staff choices. Stalin and the other elite party oligarchs of his generation "controlled" these appointments only through a loose Orgburo/Secretariat supervision that resembled rubber-stamping most of the time.

Personnel vacancies arose in a variety of ways. Party committees and state institutions requested additional staffing or prompt filling of vacancies. (Often they proposed particular candidates to Orgraspred.) Newly created organizations needed entire complements of workers. Moreover, individuals unhappy with their current assignments pleaded that they were unable to get along with their current chiefs or subordinates and requested reassignment. With the exception of the very top positions, these requests came first to Orgraspred, which studied the matter and made a recommendation to the Secretariat or Orgburo for its approval (which was nearly always forthcoming).

The simplest matters were those that involved no objections from the parties involved, all of whom were routinely consulted. If the proposed appointee's current boss had no objections, if his or her prospective chief accepted him, and if the appointee him- or herself raised no serious objections (which would have been considered bad form in party custom), the matter seemed straightforward and moved quickly ahead. After a report from Orgraspred staff, the Secretariat or the Orgburo would "approve" (*utverdit'* or *udovletvorit'*) or note simply that it had no objections (*ne vozrazhat'*) to Orgraspred's proposed appointment. Orgraspred staff had prepared a draft Secretariat or Orgburo resolution in advance for the expected brisk confirmation and signature. Thus a typical Orgraspred recommendation read, "To the Secretariat (by polling): Comrade Vitolin, member of the party since 1918, worker, his past basic work being in the organs of the police, and recently for a short time in leading soviet work. Orgraspred CC has no objections to his candidacy, and asks confirmation of Comrade Vitolin as chief of the Mari regional department of the GPU. The Mari regional party committee and Comrade Vitolin have agreed."[52]

More complicated appointments required personal adjudication by the senior oligarchs present. Sometimes organizations resisted proposals to take valuable workers from them and reassign them elsewhere; they would then ask the Secretariat or the Orgburo for a reconsideration (*peresmotr*), or they would make a formal complaint (*protest*) to try to block the transfer. Other appointments were complicated by jurisdictional and turf issues. For example, a territorial party committee might insist on its right to approve directors appointed to factories in its province even though such placements came under the purview of the state economic agency that governed the branch of production. In yet other cases, personal requests for transfer from individuals had to be discussed and vetted by the senior Orgburo or Secretariat members, especially if the person involved was of high rank and prominence.

These complicated appointments could generate different responses from the senior leaders of the Orgburo or the Secretariat, who could overrule any objections and force appointments by "ordering" them (*poruchit'*) or, more politely, "suggesting" them (*predlozhit'*)—and given Bolshevik traditions of party discipline, such a suggestion was tantamount to an order. Alternatively, they could refuse or "decline" an appointment (*otklonit'*). If the matter required discussion or confirmation by a higher or broader collection of party oligarchs, it could be tabled (*otlozhit'*) or referred upward to the Politburo (*vnesti na utverzh-denie Politburo*).[53] Whatever the final decision, however, the first step was nearly always an Orgraspred recommendation or presentation of the facts of the case.

As we shall see, Yezhov soon moved from provincial party work to Moscow. His work in Kirgizia as party secretary for cadre assignments already identified him as a personnel specialist, and his future appointment as an Orgraspred assistant in 1927 was to put him at the center of party activities in Moscow. Orgraspred was also an important part of the Stalin system because it was an incubator for future top leaders. This may or may not have been intentional, but a remarkable number of future Stalinist leaders had served time in the department or in related personnel administrations. The core of the Stalinist Politburo until 1957 all came up through the assignment apparatus: L. Kaganovich (Uchraspred chief until 1926), V. Molotov (Orgburo chairman in the 1920s), G. Malenkov (Orgraspred instructor in the 1920s). A scan of Orgraspred rosters shows other top 1930s party leaders with Orgraspred experience in the 1920s. Among future Orgraspred deputy chiefs and instructors we find Yezhov (NKVD chief); two of his NKVD assistants, Roshal' and Litvin; V. Mezhlauk (head of the Supreme Council of National Economy and Commissariat of Heavy Industry); and B. Sheboldaev, L. Petrosian, and I. Vareikis (first party secretaries of important provinces), as well as future members of the Party Control Commission Frenkl' and Meerzon.[54] Yezhov was headed for the center of things.

# FIVE

# Sorting Out the Comrades

Comrades who studied with [Yezhov] tell of his work
on a report on Marx's theory or prices. The report gave
a profound and erudite exposition of the subject.

A. FADEEV

I know of no more ideal administrator than
Nikolai Yezhov. . . . Yezhov never gives up.

IVAN MOSKVIN

Despite his earnest efficiency and apparent commitment to party work
in the provinces, it is easy to imagine that Nikolai and Antonina did not
relish staying in Central Asia for the rest of their lives. Bolshevik discipline required that party cadres go wherever they were sent without
question. Everyone recognized that provincial assignments were considered a sort of exile from the Moscow center, and even speakers at
party congresses noted this rather un-Bolshevik but common belief that
a post in Moscow was good, while a provincial assignment was some
kind of punishment.[1] In the summer of 1923, only a few months after

their arrival, Antonina left for study in Moscow at the prestigious Tim-riazev Agricultural Academy "at the assignment of the Semipalatinsk Gubkom."[2] In other words, she was "assigned" by her husband, who headed the gubkom and its cadres administration. Thus began a career in agricultural research and organization for Antonina—she would spend the rest of her days as an agricultural specialist—but it is hard to avoid the suspicion that the couple were dispatching her to Moscow to make connections and to pave the way for a permanent move there. For his part, Nikolai was also trying to move to the capital by dropping a hint to Central Committee Secretary V. Molotov, whom he met at a Moscow party conference, about his desire to come to Moscow for political study courses.

In February 1924 Yezhov thought better of his personal pleading and "careerist" conversation with Molotov, and again demonstrated his adroit Bolshevik bearing in dealing with his superiors. He wrote to Molotov, ostensibly to report local party opinion on proposed British trade concessions in Central Asia. Yezhov was negative on them, reminding Molotov of the history of English colonization and the dangerous number of exiles in the area. But the letter began with a personal note from Yezhov, in which he affirmed the correct Bolshevik selflessness:

Esteemed Comrade Molotov!

On the one hand, I would not like to bother you with this letter. And it is also simply not proper to write of such, I would say, generally understood things as in the first part of this letter, but nevertheless I decided to write.

1. At the time of the last party conference, in conversation with you I took the liberty of raising the question of the possibility of my transfer and of my wish to do it, although I did not raise this question officially in the usual way, but in the course of normal conversation with a comrade, nevertheless I consider it necessary in the same [comradely] spirit to say the following:

At the present moment, because of the general situation in the party, and chiefly because of Vladimir Ilich's [Lenin's] death, I think there that cannot be any talk of personal wishes to transfer, even more to study. If one takes into account the general difficulty of the Central Committee in selecting [party] workers on the frontiers, then it seems to me that the question becomes crystal clear.[3] I would like to say, Comrade Molotov, that at the present time each party worker must remain at the weakly defended positions of the RKP(b) (and I completely consider Kirgizia to be a weakly defended position), and therefore I think that you will not pay any attention to our conversation. Now to business . . .[4]

On the surface, this text is a bit of silliness, resembling a note one would use to undo a perhaps inebriated faux pas one had committed with the boss at a social gathering. It asked for and instigated no action and seems trivial. But it is Yezhov's style and purpose that are interesting here, both in language and in the way Yezhov represented himself.

First, we can note that Yezhov was playing the Bolshevik system of personalized politics. He was asking for a transfer not "officially in the usual way" but rather by appealing to a powerful personality, thereby short-circuiting the institutional channels. He was trying to use a personal connection, to nurture a client-patron relationship with Molotov.

His language is that of a humble plebeian petitioner. His first paragraph follows a Russian petition tradition in which one first regrets disturbing the lofty recipient but says the writer simply could not do otherwise. The subordinate then makes another implicit apology by reminding the lord of a careless incident and begs him to forget the entire matter as a matter of principle and honor. The style is supplicating, respectful, flattering, and ancient. The long, run-on sentences with many reflexive constructions and few subject-agents was typical not only of what was to become the "Stalinist" bureaucratic style but also of the actual labored prose of uneducated Russian commoners.

On the other hand, behind the flowery language and almost chivalrous posturing, there is much in the letter that is Bolshevik, couched shrewdly in the service of personal tactics. Yezhov draws on a set of cultural tools to make a text meant to do political work. First, there is no formal apology or direct personal flattery. Indeed, the entire tone of the letter is one of great events and duties that deny the personal and make individual wishes and apologies irrelevant. Bolsheviks don't linguistically abase themselves (much) with their bosses, and their democratic tradition makes explicit flattery inappropriate. They don't make personal requests for the same reason. The text itself is meant to demonstrate the fidelity of the writer to the common values of the organization—selflessness, discipline, sacrifice for the common good—and also serves as a statement of allegiance to these values. Packaged as self-abnegation, therefore, the letter really is meant to be self-recommendation.

Similarly, the underlying tactic behind the letter may have been precisely the opposite of what the text superficially says. Yezhov pretended to ask that a request be forgotten, when in fact the a real reason for writing the letter was the opposite: to remind Molotov of the incident, and of the request. Yezhov was not concerned that Molotov remembered the remark; he was really afraid that Molotov had forgotten it. The letter served to remind Molotov to keep Yezhov's request alive and current. Yezhov wanted out of Semipalatinsk. He picked a discursive strategy that affirmed his subordinate status, linguistically demonstrated his prime plebeian origins, swore allegiance to Bolshevik values and virtues, and reminded his superior of his existence and desire to be favored.

It did not work with Molotov, an experienced Bolshevik chief, who doubtless saw all this but who decided to pass the buck to another senior CC secretary whom he knew would do nothing. Molotov scribbled "for the Semipalatinsk gubkom file" and routed the letter to L. M. Kaganovich without taking any action. Molotov and Kaganovich took Yezhov at his self-effacing word and kept him in Semipalatinsk. But the failure of Yezhov's literary sally is not as important as what it shows us about power relations in the party and the uses of discursive strategies from the bottom of the hierarchy. It shows that Yezhov had learned how to play the Bolshevik bureaucratic game with some skill.

His bureaucratic talent failed to extricate him from Central Asia. On the contrary, he performed so well that his chiefs wanted him to stay exactly where he was. A performance report on him (*kharakteristika*) from

Kirgizia called attention to his initiative and good organizational abilities. He was able to orient himself quickly to local conditions, paying no attention to "trifles." Apparently he had learned from his "irascibility" and "blunders" in Mari, because now he was said to be tactful and self-critical. His self-taught, practical Marxism allowed him naturally to orient himself on political questions.[5]

Yezhov needed another route to Moscow because no highly placed patron was about to bring him to the capital. At the beginning of 1926, he found it. Shortly after the new year, the Kirgiz party committee again elected Yezhov to his leading position and voted to send him on temporary assignment to Moscow to complete a series of party courses in Marxist theory.[6] Such courses provided a means for Bolsheviks with little formal education to improve their qualifications, and performance reports on Yezhov had mentioned his lack of theoretical sophistication. Before anyone could change their minds, Yezhov presented himself at the Communist Academy in Moscow to begin study in early February. But nobody had cleared this with Moscow party leaders, and the Central Committee's Orgburo, at its meeting of 8 February 1926, resolved "to disapprove the request of Comrade Yezhov (from Central Asia) to register for Marxism courses at the Communist Academy."[7] Not easily discouraged, Yezhov remained in Moscow and persisted, and the following month he was granted admission.[8]

Party committees who dispatched a valuable worker to Moscow for study expected that the comrade would return after completion of the course and take up his former, or a better, position. After all, the sending party agency shouldered part of the expense of such education for its workers. Yezhov, however, had no intention of returning to the desert; he would never return to Kirgizia. He had finally made it to Moscow, and he and Antonina were together after nearly three years' separation. He arrived in Moscow not as the client of some powerful patron in the party who had cultivated him in the provinces and then brought him to the capital; rather, he was there despite the efforts of his superiors to keep him where he was. At this point in his life, he was nobody's creature, nobody's tool. Insofar as he had been "spotted" by high-ranking party leaders, it was as a good party worker doing a good job in a difficult place. He had a "good reputation."[9] The leaders' reflex was to continue to take advantage of his solid work in the provinces.

But now he was in Moscow by dint of his own efforts. His time in party service on the periphery stood him in good stead. He had assimilated the cultural values of the Bolshevik bureaucracy (and indeed of any bureaucracy): obedience, discipline, use of the correct political language, uncomplaining hard work, clear and subtle report writing, and self-promotion covered by modesty. By now he also had an attractive party résumé. He was a former factory worker of proletarian stock and had been a worker-activist in the most famous revolutionary factory in Russia. He had been a Bolshevik before the 1917 Bolshevik Revolution, a leader of Red Guards, and a participant in the Civil War. He had completed two difficult assignments in areas troubled by one of the Bolsheviks' biggest fears: ethnic conflict. Just as important, as part of these assignments he had mastered what was becoming the key party specialty: personnel assignment.[10] Yezhov was therefore not an insignificant party member. Even though he was not one of the party's great orators or theoreticians and had never worked in Moscow, few in the party could boast his pedigree and accomplishments. One could predict a great career for him, and he intended to make it himself.

By the middle of March 1926, Yezhov had taken up his studies at the Communist Academy in Moscow.[11] We know little about the fifteen months he studied there, except that he seems to have emerged as a student leader of sorts. An adoring (but unpublished) biographical sketch written by the Socialist Realist writer A. Fadeev a decade later, when Yezhov had already become chief of the secret police (NKVD), claimed that he threw himself into his theoretical studies with the same enthusiasm as he had applied to his party work. "Comrades who studied with him tell of his work on a report on Marx's theory of prices. The report gave a profound and erudite exposition of the subject."[12]

Given what we know about Yezhov's background and about how and when such texts were produced, we may perhaps be excused for doubting Yezhov's erudition and theoretical profundity. Nevertheless, other sources confirm that he did stand out among his fellow students. He seems to have been the representative of the student party group (*kurskom*) to the administration. In October 1926 he presented a report to Communist Academy leaders on the stipends students received. Even though most of them had families to support, no more than 40 percent of the students could receive the maximum party salary. Yezhov distinguished himself in another way. Of the 114 students currently enrolled, he had the largest family to support. He claimed eight dependents: a wife, a mother, and six nieces and nephews, five of whom were under age eighteen. Aside from Nikolai, with his monthly 225-ruble salary, and Antonina, with her 175, no other family member was earning income.[13]

Unfortunately, we know little about Yezhov's extracurricular activities and connections in the capital, but one way or another he had attracted the attention of the Central Committee's personnel administration. Ivan M. Moskvin had recently taken over direction of the Central Committee's organizational-assignment department (*Orgraspred*), the main party office for assignment and distribution of personnel.[14] Yezhov was a capable and highly regarded provincial party secretary. In July 1927 Moskvin hired him to be one of his nine assistants at Orgraspred. Even though senior party leaders preferred for Yezhov to stay in Kazakhstan, a request from so authoritative a Bolshevik as Moskvin could not be ignored, and the appointment was confirmed.[15]

At first it might seem that appointment as a personal assistant to one of many department heads in a Central Committee staff of more than 650 employees was not a great leap up the career ladder for Yezhov. After all, he had been practically running a huge province the previous year, and his new job entailed an 11 percent pay cut from his recent student stipend. Yet despite appearances, his new post placed Yezhov at the very heart of the Central Committee's activities and power, and therefore represented a huge rise in his status. In the mid-1920s, about 80 percent of the work of the Central Committee involved personnel assignment, and the vast majority of those assignments were handled by Orgraspred, with higher bodies (Politburo, Orgburo, and Secretariat) unable to discuss more than 5 percent of personnel questions and only rubber-stamping or refereeing these staff recommendations.[16]

Yezhov was confirmed by the CC Secretariat as the ninth of Ivan Moskvin's assistants for cadres assignment at Orgraspred. He joined a staff of responsible workers that also included nine deputy chiefs (*zamestitely zaveduiushchego*), seven assistants for organizational work, and nineteen responsible instructors.[17] These forty-five officials were responsible for recommending virtually all personnel appointments in the expanding party and state bureaucracies.

They apparently worked as a more or less egalitarian collective. Chief Moskvin's salary of 225 rubles per month was the same that his deputies and instructors received, and Yezhov's wage of 200 rubles was only slightly lower. Moreover, the division of responsibilities seems to have been fairly distributed. Each deputy, assistant, and instructor covered three to five areas of specialization that seem to have been based more on work load than on importance or prestige.[18]

Yezhov settled quickly into his new job and showed his superiors his customary efficiency and value. After slightly more than a month on the job, he was writing Orgraspred reports for the Orgburo on party education and other matters.[19] By September he was soliciting and receiving reports from provincial party organizations about a variety of political affairs, including checkups on political dissidents.[20] Moskvin must have found him as useful an assistant as had Yezhov's former bosses in Kazakhstan (whose work Yezhov took over), because sometime in November, after only four months as Moskvin's assistant, Yezhov was promoted over the heads of the other eight assistants to the post of deputy chief.[21] As we shall see, less than two years after that he would be running the entire personnel apparatus of the Communist Party.

The writer Lev Razgon survived years in the Gulag camps to recall his impressions of the young Yezhov at this time. Razgon grew up in Moskvin's household, where Yezhov was a frequent guest. "For some reason" Moskvin "took a liking to this quiet, modest, and efficient secretary." Razgon spent several evenings at Moskvin's table with Yezhov, whom Moskvin's wife doted over and called "little sparrow." Razgon remembered her cooing: "'Come on, my little sparrow,' she would fuss encouragingly around him, 'try some of this. You must eat more.'" Razgon recalled Yezhov as "a small slender man, . . . always dressed in a crumpled cheap suit and a blue satin collarless peasant shirt. He sat at the table, quiet, not very talkative and slightly shy; he drank little, did not take much part in the conversation but merely listened, with his head slightly bowed. I can understand how attractive such a person, with his shy smile and taciturn manner, must have been to Moskvin."

Aside from this possible attraction of personality, Moskvin thought Yezhov was a trustworthy and competent worker. He told Razgon, "I know of no more ideal administrator than Nikolai Yezhov. . . . Entrust him with some task and you have no need to check up—you can rest assured he will do as he is told."[22] Yezhov's efficient obedience would ten years later lead him to carry out Stalin's order to arrest Moskvin and Razgon, along with their wives and hundreds of thousands of others.

Moskvin found Yezhov to be a valuable worker in Orgraspred. At one point, probably in 1928, M. Khataevich was being transferred out of the Tatar regional party committee. According to one source, he wrote to Central Committee Secretary S. V. Kosior, proposing that Yezhov take his place. Yezhov, he wrote, was a "strong guy . . . who will put the Tatars in order." Moskvin, however, was successful in keeping his favorite assistant.[23]

Success at Orgraspred was not only a matter of firmness and strength. The politics of personnel appointment was sometimes complex and required negotiation and tact. To appoint someone to a new post, it was customary to secure the agreement of the candidate's current boss, his future boss, and the candidate himself. Thus, for example, in 1928 the political police (OGPU) wanted to replace a provincial secret police chief. Because such posts were on Nomenklatura List no. 1, the appointment required CC approval. But in the process of consultation, Orgraspred discovered that one of the parties objected. Yezhov drafted an "explanatory note" to the Secretariat, outlining the history of the issue and making a recommendation: "The OGPU requests that

Comrade Agrov be relieved of his duties as chief of the Viatsk city OGPU and put at the disposal of the OGPU. Comrade Shiiron, former OGPU chief in Ulianovsk city, is to replace Comrade Agrov. The Viatsk city party committee objects to the transfer of Comrade Agrov from its organization. Orgraspred CC considers the replacement of Agrov with Shiiron advisable and asks for confirmation."[24]

Like the other assistants, instructors, and deputies at Orgraspred, Yezhov was responsible for particular areas or specializations. These were somewhat fluid, but the documents suggest that he had three main areas of expertise: rural cadres for the five-year plans, studying proposals to enact a seven-hour workday, and promotions from the ranks of workers and peasants into managerial posts (*vydvizhenie*).[25] Orgraspred responsible workers were also expected to handle other issues as they came up, however, and at various times in the late 1920s Yezhov prepared recommendations on a wide variety of other issues, including personnel assignments to the Commissariats of Justice and Labor, the trade unions, and the food industry. He also wrote memorandums on party political education and supervised the formation of presidia for various ceremonial conferences.[26] Although he had no defined specialty as such, in a preview of his subsequent career he seems often to have drafted recommendations for staffing of several judicial procuracies and police (OGPU) positions.[27] These varied assignments in Orgraspred gave Yezhov and his colleagues wide experience and familiarity with many areas of the regime's activity. The tasks would stand them in good stead and help to explain why so many of them went on to higher positions in the party and state.

The fragmentary records we have do not give a complete picture of Yezhov's work at Orgraspred, but surviving transcripts of some departmental conferences do allow us to form a general impression of his approach to problems and his style of work. Orgraspred was as much think tank as personnel bureau. It regularly received written reports and heard in-person explanations from virtually all sectors of party and state activity, and it conducted a constant series of in-house conferences on many themes. The idea was apparently to build up a store of information and knowledge about how the state and the economy worked in order to be able to assign cadres more intelligently. Yezhov participated in (and often chaired) conferences on agriculture, labor, state institutions, and the specifics of party committees in various provinces.

Such Soviet conferences, following the true Russian bureaucratic style, tended to be long-winded displays of oratory replete with vague generalities, repetition of correct slogans and terminology, and little in the way of concrete proposals. It was important for everyone to go on record with as many remarks, however inconsequential, as possible. Speaker after repetitious speaker outlined the problem, summarized the (often negligible) accomplishments to date, beat his breast with self-criticism for not doing more, and then pledged to do better. The conferences resembled scripted rituals in which the point was as much to be heard speaking and to affirm values as to move problems forward. It must have been the case that at the end of the Orgraspred conferences, which sometimes lasted many hours, the participants were too exhausted to do much in concrete terms. A typical finale was the decision to go back and study the question further, appoint a new commission to look at the matter, or draft a resolution that repeated—often verbatim—previous pronouncements on the matter. That way everyone had gone on record, identified the problem, and said the right words, but no one risked going out on a limb with some new proposal that might fail or offend some bureaucratic interest.

Reading transcripts of party meetings at all levels, one gets the impression that those who would rise to prominence often took a different approach. In the 1920s leaders like Stalin, V. M. Molotov, L. M. Kaganovich, G. K. Ordzhonikidze, M. F. Shkiriatov, S. V. Kosior, and others expressed impatience with interminable talk. It was often their voices that interrupted a speaker (a hallowed Bolshevik tradition) and called on him to get to the point, stay on the subject, or provide specifics. Thus meetings of the Orgburo and the Secretariat chaired by such leaders rarely put things off and often covered more of the agenda than might have otherwise been the case. Compared with other Bolsheviks, especially those with roots in the intelligentsia, these Stalinists were men more of action than of words. Their style was practical and pragmatic; getting the job done was more important than talking about it. They were often praised as "businesslike" (*delovoi*), "firm" (*tverdyi*), or "reliable" (*nadezhnyi*), and their "Stalinist style of work" was posed as a model for others.

Stalin valued such personality types around him not only for their obedience but also for their directness and efficiency and, when it came to that, their brutality in completing an assignment. In a system where personnel staffing, or "finding the right cadres," was more important than the formal structure of institutions, those who could reliably cut to the chase and quickly and efficiently break a bottleneck rose quickly in Stalin's regime. Moreover, such lieutenants as Molotov, Kaganovich, Ordzhonikidze (and later N. S. Khrushchev, N. M. Shvernik, L. D. Mekhlis, and A. S. Shcherbakov) functioned as roving troubleshooters rather than as specialized bureaucrats. They were sent to trouble spots to organize solutions, regardless of their previous expertise or specialization, and were known for seeing tasks through to a conclusion, regardless of cost.

Molotov worked in the party apparatus and later served as prime minister and foreign minister. Kaganovich also started in the party apparatus and then had a series of positions in many fields, including railroad administration, running Ukrainian and Moscow party organizations, and building the Moscow subway. Ordzhonikidze's assignments ranged in the 1920s and 1930s from the Caucasus to enforcement of party discipline to heavy industry. Whether the hot spot was railroads, foreign affairs, agriculture, or heavy industry, Stalin often dealt with it by dispatching one of these firm businesslike troubleshooters. He apparently liked their impatience with inefficient conservative approaches, and their combination of hard work, organizational ability, and, when necessary, a brutal steamroller approach.

Nikolai Yezhov seems to have been such a type: what today we might call a "can-do" or "results-oriented" manager who got things done. We have already noted his propensity for hard work and timely fulfillment of assignments. As we shall see, his work experience would also be that of a troubleshooter, touching on a wide variety of fields and subjects. Even in the late 1920s, as a young official in his early thirties, Yezhov also showed the relentless, Stalinist steamroller quality. This is perhaps what Ivan Moskvin (who himself never became a Stalin lieutenant) meant in another prophetic remark to Lev Razgon; after praising Yezhov's ability to complete tasks, he observed, "Yezhov has only one shortcoming, although it is significant: he does not know how to stop. Sometimes you have a situation where it is impossible to do anything and you have to stop. Yezhov doesn't stop, and sometimes you have to keep an eye on him in order that he stops at the right time."[28]

We can see glimpses of Yezhov's approach to work in the minutes of various Orgraspred meetings at which he spoke. The impression is that of a young official concerned with proper and efficient organization of his department. In a meeting of a commission on verifying the composition and work of agricultural cadres, Yezhov as chair gave a succinct but detailed summary of progress to date. Without the cheerleading attestations of the task's importance or the verbose global phrases that were common to the work of such committees, he came immediately to the point. He outlined the functions of each subcommittee and prioritized the issues needing immediate decision.[29]

At an Orgraspred conference in 1928 he reflected at some length on how Orgraspred itself should be organized. Having been formed from the merger of the cadres assignment–registration (*uchraspred*) and organizational (*orgotdel*) departments, Orgraspred retained the previous departmental structures of both its predecessors. There was considerable sentiment in favor of retaining the bifurcation, because as Moskvin and others noted, assigning cadres and communicating with territorial organizations were two distinct functions. Yezhov agreed that it would be dangerous to merge both apparats into one, but he also bemoaned the overlap and lack of efficiency inherent in the current structure. He noted that when a new issue or question came to Orgraspred, it was often assigned to one of the responsible workers according to workload. But the person in charge of the issue found that various registration, assignment, and/or organizational sectors were involved, either in the past or because of the nature of the question. This made for confusion and inefficiency, and Yezhov impatiently argued for a kind of one-man management:

> What happens now, comrades? [As an assignment worker] I have a series of trade union conferences [to staff and organize]. I must tell you from experience that it happens that I have to conduct negotiations with the Organizational Subdepartment to reach any conclusion. There has been talk that such problems would be dealt with and that we need one person to do such things. . . . If things are worked out [elsewhere, in subdepartment] without my leadership, whether or not the conclusion coincides with my opinion, [as the responsible official] I will have to redo everything because I am the one who will report to the [Orgburo] commission. That is the downside [of how we do things now.] . . . If you are going to work out a question, then make it so that I am responsible for it, that I have the possibility to work it out, to cooperating as needed [with the sub-departments].[30]

Another theme in Yezhov's discourse in Orgraspred related to political adherence and obedience to the party line of the Central Committee. Pushing the need for a centralized political approach to various questions, he argued that cadres assignment officials at various levels should function as "agents" of the Central Committee. He believed that they should know the past and current decisions of the Central Committee in their essence, "not bureaucratically." After hearing a report in Orgraspred from cadres officials from the State Bank and that conservative, nonparty banking officials were trying to block party appointments, Yezhov said,

> When we hear talk about us as agents of the CC . . . many comrades imagine their role completely other than what it really is. I think that our essential strength as agents of the CC of the party must be that we perfectly know the policy of the CC of the party.

This is basic for us: to know the CC's policy in every institution, in every situation in which we find ourselves, to know the party's policy and how to push it forward. . . . This is a crucial thing. And from the report we just heard, obviously the comrades don't feel this. The basic evil here is that he [the speaker] is helpless in this crucial matter, that he essentially cannot influence the selection of personnel [in the State Bank], mainly because he himself has an extremely weak understanding of the party's policy. . . . We have to say that in the essence of the matter this kind of thing cannot move things forward one iota. We have no need for such agents, in my opinion. We have to get rid of such agents because they cannot carry out the party's policy.[31]

Yezhov argued that conservative institutional resistance to party appointments could be overcome by proper use and citation of party resolutions. If party agents at Gosbank could show "that the resolution says *this,* that the resolution says *that,* that you have this or that practical plan, then I do not think that Sheinman or Spunde could do anything against it." Otherwise, he said, you end up with bureaucracy and petty relations to party decisions, "and nothing moves forward."[32]

But his spirited defense of party resolutions was not universal, and he strongly condemned the practice of party organizations avoiding real decisions by passing vague resolutions or appointing an endless series of commissions to study problems to death. After prolonged discussion of an issue, Yezhov said,

Now some comrades here have suggested passing a resolution. Comrade Riabokon' suggests passing a resolution that would serve as a guideline. Bogomolov wants to form a commission. What a joke. We will pass ten resolutions, convene another commission, and so forth. We do not need any commissions here. Here we need concretely and directly to recognize that nothing has been done, that we need to carry out the [party's] line and make corresponding conclusions. What, every six months we hear a report and every six months repeat the same thing? Why do we waste so much energy? Not to mention how much the CC wastes energy and resources when we gather all this material and just take a resolution; we take a resolution and after six or seven months things have not moved forward one iota. . . . I suggest that we not take a resolution, but limit ourselves to the existing ones. There are enough of them. We need to verify fulfillment of the old decisions.[33]

Similarly, Yezhov was impatient with those of his colleagues who either did not work as hard as he did or thrived on covering their laziness with vague suggestions. At one Orgraspred conference a colleague of Yezhov's, one Comrade Farber, presented a report on the trade unions and the question of replacing "bourgeois specialists" for discussion at a meeting chaired by Orgraspred chief Moskvin.

Moskvin: Any additions to the agenda?

Farber: In view of the fact that a whole group of comrades have not acquainted themselves with the report, maybe it would be advisable to put off discussion of my report for a week so that comrades would be able to acquaint themselves with my materials.

Moskvin: When were the materials circulated?

Farber: On Saturday.

Bogomolov: I myself feel ready to hear Comrade Farber's report today. Even Comrade Yezhov, who only now returned from vacation, has succeeded in reading the report.

[Farber reads his report]

Yezhov: The weakest part of the report is the absence here of any concrete conclusions. This is not like discovering America, but rather a simple matter of the Central Committee giving practical help to the trade unions in the nearest future. That's the essence of the matter. . . . I think the report mainly gave a snapshot, not a bad snapshot, but the real work is yet to be done.

The basic thing is to make it concrete, to say that in such and such a time, such and such a number of [bourgeois] specialists are to be replaced, and to say exactly how replacements are to be prepared according to a concrete plan, and then to figure out where to find those replacements. . . . Of course, it's not hard to chase away hundreds of specialists, but we need to replace them with others. Such concretization should have been the task of Comrade Farber.[34]

The belief in strict obedience to Central Committee decisions also pertained the political struggles with the oppositionists. Clearly, as part of its mission to gather information on party cadres, Orgraspred was involved in identifying political dissidents, but because archival materials on this subject are so scanty, we cannot judge its extent. The only document bearing Yezhov's name from this period relating to the opposition is a memo from the Voronezh provincial party committee to "Orgraspred, Comrade Yezhov or Comrade Mogil'nyi." It reads, "In response to your request, Orgotdel of the provincial VKP(b) sends this list of oppositionists working in the Voronezh organization with short biographies (*kharakteristiki*) of them."[35]

Nikolai Yezhov's early work in the Moscow personnel apparatus of the Central Committee showed him to be his usual diligent, hardworking self, indispensable to his boss and probably again taking over much of his work. He was an excellent administrator and organizer who took an interest in making Orgraspred run efficiently. What we know of his psychology and approach to problems also suggests parallels with those of the effective troubleshooters Stalin favored. Although there is no evidence that Yezhov had yet met Stalin or that Stalin took any special interest in him, the young Orgraspred worker displayed the can-do, relentless, get-it-done-regardless-of-consequences attitude that characterized successful Stalinist lieutenants like Molotov, Kaganovich, and Ordzhonikidze.[36] He seems to have had the right personality, as well as the right biography, for the era of Stalinist dictatorship.

He also mastered new areas of expertise from party education to agriculture. In Orgraspred in the 1920s he added other elements to his résumé that would be important to his future career: his experience placing cadres in the courts, procuracy, and the secret police (OGPU), as well as his activities in keeping track of oppositionists, presaged his involvement in the horrible purges of the 1930s.

Most immediately relevant to his upward career path, however, was his newfound interest in and knowledge of rural cadres working in agriculture. By 1929 Stalin and his circle had decided to deprive the peasants of their private landholdings and launch the full nationalization and collectivization of agriculture. Up to this time, the state had supervised farming through commissariats (ministries) of agriculture at the republic level. Thus in the Russian Republic the RSFSR Commissariat of Agriculture had been in charge. But many of the agronomists and specialists in these republic-level agencies thought that the collectivization scheme was ill-advised and dragged their feet in the planning process. By the end of 1929 Stalin had decided to solve this problem with his usual strategy: using personnel appointment and the creation of a new agency to circumvent the old ones. He created an all-union-level USSR Commissariat of Agriculture to push collectivization forward.

Characteristically, the higher reaches of the new commissariat were filled with stalwart, radical party workers transferred from hard-line party disciplinary agencies, including the Workers' and Peasants' Inspection.[37] Cadres selection for the new agency was a main component of the plan because the new commissariat's selection of "correct" personnel—those willing to carry out the crash plan for collectivization—would be crucial. Who better to direct this effort than the modest, hardworking personnel specialist who had shown himself to be dedicated to obeying Central Committee resolutions to the letter? On 15 December 1929 the Politburo, upon the recommendation of L. M. Kaganovich and Ya. A. Yakovlev (the new USSR Commissar of Agriculture) appointed N. I. Yezhov Deputy Commissar of Agriculture of the USSR, "with instructions to him to work on personnel."[38]

Yezhov's move to the USSR Commissariat of Agriculture took him out of the party's formal personnel assignment system, but it did not take him away from cadre assignments. The order appointing him to his new position noted specifically that he was to be the deputy commissar "to work on personnel."[39] The new agency and Yezhov's job within it put him at the very center of Stalinist policy implementation at the time.

## SIX

# Yezhov on the Job

"CADRES DECIDE EVERYTHING"

The party leads by appointing people. Power is not power
if it cannot appoint people.

N. I. YEZHOV

Stalin's decision to end private agriculture and to force peasants into collective farms led to the most dramatic upheaval since the 1917 Revolution and the Civil War. The collectivization struggle would last from 1929 well into the 1930s; the main stages would feature violent struggles between regime supporters and peasants, tremendous confusion and chaos, and the deaths of millions due to famine and deportation.[1] The policy change of 1929 was so drastic that the Politburo found that it had no bureaucracy willing and able to implement it. When the leadership created one and cast about for a reliable, hardworking, experienced personnel specialist, they could do no better than Nikolai Yezhov.

The first three months of 1930 were given over to establishing Narkomzem SSSR and its staff. The order from newly appointed Commissar Ya. A. Yakovlev formally appointing Yezhov as deputy commissar in charge of cadres was followed by orders appointing Yezhov's deputies, creating a personnel department (*Orginstrukt otdel*) under Yezhov, and fixing salaries for the new top staff.[2]

In addition to ongoing and routine personnel appointments, much of Yezhov's year at Narkomzem was taken up in simply organizing the new agency.[3] He wrote to Avel Yenukidze, the chairman of the Central Executive Committee of Soviets (TsIK), pointing out that the new agency had no housing of its own and asking that apartments be assigned to it.[4] He was involved in creating new departments, schools, and laboratories, all with new staffs. It was a sign of the primitive nature of Soviet infrastructure that Yezhov discovered that no telephone communication existed between Moscow and Tashkent in 1930. Work on the phone line proceeded slowly, and pressure from Yezhov led to a promise from the Commissariat of Posts and Telegraphs to establish radio-telephone contact pending completion of a telephone line.[5]

In addition to the ongoing location and appointment of suitable cadres for the new agency, one of Yezhov's first major projects was the reorganization of existing training institutions (and the creation of new ones) for agricultural specialists.[6] As early as 3 February he was issuing orders for the reorganization of the prestigious Timriazev Agricultural Academy (where Antonina had studied in the mid-1920s), whose existing staff was too much prisoner of the old thinking on collectivization.[7]

During this time, Yezhov wrote a series of short articles on education that showed his radical views, which were fully in line with the radical "cultural revolution" spirit of the times. Yezhov had never been a major supporter of the mixed-economy NEP of the 1920s. In the early 1920s he had written to his friend Petr Ivanov, "NEP is annoying. Everything is extremely expensive, e.g., a pound of butter costs 8 to 10 million, sugar 8–18, etc. Bread, a pound of white, 1,200,000, rye bread 400,000, in a nutshell people are screaming 'robbery,' and me as well."[8]

We have seen that he had written to Molotov in 1924, sharply opposing the extension of economic concessions to the British in Central Asia and noting the dangerous history of British imperialism at Russian expense. Now, in the late-1920s, he wrote to celebrate the demise of old-fashioned universities in favor of the radical plan to replace them with institutes to train cadres in the specialties needed for agriculture and industry in the Stalin Revolution. Educational institutions were to become "a sort of factory" to quickly produce specialists for the economy.[9]

The decision to plunge ahead with full and rapid collectivization required expanded training facilities for politically reliable cadres to push the campaign forward. In conversation with Stalin, the dictator had "suggested" that Yezhov organize courses for higher command staff in agriculture, in order to prepare leaders for full collectivization in the provinces. Yezhov had set to work on the matter with his usual energy, but by February he was frustrated with bureaucratic foot-dragging on a matter he considered politically important. On 16 February 1930 he wrote to Molotov complaining that the movement to organize new courses was following a "catastrophic tempo."[10] His letter illustrates several important characteristics of Bolshevik administration and administrative tactics.

Yezhov blamed the "bureaucratic slowness" of several organizations, including his former Orgraspred, which he claimed was constantly submitting revised plans to the Orgburo, thereby "sabotaging" Narkomzem's educational plans. He noted that it took more than two years to finish the courses, making for inexcusable delay; more than two hundred applications had been received, but confirmation of applicants' assignments and enrollment was not forthcoming. "Therefore we insist that one thousand comrades be mobilized from party, soviet, trade union, and economic work" to enter the new courses. He asked Molotov to intervene to short-circuit the bureaucratic logjam: "Viacheslav Mikhailovich, please pose this question directly to the Orgburo, without the usual 'study' by your departments, in order to decide this question quickly."[11]

Yezhov's letter is an example of the common tactic of social blame-shifting. He blamed the delays, among other things, on the presence of non-Bolshevik "alien elements." "It is sufficient to say that in the leading composition of our regional and territorial land administrations there are 40–50 percent former SRs in order to understand how serious is the problem of preparing new leading cadres for us in agriculture." Yezhov noted to Molotov that in the few months that Narkomzem had existed, "we have sent more than seventy people to court for criminal work in land organs." As early as 10 March 1930 he had established an All-Union Action Society to Struggle with Wrecking in Agriculture and Timber.[12] He also established special sectors in Narkomzem to "struggle with wrecking."[13] Although such measures might be thought to presage his future work in the secret police, in the heated atmosphere of collectivization they were not unusual. Like most Bolsheviks, Yezhov was sensitive to the presence and presumed activity of "aliens" and "enemies" in the bureaucracy, and, as we shall see, he practically defined good personnel policy in terms of removing "them" and appointing "ours" to key positions.

Yezhov's latest letter to Molotov, in its criticism of his former boss and agency, also illustrates *vedomstvo,* or loyalty to one's agency instead of compromise or understanding of a common good or bigger picture. Yezhov fought for his agency, even though three months earlier, when he worked for Orgraspred, he might well have dragged his feet precisely in the same way he now found so intolerable in his new post. In many ways, scarce resources (especially skilled personnel) dictated that agencies battled with each other constantly, hurling accusations and denunciations of sabotage and obstructionism when they did not get what they needed. Each agency would be judged on results, more than on politeness or accommodation, and this led to competition among them for resources and for recognition, and to a corresponding tendency to denounce other bodies for obstructing them.

We saw in our discussion of the Orgburo and the Secretariat that these agencies functioned often as councils of elders: leaders of top rank and prestige who blessed proposals from below or adjudicated disputes. In this Darwinian struggle among agencies, one of the important roles of top leaders was that of referee or moderator among disputing agencies and officials. When Yezhov wrote to Molotov, he was asking a top baron to intervene, to cut across the formal existing channels, to use personal power to resolve a dispute. As we shall see, in this system of personalized power, one's rank or position in the party hierarchy did not necessarily mean a change in duties or spheres of activity. Rank, symbolized by the accumulation or holding of top positions, positioned one to resolve disputes at higher levels. When Bolsheviks spoke of the "authority" of a top leader, they meant the level at which he functioned more than the concrete office he held. And that functioning was inseparable from the role as mediator and referee.

As a new agency without personnel, Narkomzem had to staff itself with personnel drawn from other organizations, many of which resisted parting with their valuable specialists and administrators. In such cases, Yezhov often appealed to higher instances to settle the dispute. On 12 April 1930 he wrote to the Central Committee about one Dzhian, who had agreed to come to work at Narkomzem. But Dzhian's boss, Melnichansky, objected to the transfer. Yezhov wrote, "We strongly request, despite Comrade Melnichansky's objection, to assign Comrade Dzhian to us."[14] On another occasion, the Moscow Land Administration refused to release one Protasov, an agronomist, to Narkomzem. Yezhov wrote to the Moscow party committee that "we need an experienced agronomist" and asked that committee to overrule the land administration.[15] Yezhov often used forceful language in such appeals; in letters to higher party bodies, he often "categorically insisted" on personnel transfers he wanted.[16]

Yezhov was just as tough with his subordinates. He demanded that all complaint letters, even those from ordinary peasants, be answered in twenty-four hours and that reports on them be made to the Narkomzem Collegium every ten days.[17] He took Narkomzem's regional representatives to task when they failed to report in a timely fashion: in one case, he formally censured an entire organization, writing, "We regard your silence on the question of staffing district land administrations as complete negligence." Yezhov found himself using this language so often that he printed up forms containing the reproaches with blanks to be filled in with the names of offending organizations.[18] But he was also aware of the limits of paper reproaches. On one occasion, he admitted that some of his local officials were mishandling some peasants: "Writing a paper will not do any good. We will have to send some of our people there to straighten it out."[19] Ultimately, Bolshevik leadership was about sending out "our people" more than about the rule-bound procedures of a bureaucracy.

He was also a smooth bureaucrat. In early June 1930 he presided over a conference of ordinary peasants who had left the collective farms following Stalin's "Dizzy with Success" article in March. His visitors complained that local officials were refusing to give land to individual peasants. Yezhov was understanding and conciliatory, admitting that the peasants had a point. After unsuccessfully trying to convince them to reenter the collective farm, he agreed to take their complaints seriously and get to the bottom of the affair. Whether he did so is unknown. But the peasants left feeling that a powerful official had heard their grievances and would right the wrongs. Notwithstanding whether he actually did anything, his petitioners left with a smile: clear evidence of a bureaucrat's silky charm.

Once the new agricultural commissariat was on its feet, Yezhov got a new and important job. On 14 November 1930 he was given responsibility for the selection and distribution of all party personnel. That month Sergo Ordzhonikidze, a Stalin intimate, was named to head the Supreme Council of National Economy (VSNKh). As Yakovlev had done when he took over the USSR Commissariat of Agriculture, Ordzhonikidze tapped the party cadres apparatus for a deputy to handle personnel for him. Yakovlev had taken Yezhov from Orgraspred to be his deputy, and now Ordzhonikidze asked for Orgraspred chief Ivan Moskvin to move with him to VSNKh, leaving Orgraspred without a chief.

The Politburo met on 14 November to consider Ordzhonikidze's request and at this meeting sent Moskvin to VSNKh and moved Yezhov from Narkomzem back to the personnel apparatus. Orgraspred had recently been reorganized and divided into a party cadres–assignment department (Orgotdel, or organizational department) and a department for distribution of cadres to all state agencies (Raspredotdel, or distribution department). Yezhov was named chief of the new Raspredotdel.[20]

Although Yezhov had worked in the agricultural commissariat less than a year, there are no signs that his work there had been unsatisfactory. On the contrary, he seems to have done his usual efficient job and put Narkomzem personnel assignment on a firm footing. Moreover, his new position was a dramatic promotion: he now answered for cadres assignment not only in a single organization but for the entire state apparatus. Having arrived in Moscow only three years before, he had managed largely through his skill and abilities to move from the bottom to the top of the most important part of the Bolshevik bureaucracy. As Stalin would say, "personnel assignment is the most important factor."

Scholars writing on Yezhov have long sought the origins of his later police job in his early career. Thus one study implies that his 1930 work in agriculture had somehow been connected with the cruel and devastating repression of peasants during collectivization.[21] In fact, as we see in this case and others, Yezhov was a personnel specialist—by 1930, the leading personnel expert—who was assigned to whatever institution or initiative needed specialized knowledge of cadres and their qualifications. This kind of work involved personally knowing a large number of party members, knowing how to mobilize and direct their assignments, and arranging their education and job conditions. Sometimes these assignments were to institutions involved in repression, but more often they were not, and there is no evidence or reason to believe that his work at the USSR Commissariat of Agriculture during collectivization had anything directly to do with the persecution and devastation of the peasantry. Yezhov was sent wherever specialized knowledge of personnel was needed.

The latest biography of Yezhov mentions only two of his activities as head of Raspredotdel in 1930–33: his participation in a commission to set up the Dalstroi forced labor gold mining trust in November 1931 and his position as member of the central commission that carried out the *chistka* (purge, or screening) of party members in early 1933.[22]

Associating Yezhov with repressive or police activities before 1933–34 is highly misleading. First, his membership in the commission to establish the Dalstroi mining trust was standard practice. Whenever any institution was formed or reorganized, the chief personnel specialist was an essential participant. In a system based largely on personalized politics, assignment of cadres and patronage are naturally important factors. Moreover, the Bolsheviks conceived of institutions largely as collections of personalities, so for them the most essential element of any organization was staffing. Thus, as the party's chief personnel specialist, Yezhov was a member not only of the Dalstroi organizing committee in these years but also of commissions to organize or reorganize the Wheat Trust, the Commissariat of Supply, the Timber Trust, the Commissariat of Light Industry, and many others.[23] Similarly, Yezhov's participation on Stalin's 1934 commissions to reorganize the secret police (OGPU) into a new Commissariat of Internal Affairs (NKVD) had the same routine character. It was natural and common practice to include the chief personnel specialist in such reorganizations to advise on staffing, personnel policies, and the like, by no means reflecting some new specialization in repression.

Second, the vast bulk of Yezhov's work in the 1931–34 period had absolutely nothing to do with policing or repression. In these years his name appeared forty-seven times in the protocols of the Politburo. More than half of these instances (twenty-nine) reflect Yezhov mobilizing party cadres for work in industry or for higher education. He was appointed to commissions or ordered separately to propose cadres for work in the wheat, sugar, gold, construction, airplane, metal, timber, and soap industries.[24] He also recommended party cadres for appointment to the several Soviet military academies (army, navy, and air force).[25] Another twelve instances reflect Yezhov's recommendations of senior individual appointments in various commissariats.[26] The remainder of Yezhov's personnel assignment citations in the Politburo protocols pertain to Yezhov's mobilization or assignment of cadres for the regions or for delegations abroad.[27]

Third, even when Yezhov's assignments related to police activities, sometimes his commission memberships were parts of initiatives against repression. In 1931 in the Urals, he headed a commission that found that exile victims were being abused in "horrendous conditions": they were owed wages, were impoverished, and had difficulty feeding their children.[28] Yezhov also participated in the Kuibyshev Commission that sought to reform the judiciary and correct police abuses. In September a memo from Stalin proposed the formation of this commission and ordered it to "free the innocent" and "purge the OGPU of practitioners of specific 'investigative tricks' and punish them regardless of their rank." The Kuibyshev Commission prepared a draft resolution censuring the police for "illegal methods of investigation" and recommending punishment of several secret police officials.[29] In these years we find Yezhov exactly where we would expect to find the party's hard-working personnel specialist.

Yezhov's leadership of Raspredotdel again demonstrated his diligent style.[30] He paid close attention to the structure of his organization; he was a good manager. At a 1933 staff meeting he chided his staff for their excessive paperwork, their careless and narrow bureaucratism, and (as he had in the 1920s at Orgraspred) their rudeness to guests and other officials.[31]

At another staff meeting he made a long, detailed speech to his subordinates in which he carefully outlined his comprehensive restructuring plan for the personnel assignment agency into specialized subgroups, departments, and territorial specialty groups of instructors. He expected his underlings to be as conscientious as he was, and emphasized the Bolsheviks' cardinal principle of leadership: knowing "our people" and how to assign them. To his department's officials he said, "You must know each of your [territory's party] workers personally. If I call you and wake you up any time of night, you have to be able to tell me where such and such a worker works, how he conducts himself, and so forth. . . . I repeat: a responsible instructor of the CC must do this. . . . He has to know cadres not only from their files, not only personally; he has to study them daily, hourly." He also chided his subordinates for their misunderstanding of the importance of what they were doing:

Up to now, there has been this careless attitude toward working with cadres: "Cadres really aren't an interesting thing—you just have to sit, shuffle papers, read forms." That is, you have had a primitive and simplified understanding of it. You people don't understand that we really lead through people. . . . The party leads by appointing people. Power is not power if it cannot appoint people. Strength consists in the fact that we first of all keep the appointment of people and the nomenklatura system in our hands— this is the political expression of party leadership in its organizational form.[32]

In 1933 Yezhov became involved in a series of measures to regulate the membership of the party, activities that flowed naturally from his role as the party's chief personnel specialist. That role was understood to be concerned not only with personnel assignment but also with a range of other duties. We saw earlier, for example, that personnel assignment in the 1920s included close study of the work and needs of economic agencies. In the 1920s and 1930s it also included overall supervision of the party's size and composition, both internally and externally.

Internally, in early 1933, the party leadership decided to conduct a membership screening, or purge, of the party's membership. Purges had been traditional events in the party's history since 1918 and had been aimed at a wide variety of targets. Most often, the categories of people specified for purging were not explicitly related to political oppositional dissidence and included traditional targets like careerists, bureaucrats, and crooks of various kinds; members of oppositionist groups were not mentioned in the instructions.[33] This 1933 screening was part of a cyclical dynamic of party membership. In periods when the party needed more members to accomplish some task (1924, 1929–32), admission was opened to masses of new recruits. This was always followed by a pruning of the membership to weed out what the party called uncommitted "chance" elements: "The party has increased its membership the past two years by 1,400,000 persons, bringing the total to 3,200,000 (members: 2,000,000; candidate members: 1,200,000). Nevertheless, in some places this mass admission into the ranks of the party was frequently carried out indiscriminately and without thorough checking."[34]

The largest single group expelled were "passive" party members:

those carried on the rolls but not participating in party work. Next came violators of party discipline, bureaucrats, corrupt officials, and those who had hidden past crimes from the party. Members of dissident groups did not even figure in the final tallies.[35] The vast majority of those expelled were fresh recruits who had entered the party since 1929. The 1933 purge expelled about 18 percent of the party's members.[36]

The 1933 purge was managed by a specially appointed committee to oversee implementation of the operation locally, and as head of the party personnel office, Yezhov was made a member. The archival evidence does not suggest that he played a major role in the 1933 screening. His papers do contain various summary reports on the screening in various regional organizations and commissariats, but no correspondence or indications that he played an active role.[37]

Yezhov played a much greater, indeed a leading, role in checking on the backgrounds of foreign Communists, who with the rise of Fascism and National Socialism in Europe were beginning to flee to the Soviet Union in significant numbers. From January to December 1933 Yezhov had chaired a committee looking into the backgrounds of foreign Communists entering the USSR through the auspices of the Communist International (Comintern). Early in 1934 Yezhov, as head of Raspredotdel, made his report to Stalin, Molotov, and Kaganovich. He wrote that as the Fascists became stronger, especially in Germany, the stream of Communist political refugees to the USSR had become a flood. He claimed that German and Polish intelligence agencies were "turning" these political émigrés and using them as agents against the USSR, noting that in the past six months the secret police (OGPU) collegium had worked more than fifty cases of Polish infiltrators alone.[38]

Yezhov observed that there was a wide circle of Soviet agencies with the right to invite and vet foreign Communists—the Comintern, Inturist, the OGPU, and MOPR (International Organization for Aid to Revolutionaries)—and that none of them had much in the way of verification of refugees or indeed elementary record keeping. He proposed that with the exception of Communists invited on specific CC or Comintern business, the already stringent rules about entry into the

USSR be enforced for Communists as for others. Uninvited Communist immigrants were to be quarantined and checked by the OGPU, and particularly suspicious types were to be sent to camps for further investigation. No political émigrés were to be allowed to work in border areas, military factories, important electrical stations, and the like. The verification commission of MOPR (which sheltered most Communist immigrants) was to be strengthened.[39] Although Yezhov's recommendations were apparently accepted, they seem not to have been enforced in practice. As we shall see, he and the leadership would return to the question of suspicious foreign Communists in 1936.

From 1933 to 1934 Yezhov's activities began to expand in other directions. In part because the party moved away from mass personnel mobilizations, which had occupied Yezhov in the 1920s and in 1931–32, and in part as a sign of his increasing reputation as a careful and hardworking official, his portfolio grew. Now, in addition to his personnel assignment job, he began to participate in policy matters on a national scale. He took on several assignments relating to verification and checking agreements between various economic agencies, in both domestic and foreign trade.[40] He took charge of certain party investigations, including, for example, checkups on corruption in customs offices and in the aircraft industry.[41] By the end of 1933 he was signing documents as chairman of both the Aviation and Budget Commissions of the Politburo, even though he was not a Politburo member. Thus by the end of 1933 Yezhov had his finger in many pies.[42]

It is not surprising, therefore, that at the Seventeenth Party Congress in February 1934 Yezhov received appointments commensurate with his skills and activities. At that meeting he gave the report of the congress's Credentials Commission, as was expected of the Raspredotdel chief. He was also elected a member of the CC and of the newly organized Party Control Commission (KPK, the successor to the Central Control Commission), which had overall responsibility for checking and punishing infractions among party members. By March 1934 he had become a member of the Orgburo, chairman of the CC's Commission on Foreign Travel, and head of the CC Industrial Department.[43]

The Orgburo appointment was routine: it was customary for the party's personnel chief to be a member, and Yezhov took Ivan Moskvin's seat, this being the first party congress since Yezhov had replaced Moskvin in Orgraspred/Raspredotdel. Moreover, for two years as Raspredotdel chief, Yezhov had already had a major hand in senior appointments. In January 1932, for example, he had nominated the deputy commissars and members of the Collegium for the newly formed People's Commissariat of Timber, and his recommendations were approved by the Orgburo automatically without that body even meeting.[44]

On the other hand, the move to Orgburo was important in other ways. It put Yezhov on the same committee as such powerful leaders as S. M. Kirov (head of the Leningrad party organization and CC secretary), A. A. Zhdanov (CC secretary), A. V. Kosarev (head of the Komsomol), and of course Stalin himself. He joined the ranks of those who not only selected and vetted senior personnel posts; he was now part of the senior team that finally blessed or rejected appointments. He was rubbing shoulders with the top brass, some of whom he now addressed (and who addressed him) with the familiar "Kolya," or as "*ty*."[45] His reputation for knowledge and hard work now led the highest leaders— including Stalin himself—to routinely refer various matters to Yezhov for his advice. Yezhov's archive and other archival sources contain many letters and memos addressed to Stalin, Kaganovich, Molotov, and others, which they forwarded to Yezhov with handwritten margin notes like, "Comrade Yezhov! Your opinion? Kaganovich" or "to Comrade Yezhov. What's this all about? I. S. [Stalin]" or "Comrade Yezhov, what to do about this? I. Stalin."[46]

Membership on the Orgburo was a recognition of Yezhov's status; no longer merely a staffer (however powerful), he had become a visible grandee and now appeared to the party masses and general public as a powerful *boyar* of the inner circle. Party officials began to associate themselves with him. Lavrenty Beria, who didn't know Yezhov well but was good at ingratiating himself, knew a rising star when he saw one and began to address letters to "Dear Comrade Kolya!"[47]

As a senior notable, Yezhov was now a source of patronage and favors, regardless of his formal areas of responsibility, in a system of personalized politics. Bukharin wrote to him for help getting a dacha, having failed to solve the problem through the regular Moscow administration. The former oppositionist Alexander Shliapnikov wrote to him for help in arranging medical treatment. Shliapnikov's wife asked for a new job. (Yezhov wrote on her letter, "We have to help and find her work.") David Kandelaki, the Soviet trade representative in Germany, first wrote to Yezhov's wife asking her to approach her husband about a dacha for Kandelaki's mother. He then wrote directly to Yezhov, who wrote to his secretary, "Comrade Ryzhova: Take care of this and let me know ASAP!" Kandelaki's mother soon got a four-room apartment.[48]

Soviet Foreign Minister Maxim Litvinov was feeling smothered by what he considered excess bodyguard security while traveling abroad. But rather than write to NKVD chief Yagoda, who was responsible for such matters, Litvinov bypassed the police and wrote directly to Yezhov with a personal appeal for flexibility. Even though Yezhov had no formal responsibilities in this area, he intervened.[49] Also perhaps sensing Yezhov's personal power, Ivan Akulov too bypassed the police and wryly wrote directly to Yezhov:

Dear Nikolai Ivanovich,

I am forwarding you an envelope in which I received a letter. I would like to direct your attention to the extremely careless way the NKVD intercepted the letter: the envelope was ripped and the postmark all messed up. If the organs of the NKVD consider it proper to intercept letters addressed to a member of the Buro of the KPK and member of the government, perhaps they should do their work carefully.

With strong handshake, Ivan Akulov[50]

People who saw Yezhov's name in the papers wrote to him trying to establish kinship or establish long-forgotten (or imaginary) acquaintance: "Comrade Yezhov, I don't know if you remember me, but . . . "

One L. F. Sudnitsin wondered whether they were related. Another comrade wrote from Kazan, purportedly asking for nothing except to be "remembered":

> Allow me, a former Red Army man from the detachment in which you were commissar, to congratulate you on your new post and wish you all success in work and health for many years. . . . I am proud of you, my former commissar, and joyous that I knew such a person and will be even happier if you, dear Nikolai Ivanovich, would remember me and in your spare time jot down two or three words to me about yourself and your health—I could not wish for more. . . . I am not writing about myself, and will only say that after demobilization from the Red Army I became a state employee living in Kazan the whole time. Now I'm working in the Tatar supply administration, but that's not important.[51]

Other letters came from various people recalling their real or imagined party and Civil War service together.[52] Citizens now began to write to him, as they did to Stalin and the other senior party figures, with complaints and requests for assistance and personal intervention on jobs, pensions, permission to travel abroad, and the like.[53]

Nobody had petitioned Yezhov when he was working in Raspredotdel, even though he had been powerful. Everyone understood the system to be one of personal patronage and favors, and it was now logical to write him as one of the public party elders for help in solving problems and cutting across bureaucracy.

We have also seen that in the power system of the Bolsheviks, one's place in the hierarchy put one in a position to resolve disputes at a corresponding level. In fact, formal position in the Bolshevik hierarchy operated less as the ability to make or oppose policy than as a marker or credential as a judge of disputes among a certain category of officials. In Yezhov's Orgraspred/Raspredotdel work, we saw how he moderated and judged disputes about personnel at the middle provincial and central levels. Now he continued to referee disputes below the top levels, but as a member of the Orgburo and the KPK, he was now empowered to resolve personal and personnel disputes among senior party notables at a higher level than he could before. These 1930s disputes resembled the personal *skloki* (spats) of the early 1920s. Then, Yezhov was a participant; now he adjudicated them.[54]

In 1934 the KPK created a network of plenipotentiaries, each of whom was dispatched to a region or province to check on the work of regional party committees and ensure the "fulfillment of decisions," as the current phrase had it. These Stalinist *intendants,* representing an inquisitive Moscow center, almost immediately came into conflict with the local leadership in the person of the provincial party First Secretary.[55] Because a KPK plenipotentiary and territorial First Secretary were both powerful figures, disputes between them had to be adjudicated at a high level, and as a KPK and Orgburo member, Yezhov found himself in that role. Complaints from both KPK plenipotentiaries and party first secretaries landed on his desk.

From Rostov, First Secretary B. P. Sheboldaev complained in a letter to Yezhov and Stalin about the high-handed and secretive activities of a KPK representative named Brik, who according to Sheboldaev was end-running him and tattling directly to the CC. "Sometimes we find out what he is doing only when he makes a speech to the kraikom plenum!" Yezhov ruled that Brik should continue his investigations but keep Sheboldaev informed on his investigations. Later, Yezhov had to transfer Brik out of Rostov to pacify Sheboldaev. Brik's KPK replacement, one Shadunts, fared no better and also had to be rotated out. In Kazakhstan, First Secretary Mirzoian complained about KPK representative Sharangovich. In Sverdlovsk, First Secretary I. Kabakov complained that KPK representative Paparde was rude. Yezhov ruled that Paparde should continue his serious investigations of the economy in Sverdlovsk, but should be less rude and forceful. In his notes on conversations with his KPK boss, L. M. Kaganovich, Yezhov said that they would have to shift and rotate their KPK people.[56] Brik, Sharangovich, and Paparde were all rotated to other provinces to mitigate conflicts.

The worst conflict would come in Kuibyshev, when KPK inspector

Frenkel secretly informed Stalin and Yezhov of First Secretary P. P. Postyshev's "bad work" and "purely one-man style of work." Postyshev was a powerful personality. He had been a secretary of the Central Committee and was currently a candidate member of the Politburo. Postyshev retaliated by not only refusing to let Frenkel speak at party meetings but threatening him personally: "If you criticize us, we will criticize you. . . . We should give you orders and you should carry them out. . . . I have the right to give you orders and you are obligated to hear them and not to play here at independence. . . . You can write [to Moscow] if you want, but I recommend that you don't do it. It's very lofty there and you could break your legs."[57] Yezhov removed Frenkel.

This struggle between regional party first secretaries and KPK plenipotentiaries brings the personalized nature of Stalinist politics into clear focus in two ways. First, formally and by statute, the KPK representatives had a right to investigate and criticize the party secretaries. The institution of the KPK in 1934 was accompanied by Stalin's pointed criticism at the same 17th Party Congress of those regional secretaries who acted like "feudal lords," so it would seem that the KPK inspectors had not only the law but Stalin's sanction on their side. Were this a rule-bound system of prescribed powers, their criticisms should have won the day. But the regional party secretaries were in fact powerful barons. Nearly all of them were veterans and heroes of the Revolution, the Civil War, and the struggle against the opposition groups of the 1920s. They had carried out collectivization and five-year plans and were masters of their territories, controlling agriculture, industry, police, employment, and budgets in their realms. Many of them were themselves Central Committee members. By contrast, the KPK plenipotentiaries were lesser personalities who in a personal conflict, regardless of the rules and regulations, were no match for the secretary notables.

Second, the very process of conflict resolution in such cases speaks to the personalization of politics. On paper, according to the KPK statute, such conflicts were to be adjudicated institutionally by "appeal to the Central Committee." But in fact, this meant resolution by a powerful personality: a Central Committee secretary and Orgburo member like

Yezhov. In this case, it is not even clear in which institutional capacity Yezhov resolved such conflicts. He was both head of the KPK (the plenipotentiaries' boss) and Orgburo member (entitled to speak for the Central Committee). That Yezhov's formal role is not made clear in the documents speaks for itself: it was he as powerful person who resolved the conflicts, and nobody cared or asked what formal institutional position gave him the power to do so.

Yezhov's position on the Orgburo (and a year later as a secretary of the CC) put him in a position to resolve other disputes as well. In Tajikistan, First Secretary Shadunts and Second Secretary Ashurov got into a spat; Ashurov wanted more energetic investigations of "enemies," while Shadunts was more cautious. Ashurov went behind Shadunts's back, publishing embarrassing secret speeches. Shadunts retaliated by claiming that Ashurov had signed an antiparty platform. All this also landed on Yezhov's desk. He recalled Ashurov to Moscow and sharply criticized Shadunts, whom he removed a short time later. Then Shadunts went over Yezhov's head to Stalin, complaining about Yezhov's solution: "Today I was removed. It was a surprise. Yezhov said I couldn't maintain a normal situation in the Buro of the CC of Tadzhikstan." Stalin referred the letter back to Yezhov, who noted in the margin of Ashurov's note, "We have to settle this." Shadunts, understanding that Yezhov would be the final judge, wrote a conciliatory letter to Yezhov, admitting his "mistakes." Yezhov decided to receive him personally and found him another position.[58]

In addition to finding himself a higher-level referee, Yezhov continued his basic personnel assignment work. As head of Raspredotdel, he had made recommendations to the Orgburo. Now, from the Orgburo, he confirmed appointments himself or, if they were very high ranking, recommended them to Stalin, who as far as we can tell always accepted Yezhov's suggestions. Often, like the personal spats, these appointments required negotiations, and Yezhov was good at these. In March 1935 he wrote to Stalin (who reserved senior territorial party appointments for himself): "Comrade Stalin. I summoned Pshenitsn. He agrees to become Second Secretary in Sverdlovsk. I had a telephone conversation with Kabakov [Sverdlovsk First Secretary]. He is very satisfied with Stroganov [the outgoing Second Secretary] being placed at the disposal of the CC. He agrees with the candidacy of Pshenitsn, and asks for quick approval." Stalin approved.[59] Sometimes Yezhov was more direct: "Comrade Stalin. To name Kalygin to work as secretary of Voronezh city party committee. Riabinin agrees. Comrades Kaganovich and Molotov agree. I ask your approval. Yezhov." Stalin approved.[60] In all such cases, Yezhov confidently included with his note to Stalin a pretyped draft resolution of the CC approving the request he was making. These drafts became the formal CC orders when Stalin approved — which he did routinely.[61]

By the end of 1934 Yezhov had become a member of the inner circle of the Stalinist leadership, with the broad portfolio and refereeing powers that such leaders enjoyed. His duties — personnel allocation, regulating party size and composition, and participation in various commissions — were vast, and there is every reason to believe that he was among the hardest-working and most efficient leaders. To this point, he was not particularly concerned or associated with police or security matters, and had political developments continued along their normal course, he probably would have worked to a ripe old age along with Molotov, Kaganovich, Mikoian, Kalinin, and others of Stalin's inner circle.

But on the first day of December 1934 an event took place that would put Soviet history on a new and horrible path. The Politburo member and Leningrad party chief S. M. Kirov was shot to death in the corridor outside his office by Leonid Nikolaev, an unbalanced and disappointed office seeker. The assassination sent shock waves through a leadership already (and always) anxious and afraid of conspiracies of foreign agents, peasants, White Guards, former oppositionists, and others.[62] Fearing that some kind of coup might be in progress, Stalin and his lieutenants did what they had done several times before when they thought the regime was in danger or needed quick brute force. As they had done in the past in retaliation to perceived attacks, the Politburo quickly drafted a Draconian law. The "Law of 1 December 1934," or the

"Kirov Law," gave the courts the right to pass and carry out death sentences without the participation of the accused and without appeal.[63]

Stalin immediately went to Leningrad to see for himself what had happened. Yezhov was among the small group he took along with him, and Stalin would leave him there for three weeks to oversee the investigation of Kirov's murder. This train ride would catapult Yezhov into police matters, make him the most powerful person in the Soviet Union except for Stalin, and eventually cost him his life.

Yezhov in 1916. RGASPI

Yezhov (standing), 1916. RGASPI

Graduates of Radio Specialists, Kazan, 1920. Yezhov is at the center of the front row. RGASPI

Yezhov (on platform, right) addressing a mass meeting after suppression of Bukhtarma revolt, Kazakhstan, 1923. RGASPI

Yezhov (second from left, front) at a mass meeting after suppression of Bukhtarma revolt, Kazakhstan 1923. RGASPI

Yezhov (seated, at right) with Kazan comrades, 1926. RGASPI

Molochnyi Lane, no. 20, Yezhov's apartment from 1927. J. Arch Getty

Stalin (far left) and Yezhov (far right) with Politburo members,
May Day Parade, 1935. RGASPI

Sergo Ordzhonikidze (left) and Yezhov, 1936. RGASPI

Left to right: Yezhov's adopted daughter Natalia, Yezhov, Yezhov's second
wife, Yevgenya, Sergo Ordzhonikidze, Ordzhonikidze's wife,
Zinaida, unknown person, 1935. RGASPI

===

# SEVEN

# Yezhov and the Kirov Assassination

*Judging from what I saw in Leningrad, I must say that those people
do not know how to conduct an investigation.*

N. I. YEZHOV

At 4:30 P.M. on 1 December 1934, Leonid Nikolaev, a troubled young
man who had been expelled from the party, walked into Leningrad party
headquarters at Smolny, climbed the stairs to the office suites of city
party leaders, and shot to death Serge Kirov, Leningrad party chief, secretary of the Central Committee, Politburo member, and Stalin's close
collaborator. When party officials rushed out of their offices, they saw
Kirov bleeding on the floor; beside him lay Nikolaev, who had fainted
after unsuccessfully trying to shoot himself. NKVD security agents came
running, doctors were summoned, and Kirov was taken into his office,
where he soon died on the sofa. Party officials placed a call to Stalin in
Moscow. When Stalin heard the shocking news, he quickly assembled a
team of senior officials and boarded a fast train to Leningrad.

We can only imagine what ran through the minds of the leaders as
they sped to the scene of the killing. How could this have happened?
Politburo members were guarded by an entire section of the NKVD.

The strange incompetence of the Leningrad police in failing to prevent the assassination was alarming, if not suspicious. Who could have done it? The traditional counterrevolutionary "enemies" were former White Guards and foreign agents, and these possibilities must have run through their minds. There was also the chance that oppositionists, in the persons of present or past party members, could be involved; Stalin was keen to explore this particular variant.

Stalin would later use the Kirov assassination as a justification for persecution of his enemies. In fact, some historians believe that he worked through the NKVD to organize the assassination for this very purpose. The question is of more than antiquarian interest for two reasons. First, if Stalin was involved, it would be possible to argue convincingly that he had a long-range plan to launch a terror of the elite and, indeed, of the entire Soviet Union. If, on the other hand, the assassination was not his work, other explanations for the terror would have to be sought besides the framework of a grand plan. Debates about Stalin's possible involvement in engineering the Kirov murder have been fierce but inconclusive because of the lack of official documentation and because official statements in the Soviet period were vague and contradictory.

In his speeches to party congresses in 1956 and 1961, Nikita Khrushchev hinted that indeed "much remained to be explained" about the assassination, although he stopped short of actually accusing Stalin. In the 1980s a new official investigation into the assassination was chaired by Politburo member Alexander Yakovlev, an intimate of Soviet leader Mikhail Gorbachev. Assembling an interagency team from the Communist Party, the KGB, and other bodies, this committee reexamined the evidence. But like all previous investigators, the Yakovlev commission failed to produce a report. Their efforts dissolved into mutual recriminations among the members that leaked into the press, as Yakovlev pressed for a conclusion implicating Stalin while several of the staff researchers argued that the evidence pointed the other way.[1] Despite the high-level political advantages of implicating Stalin in the Khrushchev and Gorbachev years, no official investigation by even the most anti-Stalin Soviet administrations had accused Stalin of the crime, though he was directly accused of murdering many equally famous politicians.[2] The leading scholars on opposition to Stalin in the 1930s now make no judgment on the matter, and the memoirs of V. M. Molotov (perhaps unsurprisingly) observe that Kirov was never a challenger to Stalin's position. The most recent scholarly work on the Kirov assassination from a Russian scholar, based on Leningrad party and police archives, concludes that Stalin had nothing to do with the killing. It seems safe to say that the question is still open.[3]

A full examination of the Kirov assassination is beyond the scope of this book. Here we are concerned primarily with Yezhov's role in the investigation, which is well documented in his archive. Although the "motive" and "means" for Stalin to kill Kirov are unclear and disputed, an examination of these materials may shed light not only on Yezhov's role but on the assassination itself. In other words, if we make no assumptions about Stalin's purported motive and means to kill Kirov and thus suspend a priori judgment on his role in the killing, investigating Yezhov's investigation could tell us a lot about whether his inquiry was a cover-up or not.

When Stalin and his entourage arrived in Leningrad, they knew nothing of the circumstances of the crime, but they certainly had reason to wonder about the competence (or complicity) of Leningrad's NKVD. As a Politburo member, Kirov should have been heavily guarded by competent NKVD officers. That an assassin could get close enough to Kirov and shoot him with no one present surely made the Politburo members suspicious of those charged with Kirov's security. With unknown culprits and possible police complicity, it would be a complicated investigation and one hard to run objectively. It was necessary to find a professional policeman to investigate the circumstances of the killing, but with the local police under suspicion, it made no sense for the Leningrad NKVD to investigate itself.[4] Someone else had to be found who was not tied to Leningrad police cadres and who also intimately knew the backgrounds of party cadres to look into the possible involvement of party members. Stalin's solution was to quickly take the

Leningrad NKVD out of the investigation altogether and put Yezhov, a party man specializing in personnel files, in overall charge, with particular responsibility for looking into the possible involvement of both the local NKVD and former oppositionists. This would therefore be a party-controlled inquiry. To conduct the technical investigation of the murder itself, a job requiring police expertise, he selected Yakov Agranov, a deputy commissar of the NKVD, but with no personal ties to his Leningrad colleagues and no close ties to Genrikh Yagoda, chief of the USSR NKVD.[5] Agranov was a secret police veteran, having joined the CHEKA in 1919 and subsequently serving in various police departments involved in "especially important" political cases. He had been a secret police (OGPU) deputy chief since 1931 and deputy commissar of the NKVD since the formation of that organization in 1934.[6]

Stalin fired Leningrad NKVD chief Filip Medved and replaced him with Leonid Zakovsky, a veteran policeman whom he transferred in from his NKVD post in Belorussia. Stalin had brought both Yezhov and Agranov with him on the train to Leningrad; Zakovsky arrived in the city shortly thereafter.

Yezhov was given overall supervision of the investigation of the Kirov assassination and was charged by Stalin with pursuing an investigative line aimed at Zinovievists. All of Agranov's investigative reports and Zakovsky's subsequent punitive operational reports were copied to Yezhov, as well as to their NKVD chief, Yagoda. Yezhov had the rank and prestige to overrule anyone on the scene if necessary and had a direct channel to Stalin. Already on 3 December the well-organized Yezhov had drafted a "plan" for his tasks in his notebook. They included:

1. Direction of the investigation;
2. Borisov affair;
3. Nikolaev affair;
4. The affair of Nikolaev, Draule and others;
5. On families of those arrested;
6. List of Zinovievists;
7. Continuation.[7]

In the immediate aftermath of the killing, and separate from Yezhov's investigation, the regime's reaction was locally savage but spasmodic and unfocused. As they had done during the Civil War, the police immediately executed groups of innocent "hostages" with no connection to the crime. According to Bolshevik "us" vs. "them" thinking, the world forces of counterrevolution ("they") had with the Kirov killing collectively launched an attack on "us." Therefore "we" are justified in retaliating against "them." Several dozen opponents, labeled as "Whites" and already languishing in prison, were summarily executed in cities around the Soviet Union.[8]

Several thousand persons in Leningrad, described as "former people" (nobles, prerevolutionary industrialists, and others) were evicted from the city.[9] This mass deportation was the job of the new Leningrad NKVD chief Zakovsky. In late February 1935 Zakovsky enthusiastically reported that his Leningrad NKVD had expelled 11,095 persons from the city (see Table 7.1).

NKVD chief Yagoda wrote to Stalin on 26 February, rather belatedly pointing out that Zakovsky wanted to carry out "mass operations" in Leningrad. Yagoda agreed that those with incriminating materials

TABLE 7.1

### "Former people" expelled from Leningrad, December 1934–February 1935

| Expellees | Number |
| --- | --- |
| Families of those shot for terrorism | 941 |
| Former aristocrats and princes | 2,360 |
| Former tsarist military officers | 1,545 |
| Former large merchants, speculators, landowners | 5,044 |
| Former tsarist police officers | 620 |
| Upper and middle clergy | 585 |
| Total | 11,095 |

Source: Zakovsky report 16 February 1935, RGASPI, f. 671, op. 1, d. 148, ll. 1–14. These figures are incomplete, as the operation continued sporadically through March, during which time Zakovsky reported regularly.

against them should be deported to the provinces and particularly that Leningrad educational institutions should be purged of "socially dangerous elements." But he pointed out that many of these targets were connected to western circles through the intelligentsia, and he observed that a sudden mass operation could generate unfavorable propaganda abroad. He advised stretching the operation out, doing it gradually over two to three months.[10] As we have seen, however, Zakovsky's mass operation was already in full swing by then, and it had Yezhov's explicit support.[11] This would not be the last time that Yezhov and Yagoda disagreed on operational measures that Yagoda was supposed to be responsible for. And it would not be the last time that Yezhov undermined Yagoda by siding with one of his deputies.

Zakovsky also stepped up NKVD "unmasking" of various purported conspiracies, as always copying everything to Yezhov. He "unmasked" a series of newly discovered counterrevolution organizations in Leningrad. With names like The Russian Party of Fascists, Land and Liberty, and The Brotherhood of Avvakum, these small-scale organizations printed anti-Soviet pamphlets and manifestos, criticized Soviet policy, conducted unauthorized religious services, and the like. In some cases, a couple of pistols were confiscated. In December and January alone, Zakovsky's agents arrested 502 participants in 94 underground groups, plus 782 individual counterrevolutionaries; 1,284 persons in all. Of these, 83 groups were categorized as "fascist-terrorist" and 11 labeled as "Trotskyist-Zinovievist." Zakovsky made a more serious case by arresting active-duty Red Army officers suspected of Zinovievist connections in Leningrad, including 25 commanders, 34 military cadets, and 4 border guards.[12] By the end of February 1935, 843 accused former Zinovievists were under arrest.[13]

On the afternoon of 1 December the assassin Leonid Nikolaev was already in custody, having been apprehended at the scene of the crime. The same day, before Agranov's arrival, the local NKVD had detained Nikolaev's wife, Mil'de Draule, and Kirov's bodyguard Borisov. The next day, several former Leningrad oppositionists whom informers had named as Nikolaev's friends were also taken into custody, including former Zinoviev supporters Kotolynov, Shatsky, and Rumiantsev.[14]

Nikolaev's wife was the first to be interrogated, at 7:10 P.M., just two and a half hours after the shooting. In the first of many Leningrad NKVD bungles, her written statement was misdated. In that statement she said that her husband had been unemployed, lazy, and despondent. She said that he used to have a gun but had turned it in some time ago. In subsequent interrogations, she changed her story, saying that Nikolaev had kept a diary and that she had helped him write it. In a third interrogation she admitted that she knew he had a gun and that he was planning to shoot someone.[15]

The same day, Leningrad NKVD officials interrogated Borisov, who had been straggling behind Kirov when he was shot. Borisov was unable to explain why he had not been close to Kirov at the crucial moment. And in another display of the Leningrad NKVD's incompetence that would arouse suspicion, Borisov had not even been searched when he was interrogated. One interrogator became alarmed and yelled at the other, "You need to watch the old guy, he has a gun!" Borisov was then disarmed, and in yet another sign of Leningrad NKVD carelessness, it was discovered that his gun had been unloaded at the time he was supposed to be protecting Kirov. If this were not enough to make Stalin suspicious of the Leningrad police, Borisov was killed in a traffic accident while in Leningrad NKVD custody, before Stalin and company could talk to him.

It was only then that Agranov arrived and took over the criminal investigation from Leningrad's keystone kops. He organized simultaneous separate interrogations of the assassin Nikolaev, his wife, and the several arrested members of the former Zinovievist Leningrad opposition. Yezhov sat in on these interrogations, and his notebook contains a list of the accused and the rooms in which they were being questioned.[16] Nikolaev began talking freely from the start.[17] He admitted to having planned the killing for some time because he blamed Kirov for persecution of the Zinoviev group and his resulting unemployment. He said that he had initially planned the killing alone but had then talked to Kotolynov and others, who at first tried to dissuade him. According to Nikolaev, they wanted to kill someone higher up, like Stalin, but they later approved his plan. Nikolaev also admitted to contacts with the Latvian consul in Leningrad, whom he correctly picked from a photo array. Supposedly the consul had funneled money into the plot through Nikolaev.

Agranov and his assistants conducted lengthy and grueling interrogations of Nikolaev's oppositionist friends Kotolynov, Shatsky, and Rumiantsev, along with several others of their cohort, and of Zinoviev and Kamenev themselves.[18] The thrust of these interrogations, as might be expected, was to get the accused to admit to membership in a conspiracy that organized the Kirov assassination using Nikolaev as the tool. In what has now become a well-studied scenario, some of them confessed fully, either from party loyalty or after physical pressure. Those who had not confessed were then confronted with the confessions and were worn down. These interrogation transcripts vary. In some cases, the accused refused to confess to belonging to any conspiracy and maintained his or her innocence through the drumhead trial that followed.[19] Some admitted to maintaining contacts with other former oppositionists but denied that such contacts constituted a criminal or "counterrevolutionary" organization. As Zinoviev told his interrogators:

Zinoviev: Nevertheless there is a difference when people happen to spend the night with each other and being in an organization.
Interrogator: Your answer is not serious.
Zinoviev: People were associated with each other for years without carrying out any counterrevolutionary work. You can't mix them all up into one club.[20]

Others admitted to belonging to a "counterrevolutionary organization" but not to knowing of Nikolaev's plans. One of these, Kotolynov, presaged the confession scenario of the three later Moscow show trials by saying that even though he did not know of terrorist plans, the "algebra" of such an organization was such that others would be encouraged to take criminal action.[21] One of these suspects even thanked his interrogators for teaching him the error and implications of his ways. Another group admitted to the full accusation: belonging to a criminal conspiracy that organized the assassination.

On the issue of finding broader and higher-level oppositional involvement, Yezhov was only partly successful. All of the lower-level Zinovievist defendants at the Nikolaev trial were found guilty of conspiracy and shot. But after one month of questioning, Agranov had to report to Stalin that he was not able to prove that Zinoviev and Kamenev themselves had been directly involved in the assassination, and on 13 January the Politburo concurred: "The investigation did not find any facts that would substantiate the claim that members of the Moscow center [meaning Zinoviev and Kamenev] helped organize a terrorist act against Comrade Kirov."[22] So in the middle of January 1935 they were tried and convicted only for "moral complicity" in the crime: that is, their opposition had created a climate in which others were incited to violence. Zinoviev was sentenced to ten years in prison, Kamenev to five.

Yezhov's notes show that already from the second day after the assassination, he was looking into the records of former Leningrad oppositionists, both those exiled earlier and those still in the city. But once the focus was strictly on lower-level members of the Zinoviev opposition, Yezhov went to work. According to his report to Stalin in February 1935, there were roughly 2,500 former Zinovievists in Leningrad, of whom 1,200–1,300 had been "active functionaries." The remaining 1,200–1,300 had perhaps voted "incorrectly" once in the past but had left the opposition; Yezhov proposed leaving them alone.

Of the 1,200–1,300 "active" Zinovievists, Yezhov reported that between 1 December 1934 and 20 February 1935, he had ordered the arrest of 283. With his trademark bureaucratic precision, Yezhov divided the remaining thousand into four groups. His taxonomy was:

1. Former party members who had been expelled and not readmitted to the party. These should be exiled from Leningrad "voluntarily": each should report to an NKVD officer who

would allow him or her to leave for a new city of their choice (excepting places where wives of arrested Zinovievists were exiled). This group initially consisted of 200 persons, later increased to 265.

2. Party members who had been expelled for opposition and subsequently readmitted to the party. Such people might still be "dangerous" and should undergo a new verification (*proverka*). If reexpelled, they could appeal. Initially 463 persons, later revised to 626.

3. Party members who would be permitted to remain in the party but not in Leningrad because they were suspicious, because Leningrad party members did not want them around, or because they might group together again. These should be reassigned to party work in other regions. Initially 325, later 365.

4. Party members who had left opposition long ago and who therefore could remain in Leningrad. These should be put on a list for possible observation. Initially 200, later 270.[23]

In his archive, Yezhov kept exact and voluminous records on the implementation of measures against Leningrad oppositionists. He saved files full of memos from the Leningrad police (*militsiia*) on Leningrad oppositionists' moves to other cities, records of the Leningrad obkom's and KPK's expulsions of oppositionists from the party, and various miscellaneous notes on party expulsions.[24]

As a thorough personnel specialist, Yezhov also began to create a database of Leningrad oppositionists. Consisting of lists and card files (*kartoteki*), this database included biographies and short appraisals (*kharakteristiki*) of several categories of Zinovievists. His lists of former Leningrad oppositionists ran to nearly two thousand pages and included names and appraisals of confirmed and suspected oppositionists, including notes on each person's possible connection to Zinovievists and the source of the information. From these lists and from other sources, Yezhov began to assemble a card file of "personnel registration cards" on former oppositionists expelled from Leningrad. More than 450

cards in all, they were divided into two "volumes": family names A–L
and M–Ya.[25] He did this to follow up on implementation of his orders
about expulsion and/or exile and to be able to keep track of individual
oppositionists. We can also be certain, however, that when the regime
turned to terror in the years that followed, these lists were used for
more sinister and even fatal purposes.

In addition to following the oppositionist investigative trail, Yezhov
and Agranov tried to evaluate possible Leningrad NKVD complicity in
the killing, but their aggressive investigation turned up nothing but incompetence. Nikolaev said that he had made two previous attempts to
shoot Kirov: one on 15 October and the other on 14 November. On the
latter occasion, Kirov's train was moving too fast, and on the former
Nikolaev had decided not to shoot because he didn't want to hit an aide
who was accompanying Kirov. On the 15 October attempt, Nikolaev's
strange behavior on the street had led Kirov's Leningrad NKVD security men to detain him for questioning. According to Nikolaev, they
asked him whether he had a gun. He had his pistol in his pocket but answered no and was released. He was never searched.

Nikolaev's interrogators pressed him repeatedly on two points:
where did he get the pistol, and whom in the Leningrad NKVD did he
know personally? It is almost as if the interrogators were trying to support the theory that someone in the NKVD had provided Nikolaev
with the gun and aimed him at Kirov. Over multiple interrogations,
Nikolaev's story remained consistent: he had owned the gun legally
since 1918, had purchased the bullets himself in 1932, and had taken target practice in the forest. He was casually acquainted with three low-
level Leningrad NKVD officers through family connections. Verification by Agranov and his team produced nothing suspicious in all this.

Another line of inquiry that Yezhov and Agranov pressed had to do
with purported signals of terrorist plans against Kirov that had been ignored by the Leningrad NKVD. Yezhov wrote to Stalin that he had
found an NKVD file containing statements from party members about
"terrorist moods" relating to Kirov.[26] A certain Volkova had weeks before the assassination warned the Leningrad NKVD about the existence

of a "counterrevolutionary terrorist organization" that was organizing assassinations. Agranov and his team questioned Leningrad NKVD officer Baltsevich about why he had not followed up on Volkova's warnings. Baltsevich was pressed relentlessly to admit that he had been derelict (or worse) in not pursuing Volkova's leads, but he insisted that he had done his duty. He said the consensus among his NKVD team was that she was mentally unbalanced. He said that Volkova admitted that she was a wholesale slanderer; she had been crazy enough to implicate senior Leningrad NKVD chiefs Yanishevsky and Zverev as members of the nonexistent counterrevolutionary plot. When Volkova claimed to Agranov's investigators that she had retracted her charges only under pressure from Baltsevich and his team, which had consigned her to a mental institution to shut her up, Baltsevich angrily shouted, "No!" She had been put there for observation, Baltsevich said, to verify her mental condition.[27]

Nikolaev's NKVD friends turned out to be innocent social contacts. The Volkova lead went nowhere; she turned out really to be mentally unbalanced. Nikolaev's pistol had not been given to him by the NKVD. Finally, after an exhaustive inquiry and a detailed autopsy, Yezhov and Agranov told Stalin that the "death of Borisov was the result of an unlucky accident in connection with an automobile accident," not part of any Leningrad NKVD coverup.[28]

Although Yezhov turned up no incriminating evidence against the Leningrad NKVD, he made a strong case for incompetence bordering on the criminal.[29] The top leaders (Leningrad NKVD chief Medved and his deputies Zaporozhets, Fomin, Yanishevsky and Baltsevich) were removed for incompetence. Medved and Fomin were soon convicted of "criminal neglect of leads regarding plans for a terrorist act against Kirov" and sentenced to ten years each in prison.[30] If Stalin had procured Kirov's assassination through the Leningrad NKVD, it seems unlikely that Yezhov would have so aggressively and openly pursued the possibility in his investigation. Nor is it likely that the top Leningrad NKVD leaders, who would have participated in such a plot, would have been left alive to tell the tale.

Yezhov then supervised a purge of Leningrad NKVD ranks. Yezhov was convinced that those ranks were full of "clutter" (*zasorenost'*): dubious, unprofessional, useless people. So the remainder of those checked were verified only by their files—Yezhov was good at files—and were disciplined for "compromising data, socially alien origins, membership in an opposition, moral corruption, or other infractions." By the end of February 1935, Yezhov had checked the files of 2,747 Leningrad NKVD officers, 978 from state security and 1,769 from other detachments (reserves, border guards, and firemen, for example). Of the 978 state security officers, Yezhov removed 157 (see Table 7.2).

Yagoda tended to attribute the problems in the NKVD not to "clutter" but to inexperience. He complained that of thirty-eight thousand NKVD officers, only about one-fourth had served more than six years. Educational levels were low. In the next few months, he opened ten new schools to provide two-year courses for NKVD officers.[31]

Yezhov also wrote a detailed report to Stalin on 23 January 1935, ostensibly about his overall impressions of the work of the Leningrad police. But he transformed the report (which he reworked through several drafts) into an indictment of the NKVD in general. He also proposed to purge still more of the NKVD officers.[32]

TABLE 7.2
**Yezhov's purge of Leningrad NKVD security officers**

| Action taken | Number |
| --- | --- |
| Sent to work in Gulag camps | 50 |
| Transferred from state security | 47 |
| Fired | 21 |
| Transferred from Leningrad | 20 |
| Convicted in court | 17 |
| Arrested, not convicted | 2 |
| Total | 157 |

*Source:* Yezhov to Stalin, 23 January 1935, RGASPI, f. 671, op. 1, d. 118, ll. 48–49.

This document is a landmark in Yezhov's career because it represents his first open salvo in his campaign against NKVD chief Yagoda, a campaign that he was to prosecute relentlessly for the next eighteen months, until Stalin gave him Yagoda's job. We cannot know whether Yezhov was consciously angling for the NVKD job from the beginning, but it is clear that he began to wage a campaign of criticism and innuendo against Yagoda's performance. It seems equally clear that the initiative for the anti-Yagoda movement came from Yezhov himself. For example, his report would show that Stalin was largely uninformed about NKVD practices and structures. The extent to which responsibility for that crime might fall on Yagoda and the NKVD generally was in Yezhov's hands, since he was Stalin's representative and informant on the killing. And it was Yezhov who started it, with no known prodding from Stalin:

> In the process of discussing the investigatory materials on the cases of Zinoviev, Kamenev, and others, certain specific deficiencies in the work on the Leningrad NKVD were touched on. Because these partial deficiencies do not give a full picture, I decided to write this memo in the hope that it might be useful to you in correcting the work of the ChK [secret police] generally. It seems to me that the deficiencies of the Leningrad ChK with respect to the characteristics of Leningrad chekists (composition of people, familyness, absence of operational work, etc.) are signs of a broader problem. These deficiencies evidently exist not only in Leningrad but in other places and in particular in the central apparatus of the NKVD.[33]

According to Bolshevik discursive and social conventions, this was a bold personal attack on Yagoda. Of course, as an Orgburo member Yezhov had the rank and status to make such an assault. Nevertheless, such open offensives by one of Stalin's subordinates against another usually signaled a major struggle behind the scenes. So when Yezhov personally "decided" to write to Stalin about problems in the "central apparatus" of the NKVD at a time when a Politburo member had been assassinated, he opened a major front against Yagoda.

His memo to Stalin was pessimistic and highly critical, sharply disparaging both the Leningrad and the central NKVD on the misuse of agents and informants, investigations, and personnel. He complained that the network of agents and informants was bloated, unresponsive, inefficient, and so carelessly recruited that double agents could easily penetrate it. He provided detailed information about the size of the informant network and how it operated. On paper, the network of unpaid NKVD agents (*rezidenty*) and civilian informants was impressive, as Table 7.3 indicates.

But Yezhov noted that not only the informants but NVKD agents themselves were carelessly recruited and inadequately vetted. Agents recruited each other, often in batches according to planned quotas, without any background checking by superior officers. The unpaid agents were the only ones who knew their informers; the NKVD knew only the agents, who were controlled not by NKVD department chiefs but by their deputies. All this was hopelessly sloppy and loose, Yezhov argued, making it easy for foreign intelligence agents to place their people in the network. As an example, Yezhov cited the case of one Zalozhev, recruited to work in the Government Garage by the Special Department of the OGPU—that is, by one of Yagoda's central departments. Zalozhev had "turned out to be a terrorist," and only luck had prevented him from harming members of the government.[34]

Yezhov advised establishing precise order about who had the right to recruit and control agents in each department. Recruiters of agents who turn out to be spies or terrorists should be held accountable. Finally, the bloated network of agents should be sharply pruned; otherwise control of it was impossible.[35]

Yezhov also criticized the work of NKVD investigators. In general, he said, there was no independent professional apparatus for investigations. The same officers ran agents and informers as investigated cases, so they were able to fabricate and polish the cases as they liked. These officers were information gatherers and good at conducting searches,

## TABLE 7.3
## Numbers of NKVD agents and informers

| Province/Territory | "Rezidenty" (agents) | Informants |
|---|---|---|
| Moscow | 3,625 | 41,483 |
| Leningrad | 2,693 | 21,284 |
| Ukraine | 2,450 | 23,890 |
| SKK | 1,225 | 13,382 |
| AChK | 1,051 | 10,145 |
| Stalingrad | 473 | 5,522 |
| Saratov | 120 | 1,200 |
| Zakavkaz | 402 | 6,248 |
| DVK | 190 | 2,700 |
| Belorussia | 943 | 14,003 |
| Western | 725 | 7,387 |
| IPO | 885 | 7,827 |
| Tataria | 640 | 5,624 |
| Crimea | 342 | 2,621 |
| Kazakhstan | 962 | 10,424 |
| Bashkiria | 707 | 6,048 |
| Sverdlovsk | 542 | 5,193 |
| Cheliabinsk | 595 | 6,200 |
| Northern Krai | 1,123 | 11,942 |
| Middle Volga, Orenburg | 1,397 | 12,972 |
| Voronezh, Kursk | 1,886 | 18,730 |
| East Siberia, Krasnoiarsk | 630 | 6,091 |
| Kirov, Gorky Krais | 636 | 3,712 |
| West Siberia, Omsk | 1,919 | 18,452 |
| Kirgizia, Uzbekistan, Tadzhikstan, Turkmenistan, Karakalpak | 1,389 | 16,617 |
| Totals | 27,550 | 279,697 |

*Source:* Yezhov to Stalin, 23 January 1935, RGASPI, f. 671, op. 1, d. 118, l. 40.

but not competent investigators. "Judging from what I saw in Leningrad, I must say that these people do not know how to conduct an investigation."[36] Yezhov did not say that Yagoda had ignored agent recruitment, organization of investigations, and the composition of his cadres. He did not need to.

Despite his scarcely veiled attack on Yagoda, Yezhov was careful not to violate protocol and etiquette too much. He made a show of consulting with Yagoda before addressing a meeting of regional NKVD chiefs to brief them on the disorder and incompetence he had found in Leningrad and written about in his memo to Stalin. It was, of course, a major embarrassment for Yagoda to have an non-NKVD "outsider," however authoritative, criticize the work of the NKVD and by implication Yagoda's leadership. Such a speech could only diminish Yagoda's prestige and authority with his own men. Therefore Yezhov first asked Yagoda for permission and told Stalin it would be improper to make the speech without the dictator's express order. Stalin gave his approval. In this light, the humiliated Yagoda had no choice but to agree, and Yezhov addressed the assembled NKVD regional chiefs in Yagoda's embarrassed presence.[37] He reiterated to them the criticisms he had made in his letter to Stalin, adding that they lacked professionalism. Among other things, they were too close to the local party committees, often acting as plenipotentiaries for them rather than as independent agents.[38] Security was far too lax; anyone with a party card could enter government buildings. Actually, security had never been tight before the Kirov killing. As late as the end of 1930 the Politburo had to pass a resolution "to oblige Comrade Stalin to immediately stop walking around the city on foot."[39]

Yagoda deeply resented Yezhov's meddling in his bureaucratic bailiwick. He complained to his subordinates about it, and hinted that they should frustrate Yezhov's efforts. He told his assistant Deputy NKVD chief Molchanov that he was worried that Yezhov might uncover NKVD mishandling of old cases and told Molchanov not to talk business with Yezhov without Yagoda's permission. When Molchanov did so anyway, Yagoda exploded. Molchanov later related, "He screamed at me, demanding to know why I had not sought permission from him" before talking to Yezhov. "He told me that Yezhov was not the Central Committee, that his orders were not directives, and that only he—Yagoda—had the right to deal with the Central Committee on questions of the NKVD's work."[40] When Agranov told his boss Yagoda that a certain measure should be coordinated with Yezhov, Yagoda raged at him too, "If you are not the boss in your own house, then go ahead and coordinate your work with him." Agranov also later noted that by the middle of 1935 Yezhov was starting to bypass Yagoda and giving direct orders to the NKVD chief's lieutenants, and by that time they were starting to choose sides between Yagoda and Yezhov. As long as Yezhov's inquiries had Stalin's backing, there was little Yagoda could do.[41]

Yezhov's painstaking investigation of the Leningrad NKVD makes no sense as an attempt to cover up their (and thereby Stalin's) supposed complicity in the assassination. It was too thorough. It was rather an attempt to embarrass Yagoda. Although he did not accuse Yagoda personally of complicity in the Kirov killing (he would do so later), he was suggesting that chaos in the central NKVD apparatus—which was Yagoda's personal responsibility—could have very dire consequences, as the recent Kirov events showed. It did not take a genius to see that Yezhov's implication was that Yagoda's performance created a situation in which the regime, and the lives of Stalin and other Politburo members, were in danger. In terms of implications and possible consequences, therefore, the matter was very serious; Yezhov was throwing down the gauntlet to Yagoda.

The overall public lesson of the Kirov killing was that the former "left" opposition, particularly that led by Zinoviev, was still dangerous. From party meetings to the nonparty press, a new campaign took shape against these dissidents. At the grass roots of the party, a virtual witch hunt ensued in which anyone with the slightest past connection to the Zinoviev or Trotsky oppositions was likely to be expelled. Former oppositionists publicly repented their past sins, and current party members called for their heads.

In its own counsels, the Stalinist leadership established a particular interpretation of the Kirov affair, which it promulgated to the party in an 18 January 1935 closed letter to party organizations on the Kirov killing. The assassination had been the work of disgruntled, younger, low-level oppositionists. The senior members Zinoviev and Kamenev did not know of the assassination and did not organize it, but their dissidence and contacts with former followers had facilitated the crime by providing "moral justification" for the act of terror.[42] There is no reason to think that party leaders did not believe what they said, because their private texts matched their public ones.

It was a sign of Yezhov's status that he was given the task of drafting the circular letter in January 1935 to all party organizations on "Lessons learned from the events connected with the villainous murder of Comrade Kirov."[43] In the letter Yezhov sought to educate party members about the continuing danger posed by "two-faced" oppositionists who claimed to support the party but worked against it:

> Now that the nest of villainy—the Zinoviev anti-Soviet group— has been completely destroyed and the culprits of this villainy have received their just punishment—the CC believes that the time has come to sum up the events connected with the murder of Comrade KIROV, to assess their political significance and to draw the lessons that issue from an analysis of these events. . . .
>
> 1) The villainous murder was committed by the Leningrad group of Zinoviev followers calling themselves the "Leningrad Center."
> 2) Ideologically and politically, the "Leningrad Center" was under the leadership of the "Moscow Center" of Zinoviev followers, which, apparently, did not know of the preparations for the murder of Comrade KIROV but which surely knew of the terrorist sentiments of the "Leningrad Center" and stirred up these sentiments. . . .
>
> As for the Leningrad Party organization and especially the organs of the NKVD in Leningrad, it has turned out that cer-

tain of their links [*zven'ia*] have been infected with a sense of complacency dangerous for the cause and with a negligence in matters of security unbecoming a Bolshevik. . . .

5) The teaching of party history to members of the party ought to be raised to a level worthy of the party. This includes the study of each and every antiparty group in the history of our party, its methods of struggling against the party line, its tactics, and— all the more so—the study of the tactics and fighting methods of our party in its struggle against antiparty groups, tactics, and methods which made it possible for our party to overcome and crush these groups.

Although the January 1935 letter turned up the heat on present and former dissidents, it was not a call for terror. The implication of the first sentence—that "the nest of villainy . . . has been completely destroyed"—is that there were no further nests of villains. Zinoviev and Kamenev would not be charged with direct organization of the Kirov killing for more than a year and a half, and then only on the basis of "new materials" unearthed in 1936. The January 1935 letter identified the "followers of Zinoviev" (but not Zinoviev himself) and other former oppositionists as counterrevolutionary enemies. This political transcript was read out at all party organization and cell meetings. It proved to be a bit of an embarrassment in 1936, when it was announced that the nest had not, in fact, been "completely destroyed."

Privately, Yezhov began in early 1935 to write a book entitled "From Factionalism to Open Counterrevolution (On the Zinovievist Counterrevolutionary Organization)." In the 1935 draft of the manuscript, which he circulated to Stalin and other top leaders for their comments, he maintained that continued opposition to the party line—by Zinoviev, Kamenev, and others—inevitably led to counterrevolution and terror by inspiring others, even if they were not the direct organizers of the killing.[44]

During the rest of 1935 the party's strategy followed this assessment: that the problem and danger had existed primarily in the unknown lower ranks of the party, but that they were facilitated by more prominent people whose attitudes or carelessness made them unconscious enablers of those who might turn to violence. Accordingly, three strategies would be used to deal with the problem: a traditional screening of the general party membership, a campaign of political education to teach party members the danger of opposition, and the promulgation of "lessons" about complacency higher up.[45]

# EIGHT

# Enemies Large and Small

For all we know, a certain liberalism may have been shown
with respect to individual party members.

N. I. YEZHOV

In the investigation of the Kirov assassination Yezhov had demonstrated his willingness to relentlessly pursue any hint of disloyalty. For him, as for Stalin, it was a matter of the party "us" vs. the oppositionist "them," and he put his personnel expertise to good use in checking former oppositionists and compiling files on them. Events of 1935 would again demonstrate Yezhov's indefatigable capacity for work, as well as Stalin's trust in him to handle important matters. Yezhov took the lead in two of the most important party initiatives of 1935: a new screening of party members and the grilling of A. S. Yenukidze, Secretary of TsIK. With his meticulous handling of the Kirov assassination investigation, Yezhov had once again shown his efficiency.

As a sign of his growing status, in February 1935 Yezhov became a secretary of the Central Committee, taking the place vacated by the late Kirov. He became cochairman, with A. A. Andreev, of the Orgburo; together they set the agenda for that body, which in turn set the agenda for the Politburo.[1] Yezhov continued his work as the party's personnel chief: Raspredotdel had been reorganized into a Department of Leading Party Organs (ORPO), and Yezhov became its head in February 1935; later that month he took over leadership of KPK from Kaganovich.

Despite his increased top-level responsibilities, he continued to participate in a variety of other initiatives. He was everywhere at once: in the first half of 1935 he continued to be involved in education questions, aviation, and other matters. During that time he gave speeches to conferences of timber harvesters, outstanding collective farm workers, geologists, and even chauffeurs.[2] He chaired commissions of the Orgburo and the Politburo on paper production targets, party salaries, the allocation of dachas to party leaders, business trips abroad for government officials, and the dissolution of the Society of Old Bolsheviks.[3]

In Moscow in the early summer of 1935, 110 employees of the Kremlin service administration (including Kamenev's brother) were accused in the "Kremlin affair" of organizing a group to assassinate government officials in the Kremlin. Two were sentenced to death and nine others received nineteen years each in prison; the remainder received prison or camp terms of five to ten years.[4] Yenukidze—Secretary of the Central Executive Committee of Soviets (TsIK), chief of the Kremlin administration, and longtime Stalin friend—was accused of carelessness that amounted to aiding and abetting the "terrorists."

Avel Yenukidze, as Secretary of TsIK, was responsible for administration of the Kremlin. The arrests of Kremlin employees obviously cast suspicion on Yenukidze's supervision. The suspicion was compounded by Yenukidze's softhearted tendency to aid old revolutionaries who had run afoul of the Bolsheviks.

On 22 March 1935 Yezhov had received a letter from one Tsybulnik, a Central Committee worker in that body's Secret Department. The letter alerted Yezhov to the existence of "anti-Soviet elements" in the apparatus of TsIK. Tsybulnik noted that there had been "signals" about suspicious elements in TsIK since 1933 but that they had been ignored.[5] Yezhov ordered his secretaries to send copies of the letter immediately to the NKVD and KPK, and within two days Yezhov had convened a working group from his KPK to investigate Yenukidze's apparatus and leadership, again bypassing Yagoda's NKVD.[6] Within a week, Yezhov's group had investigated TsIK finances and personnel policy and reported to Stalin, recommending that Yenukidze be disciplined for carelessness and corruption and that the NKVD commandant of the Kremlin, Karl Peterson, also face "party responsibility."[7] In the course of his investigations, Yezhov displayed his usual efficiency, which here was relentless, if not ruthless. He later reported that of 107 workers whom he "checked" in the TsIK Secretariat, only 9 could be left in their positions.[8]

Already in late February 1935, Yezhov had begun to supervise an investigation into the backgrounds and loyalties of TsIK employees, many of whom were "suspicious" nonparty people. Numerous workers in Yenukidze's Kremlin apparatus, especially from the Kremlin Library and including Kamenev's brother, were arrested and interrogated by Yezhov's partner from the Kirov investigation, Yakov Agranov. Zinoviev and Kamenev were brought from prison and reinterrogated. Minutes of these numerous and lengthy interrogations were forwarded to Yezhov through Yagoda, sometimes daily, from 3 March until at least 5 May. By April, Agranov had started to bypass his formal superior Yagoda and was sending the transcripts directly to Yezhov.[9]

Yezhov made his debut as a visible player in the Central Committee at the June 1935 plenum, where he delivered the official accusation against Yenukidze. He began not by criticizing Yenukidze but rather with a lengthy dissertation on the crimes of Zinoviev and Kamenev.[10] To this point, they had been accused of only "moral complicity" in the death of Kirov. Now, however, Yezhov for the first time accused them of direct organization of the assassination and introduced the idea that Trotsky was also involved from his base in exile. Despite Yezhov's claim to the contrary, this was a radical new theory and one that could give no comfort to political dissidents. "Facts show that during the investigation of the circumstances surrounding the murder of Comrade Kirov in Leningrad, the role of Zinoviev, Kamenev, and Trotsky in the preparation of terroristic acts against the leaders of the party and Soviet state has not yet been fully revealed. The latest events show that they were not only the instigators but in fact the active organizers of the murder of Comrade Kirov, as well as of the attempt on the life of Comrade Stalin that was being prepared within the Kremlin."

Yezhov's assertion was at least an exaggeration if not an outright lie. In the interrogations, Agranov and his assistants had secured testimony from Kremlin employees (including Kamenev's brother B. N. Rozenfeld) that they had received "terrorist instructions" from Zinoviev and Kamenev.[11] The interrogators then pressed Zinoviev and Kamenev in detail about their activities since 1932, trying to catch them in inconsistencies and confronting each with incriminating statements from the other. They succeeded in getting each to criticize the other and express doubts about the other's activities and loyalty. First Kamenev claimed that Zinoviev was more guilty and tried to limit admission of his own counterrevolutionary activity to the period before 1932. Zinoviev denied this at his own interrogation: "I must state to the investigation that the evidence which Kamenev gave, that over the past two years he conducted no counterrevolutionary activity, is a lie. In reality, there was no difference between my and Kamenev's counterrevolutionary activities. This relates to our relations to the Central Committee and particularly to our relations with Stalin. . . . Kamenev was no less harmful to the party and its leadership than I was before our arrest."[12]

Confronted with Zinoviev's testimony, Kamenev again tried to distance himself from his former collaborator:

Interrogator: We show you evidence of arrested G. E. Zinoviev given on 19 March which shows that you along with him conducted counterrevolutionary activity right up to the time of your arrest in connection with the murder of Comrade Kirov.
Kamenev: I deny this testimony![13]

Both Zinoviev and Kamenev steadfastly denied ordering, encouraging, or even knowing about any terrorist plans. They would admit only, as they had after the Kirov killing, that their opposition may have created an atmosphere in which others might be inspired to act.[14] As

Kamenev told his interrogators in a rather contorted formulation: "On me lies responsibility that as a result of the situation created by me and Zinoviev in our counterrevolutionary activities, a counterrevolutionary organization arose, the members of which intended to commit foul evil—the murder of Stalin."[15]

Thus the only evidence Yezhov had for his far-reaching claim was the dubious testimony of minor figures who had cooperated with their interrogators only after lengthy and exhausting police interrogations.

Yezhov then turned to Yenukidze and said that despite numerous warnings about anti-Soviet elements and sentiments among his employees, Yenukidze had taken no action. To Yezhov, Yenukidze's passivity "border[ed] on treason against the interests of Party and country. . . . Comrade Yenukidze must be punished in the most severe way because he bears responsibility for the events [*fakti*] that occurred in the Kremlin. Comrade Yenukidze is the most typical representative of the corrupt and self-complacent Communist who not only fails to see the class enemy but in fact affiliates himself with him, becomes his involuntary accomplice [*posobnik*], opening the gates to him for his counterrevolutionary, terroristic acts." Yezhov concluded his speech by formally proposing to expel Yenukidze from the Central Committee.[16]

Yezhov's speech had three political implications. First, it introduced a new version of Zinoviev and Kamenev's guilt, depicting them as not only enablers but organizers of the Kirov assassination. Yezhov's claims about Zinoviev and Kamenev were a kind of trial balloon (Yezhov's or Stalin's). Oddly enough, it was unsuccessful. Stalin did not speak in support of Yezhov's theory. This in itself was not strange; Stalin often used others to make his points while remaining silent. But this time, the usual speakers at the plenum did not strongly back Yezhov. Despite Yezhov's accusations, no capital charges would be brought against Kamenev and Zinoviev for more than a year, when they were brought to trial for the crime.

There could be two possible explanations for the failure of Yezhov's initiative against Zinoviev and Kamenev in June 1935. On the one hand, there could have been quiet opposition in the Central Committee that forced Stalin to stay his hand. Or it may well have been Stalin himself who was unsure about what to do with Zinoviev and Kamenev. He might have allowed Yezhov to float his trial balloon, then left him dangling by telling him that it was possible to follow up only if Yezhov could prove the charges. On numerous occasions, in order to condemn prominent oppositionists, Stalin insisted on "proof" in the form of their own confessions.[17] It would take Yezhov a year to get that "proof" by forcing Zinoviev and Kamenev to confess.

The second political implication and, for Yezhov, useful by-product of his sally against Yenukidze was the further embarrassment of Yagoda and the NKVD. Although Yezhov gave some credit to the police for warning Yenukidze of the danger in his staff, the fact remained that it was Yezhov, not Yagoda, who made the indictment at the plenum. It was the party, not the police, that was blowing the whistle on the traitors. Yagoda sensed that he was under attack here no less than Yenukidze, so he tried to be more Catholic than the pope and made a hysterical and vicious speech against Yenukidze and proposed punishment more severe than had Yezhov: expulsion not only from the CC but from the party:

I think that by his speech Yenukidze has already placed himself outside the bounds of our party.

What he said here, what he brought here to the Plenum of the Central Committee, is the pile of rubbish of a philistine. . . . For a long time now Yenukidze has been the gravitational center for elements that are hostile and [class]-alien to us. . . . If we follow the thread of facts from 1928 to the events of 1935, we are compelled to state that Yenukidze not only helped the enemy but that he, from an objective standpoint, was also an accomplice of the counterrevolutionary terrorists. . . .

But let us assume that the NKVD really did not raise these questions with Yenukidze. Did Yenukidze show the most elementary vigilance on his side? . . .

In fact, Yenukidze, having taken under his wing people whose

removal we had demanded, had undermined our work and demobilized those of our officials who were engaged in the work of
checking up on these people. Yenukidze did this because, as Secretary of TsIK, he enjoyed sufficient authority among us.

What is more, Yenukidze not only ignored our signals but introduced into the Kremlin his own parallel "GPU," and, whenever
he recognized one of our agents, he immediately banished him.

Of course, none of this removes responsibility from my shoulders.

I admit my guilt in that I did not in my time seize Yenukidze by
the throat and did not force him to kick out all those swine.

Everything that Yenukidze has said here is nothing but unadul-
terated lies.[18]

Just before the plenum Yenukidze had handwritten a letter to Yezhov
saying that he could not remember a single instance in which he had
proposed hiring someone whom the NKVD questioned.[19] At the
plenum, Yenukidze expressed his regret that Yezhov had not mentioned
the letter, and in his own defense he tried to blame Yagoda and the
NKVD, making explicit Yezhov's more veiled criticism of Yagoda, forcing the besieged police chief to defend himself:

Yenukidze: Every candidate for employment in the Kremlin
would first undergo a predetermined probationary period and
only then would he be enrolled on the staff. The probation was
carried out with the participation of organs of the NKVD. No
one was hired for work in the Kremlin without their security
clearance. This applies to all officials without exception.
Yagoda: That's not true.
Yenukidze: Yes, it is.
Yagoda: We gave our security report, but you insisted on hiring.
We said not to hire, and you went ahead and hired.
Yenukidze: Comrade Yagoda, how can you say that?[20]

The third implication of Yezhov's initiative against Yenukidze was to offer the public lesson that prominent leaders, even if not implicated in conspiracies like the Kirov killing, could through inaction function as enablers of the terrorists. It fell to L. M. Kaganovich, as a real insider, to provide this "lesson" of the Yenukidze affair. In the process, he cast another shadow on Yagoda's NKVD:

And you people think that the party can let a Communist holding such a responsible post go unpunished?. . . .

No, Comrade Yenukidze, you are responsible for the Central Executive Committee apparatus. In your selection of personnel, you approached the matter in an unbusinesslike, unparty, un-Communist manner. And for us this aspect of the matter is of foremost importance. . . .

If you are sincere, Comrade Yenukidze, about your readiness to accept punishment so that others can draw their lesson from it, then you ought to have analyzed your situation more honestly, you ought to have told us how enemies had wormed their way into the apparat, how you gave cover to good-for-nothing scoundrels. Instead, you slurred over the matter and tried to prove that nothing out of the ordinary had taken place. [Voices: That's right!]

We must expose, uncover, to the last detail, this whole affair, so that it can serve as a lesson to all Communists who suffer from opportunistic complacency, a subject discussed by the Central Committee in its letter concerning the murder of Comrade Kirov.

Our party is strong by virtue of the fact that it metes out its punishment equally to all members of the party, both in the upper and lower echelons.

This matter, of course, is important not only as it pertains to Yenukidze but also because we undoubtedly have in our party people who believe that we can now "take it more easily": in view of our great victory, in view of the fact that our country is moving forward, they can now afford to rest, to take a nap.[21]

Kaganovich also revealed that the inner leadership, including Stalin himself, was having difficulty deciding what to do with Yenukidze. Various punishments had been discussed. Yezhov's personal papers contain three draft decrees on Yenukidze prepared before the meeting.[22] The first proposed only removing him from the TsIK position and appointing him TsIK Secretary in Transcaucasia. By the third draft, because of "new facts coming to light," the punishment had been escalated to "discussing Yenukidze's Central Committee membership." This was the proposal that Yezhov brought to the meeting: expelling Yenukidze from the Central Committee.

But just as Yezhov's accusations against Zinoviev and Kamenev had had only limited success, his proposed punishment of Yenukidze also created an awkward scene. The Bolsheviks set great store on unanimity, especially in the Central Committee, but Yezhov did not get it for his suggestion. Yezhov had moved to expel Yenukidze from the CC, reflecting the Politburo's prior decision. But the increasingly angry nature of the discussion at the plenum led to a second, surprise motion to expel him from the party altogether. At the end of the plenum, both proposals were put to the vote. Yezhov's motion passed unanimously, and the second motion to expel Yenukidze from the party altogether also passed, albeit on a split vote.[23]

The split vote (itself an extreme rarity in the Central Committee) was not something the top party leadership wanted to broadcast to the party rank and file. In the version of the plenum minutes printed for distribution in the party, the event was portrayed differently. History was rewritten to make it seem that there had been only one proposal and that the ultimate decision, to expel Yenukidze from the party, was based on Yezhov's motion.[24]

Stalin himself showed ambiguity about what to do with Yenukidze. After his preplenum indecision and the split vote at that meeting, Stalin changed his mind again. In September 1935 he wrote to Kaganovich that NKVD materials suggested that Yenukidze was "alien to us, not one of us [*chuzhdyi nam chelovek*]".[25] But at the first plausible opportunity, two plenums later in June 1936, Stalin personally proposed that Yenukidze be permitted to rejoin the party.[26] Then a few months later he approved Yenukidze's arrest and subsequent execution for espionage.

Aside from the year's delay between the Yenukidze affair and the actual terrorism accusation against Zinoviev and Kamenev, there are other signs at this time that Stalin was not prepared to go as far as Yezhov in prosecuting leading oppositionists. Yezhov had just finished his ponderous book manuscript "From Fractionalism to Open Counterrevolution (on the Zinovievist Counterrevolutionary Organization)," and he asked Stalin to edit it. Stalin was apparently unable to get through more than about fifty pages of Yezhov's masterpiece, but in several phrases in the initial sections he did edit, he changed Yezhov's characterization of Zinoviev and Kamenev as "counterrevolutionary" to the less harsh "anti-Soviet and harmful to the party."[27]

Central Committee members took several lessons from Yezhov's speech and the discussion of it at the June 1935 plenum. First, they were introduced to the idea that the guilt of Zinoviev and Kamenev might be greater than previously thought. Second, Yezhov had become a visibly important player: he had brought down the Secretary of the Central Executive Committee and stepped forward as the herald of a modified (albeit temporarily unsuccessful) narrative. Third, Yagoda and the NKVD had been discredited. Fourth, and most uncomfortable for CC members, one of the highest-ranking members of the elite (and a personal friend of Stalin's) had violated discipline. For some members of that elite, this action must have been personally disquieting: if Yenukidze could fall, no one was safe. For others, however, the lesson was that the dangers and threats of the new situation had infected even the inner circle of the *nomenklatura*.

Yezhov's debut in the role of hatchet man against "enemies" was not an unqualified success. Not only was his main "thesis" on Zinoviev and Kamenev ignored, but the proposal he put forward on Yenukidze was superceded. Given that everyone must have assumed that his recommendation on Yenukidze had been approved by Stalin and the Politburo beforehand, the impression created was that Yezhov's authority had been taken down a peg at the moment of his triumph. Still, he had presided over the demotion of a very high ranking leader, and in the process had cast doubt once again on Yagoda's NKVD leadership.

As we have seen, the Stalin leadership took two "lessons" from the Kirov assassination: that prominent persons (like Zinoviev, Kamenev, and Yenukidze) could be enablers of terror, and that the main danger came from lower-level rank-and-file hotheads who were either present or past members of the party. Accordingly, in the middle of 1935 another party membership screening operation, or purge, was undertaken: the verification (*proverka*) of party documents. Yezhov was entirely in charge of this operation, which turned out to be less than successful, if not a complete failure.

Actually planned long before the Kirov assassination, this purge was in the tradition of party screenings since 1921 and was designed to rid the party of "ballast": corrupt bureaucrats, those who had hidden their social origins or political pasts, those with false membership documents.[28] The fact that Kirov's assassin had a party card and thus access to Leningrad party headquarters gave new impetus to the stalled plans to screen the party membership, and in April 1935 Yezhov chaired a committee that included Shkiriatov, Malenkov, Kosarev, and four others that met to plan the membership verification.[29] In writing the 13 May 1935 order for the operation ("On Disorders in the Registration, Distribution, and Safekeeping of Party Cards and on Measures for Regulating this Affair"), Yezhov dutifully characterized the verification as a nonpolitical housekeeping operation to bring some order to the clerical registration of party membership documents.[30] Although the announcement of the proverka did not specifically call for the expulsion of former oppositionists, it was inevitable that many of them would be targeted even in a traditional background screening, and Yezhov constantly tried to put this spin on it. He personally conducted the proverka. He authored the central directives and closely monitored local and regional compliance.[31] He held a series of periodic conferences of both central and regional party leaders during the operation and produced regular summary reports (*svodki*) for Stalin.[32]

Yezhov tried to give the 1935 operation a combative stamp by calling for verifiers in the party organizations to concentrate on expelling ideological enemies of all kinds. His remarks to a closed meeting of party personnel officials emphasized the hunt for enemies. As he told regional party secretaries at a conference on 25 September 1935, "Everywhere the same methods are practiced by Trotskyists who have held out in our party. Trotskyists try at all costs to remain in the party. They strive by every device to infiltrate the party. Their first device is to remain at all costs in the party. . . . He always has in reserve a registration card, approaches another organization and is registered. Such people are expelled three or four or even five times each. They move from one organization to another—we have quite a few people like that. Trotskyists try at all costs to keep their party card."[33]

He bombarded party leaders at all levels with stories of enemies who had entered the party.[34] But despite Yezhov's concentration on Trotskyists and other enemies, the results of the verification, like previous party screenings, struck hardest at rank-and-file party members with irregularities in their documents, most of whom were charged with nonideological offenses having to do with malfeasance or "alien" class background. As a percentage of total expulsions, very few oppositionists were expelled. Two reports, one from Yezhov's 1935 report and another from an internal Central Committee memo written by G. M. Malenkov, are summarized in Table 8.1 and show the categories expelled. In Yezhov's 1935 operation only 2.9 percent of those expelled were oppositionists.

Yezhov constantly complained that local party leaders responsible for the proverka did not take the operation seriously, that they trusted its implementation to subordinates, or that they underestimated the need for vigilance. Frequently during the summer of 1935, he stopped the verification in a given region, issued a CC order denouncing the party leadership there, and ordered them to begin again.[35]

There were two problems preventing the smooth implementation of the verification operation Yezhov wanted. First, in a departure from previous practice, Yezhov entrusted the screening to party committees

TABLE 8.1

**Reasons for expulsion, 1935–36 (% of all expelled)**

| Reason | Yezhov 1935 report | Malenkov 1937 memo* |
|---|---|---|
| Spies | 1.0 | 0.9 |
| Trotskyists/Zinovievists | 2.9 | 5.5 |
| "Swindlers" | 7.9 | 8.0 |
| Former Whites, kulaks, etc. | 19.1 | 27.5 |
| Moral corruption | | 20.6 |
| Incorrect documents | | 15.6 |
| "Other" | | 17.7 |
| Unexplained | 69.1 | 4.2 |

*Sources:* RGASPI, f. 17, op. 120, d. 177, ll. 20–22; op. 120, d. 278, l. 2.

*Includes persons expelled in 1936 after the completion of the proverka.

themselves.[36] His quite reasonable idea was that local party leaders knew, or should get to know, the party members in their organization by conducting the screening of party members individually and in person.

But local and regional officials had territories to run and economic targets to meet. Their administrations contained subordinates who had to be qualified and loyal to the local leader. Because previous membership in the Trotskyist or Zinovievist organizations implied party membership dating back to the twenties, ex-oppositionists still in the party were likely to have worked their way up from the rank and file into leadership positions in local political machines by 1935. Yezhov's call for vigilance, therefore, was implicitly a demand for local leaders to purge their own "family circles" of capable officials, an idea that they must have disliked. This resulted in some of them expelling too few, according to Yezhov's standards. There was also a natural tendency of local party secretaries to deflect the purge downward to the rank and file, resulting in batch expulsions of too many. From Yezhov's point of view, by entrusting the purge to party organizations themselves he was giving them the chance to put their own houses in order.[37] Instead, they protected their own and displayed their "vigilance" by expelling large numbers of helpless party members outside the local elite leadership families. This meant that Yezhov frequently had to intervene against local party secretaries to force them back on the track he wanted.[38]

They were able to do this because of the second fundamental problem with the proverka: vague instructions allowed the locals to interpret and implement the operation in ways that suited them. As we have seen, the original order for the screening had not even mentioned rooting out oppositionists but had rather characterized the goals of the operation in terms of cleaning up party files, restoring order to the membership cards, and ridding the party of (nonideological) "ballast": careerists, crooks, those not paying dues, those losing their party cards, and other "chance elements."[39] So when Yezhov pressed local party secretaries to go after locally prominent former dissidents who were valued members of local elites, the secretaries were able implicitly to invoke the proverka's original instructions to justify mass expulsions of rank-and-file "ballast."

This friction between central and local party leaders explains why the proverka, originally planned for June–August 1935, was never finished and had to be overtaken by a replacement operation, the Exchange of Party Cards in 1936. The mass, inconsistent, and chaotic expulsions of the proverka also produced a huge number of appeals and complaints that were still being cleaned up in 1937. As late as February 1936, Yezhov was still castigating some regional party leaders. He refused to confirm the completed proverka in Sverdlovsk, for example: "Really we don't know how many members and candidates we have there. We asked three times for data. You sent reports, but we doubt the data. . . . After several of these conferences I see that we didn't sufficiently explain how to do this concretely."[40] Yezhov had little to brag about with the proverka.

Another structural problem with the proverka had to do with institutional conflict, particularly the role of the NKVD. Privately, to Stalin, Yezhov never missed an opportunity to criticize Yagoda's secret police. More than once in his summary reports to Stalin on the proverka,

Yezhov noted that the NKVD was "standing aside" or "not sufficiently active" in the struggle with oppositionists.[41]

But publicly Yezhov was respectful toward the NKVD. According to his final report on the proverka, as of December 1935, 9.1 percent of the party's members had been expelled, and 8.7 percent of those expelled had been arrested; he gave a corresponding figure of 15,218 arrests out of 177,000 expulsions, or a little less than 1 percent of those passing through the verification.[42] The level of arrests varied considerably from province to province, and there is strong evidence that relations between party and police were not always smooth. Some local party leaders complained about police interference in the party's political turf.

In fact, three different agencies were involved in the proverka: party organizations, the NKVD, and the Procuracy (which had to approve any arrests). In the course of the proverka, party organizations verified their membership. At the same time, local NKVD units passed along information to the party committees on suspicious party members who had somehow attracted police notice.[43]

Official resolutions and reports piously and confidently stressed the

TABLE 8.2
**Party Expulsions and Police Arrests, 1935**

|  | Party organization | | |
| --- | --- | --- | --- |
|  | Ukraine | Ivanovo | Western |
| Number of persons about whom the NKVD sent information to party organizations: | 17,368 | 3,580 | 3,233 |
| Number and % expelled by party orgs. | 6,675 (38%) | 1,184 (33%) | 1,337 (30%) |
| Number and % arrested by NKVD | 2,095 (31%) | 261 (22%) | 312 (23%) |
| % ultimately arrested | 12% | 7% | 10% |

*Sources:* RGASPI f. 17, op. 120, d. 184, ll. 63–66; d. 183, ll. 60–65, 92.

close cooperation between the party and police.[44] Such reports were meant to display unanimity for the middle party leaders. But behind the scenes, the story was different, and Yezhov once again displayed the essential function of Bolshevik leaders at any level: that of referee and moderator. He noted privately that cooperation between party and police organizations was not good. Party organizations had been reluctant to concede a political monitoring role to the NKVD, preferring instead the former system in which the NKVD investigated state crimes not involving members of the party and left political offenses to the party organs. The information in Table 8.2 shows, in fact, that party and police organizations worked badly together and frequently disagreed on who was "the enemy." Of the suspicious persons referred to party organizations by the NKVD, about one-third were expelled from the party. Of those, fewer than a third were arrested by the NKVD.

Yezhov also demonstrated his refereeing skills at a September 1935 conference of regional party secretaries and is worth quoting at length:

The problem here is not that of directives. We are, perhaps, a little guilty ourselves in this matter. The top brass are also human, and we haven't given attention to this matter in time. But I think that here we are dealing with people who simply do not understand what's at issue; I mean certain officials who have gotten the NKVD involved where it is not needed, who have dumped work on the NKVD that they should have done themselves and who, on the other hand, do not permit the NKVD to concern itself with that which the NKVD should concern itself with.

I want to talk about the division of labor and about the mutual relationship that ought to normally arise between [the NKVD and the party organizations].

First, I want to say that the matter comes down to this, that you conducted the verification. But in verifying a member of the party, the authenticity of his party documents—that is, his entire past and present—you may run across a swindler, an adventurist, a scoundrel, a spy, and so on. You may have some grounds for suspicion, so you finish the case and then you hand over this person to the NKVD. [Voice: But the procurator doesn't always give his approval.]

You are a true bureaucrat. Excuse me, but the way you are conducting your verification in Eastern Siberia shows that it is the procurator who is boss at your place and not you. Perhaps we'll entrust the verification process, then, to your procurator, if that's what you want! The territorial committee cannot make the procurator give his sanction—you are talking nonsense. And secondly, it is not the procurator who sanctions the arrest of a party member but the secretary of the territorial committee. The secretary of the territorial committee coordinates his work with the NKVD when deciding whom to arrest. If you are afraid of taking on the responsibility, we'll reassign the task to the procurator. If you want a party member to be arrested, don't you think you can have it done yourself? . . .

In practice, there are differences of opinion here. Either you send people to the NKVD about whom there are no doubts—you just simply need to have him arrested, to have him convicted—or else you send to the NKVD people who have nothing to do with the matter in question, and often you send all of them to the NKVD. . . .

You [the party] should organize your work with the NKVD in such a way that full daily contact is established with it, so that you can unmask a certain person. . . . And there is no need, no purpose to arrogating their work to ourselves. What is needed is a definite relationship to these [NKVD] organs. . . . And the heart of the matter lies in this, that you establish contact with the NKVD in a way that will make possible unified work.[45]

The messy and confusing screening generated another problem: massive appeals from expelled members. Party rules allowed for someone expelled from the party to appeal that decision, first to the local or regional party committee and eventually to Moscow's KPK if necessary.

With thousands of members being expelled in the proverka, the number of appeals mounted quickly. In September 1935 Yezhov had tried to restrict the appeals process by telling regional party secretaries to speed up the process:

> Concerning the question of appeals [of those expelled from the party] and time periods for appeal: I believe that we will have to establish one general appeals time period for all party organizations. . . . Because if we permit a member of the party who has been expelled and whose party card has been taken from him to continue his appeals for six months, a year, two years, or three years and so on, it goes without saying that we shall never be rid of these appeals. . . . Besides, for all we know, a certain liberalism may have been shown in respect of individual party members, a liberalism which we have plenty of in our Party Collegium. . . . Of course, if you have no doubts whatsoever regarding the materials of the case in your possession, then you may hear the case without summoning the appellant.[46]

Moscow party leaders were concerned that the mass expulsions could create embittered enemies among ex-party members.[47] By the end of 1935 the Central Committee staff was investigating the numbers of expelled and finding that some party organizations had as many former members as current members.[48] Moscow party officials not only kept an eye on those expelled, they checked into their moods.[49]

The Proverka of 1935 was followed in early 1936 by the Exchange of Party Documents. At the December 1935 plenum of the Central Committee, Yezhov reported on the completion of the proverka, which had begun in May 1935 and was to have been completed in three months. As it happened, its term was extended for another three months, and as Yezhov spoke in December it still had not been completed. Despite Yezhov's claims for its success, the need to launch yet another screening, the Exchange of 1936, testified to the failure of the initial effort and was a bad mark against Yezhov. He was also the target of considerable criticism, including some from Stalin, about the number of appeals and complaints.

Appeals that had been pouring in to central party bodies were being processed unevenly, and the June 1936 plenum of the Central Committee took up the question. *Pravda* noted that Yezhov had given a report and that decisions were reached on the basis of his report as well as on "words from Comrade Stalin."[50] No corresponding Central Committee resolution was published, but a series of press articles in subsequent days reported that lower-level party officials had taken a "heartless attitude" toward party members, had expelled many of them for simple nonparticipation in party life, and had been slow to consider appeals and readmissions of those wrongly expelled.[51]

Careful readers of even this minimal public text could discern the outlines of something curious. The press formulation "on the basis of Comrade Yezhov's report and words from Comrade Stalin" was unusual. It suggested that somehow Yezhov's speech was not sufficient or completely authoritative: additional "words" from Stalin had been required. These additional words had been a criticism of Yezhov.

When Yezhov reported on the proverka operations, Stalin complained about the numbers expelled in Yezhov's operation and Yezhov defended himself by pointing out how many enemies had been ejected:

Yezhov: Comrades, as a result of the verification of party documents, we have expelled over two hundred thousand party members.

Stalin: That's quite a lot.

Yezhov: Yes, quite a lot. I'll talk about it. . . .

Stalin: If we expel thirty thousand — (inaudible), and if we also expel six hundred former Trotskyists and Zinovievists, then we would gain even more from that.

Yezhov: We have expelled over two hundred thousand party members. Some of the expellees, Comrades, have been arrested.[52]

In the final version of the plenum transcript, prepared for party members' consumption, Stalin's criticism of Yezhov's operation was muted:

> Yezhov: You know, Comrades, that during the verification of party documents we have expelled over two hundred thousand Communists.
> Stalin: That's quite a lot.
> Yezhov: Yes, that is quite a lot. And this obligates all party organizations all the more so to be extremely attentive to members who have been expelled and who are now appealing.[53]

As we have seen, in his remarks to regional party secretaries the previous September, Yezhov had taken a rather hard line on appeals from expelled party members. He had complained that "a certain liberalism may have been shown in respect of individual party members." A few months later, in March 1936, he had again complained about excessive appeals, noting that it had become a "whole industry" in which lawyers charged twenty-five rubles per appeal.[54] Now, however, in June 1936, Stalin suggested a much more attentive attitude toward appeals:

> But let me raise a question: Is it not possible for us to reinstate some or many of the appellants as candidate members? . . . To this day, a certain, if I may say so, wholesale attitude towards party members has held sway among party leaders. They expel you. You appeal. . . . For this reason, it would be a good idea if the Org-buro of the CC [that is, Yezhov] clarified this as soon as possible, if it explained that it doesn't follow from the party rules, from the traditions of the Bolshevik Party, that a party member who has been expelled could not be reinstated as a candidate member or a sympathizer. This, after all, will allow a man to retain certain spiritual and organizational ties with the Party. This opens up real prospects for him.

At his September conference, Yezhov had also set a firm deadline by which all appeals had to be considered. Now Stalin openly questioned the practice:

> Stalin: Naturally, appeals must be handled in timely fashion, without dragging them out. They must not be put on the shelf. This goes without saying. . . .
>
> Shubrikov: . . . According to instructions issued by the CC [that is, by Yezhov], this work should have been completed by the twentieth of May.
>
> Stalin: Perhaps it was a mistake, then, to have set a deadline?[55]

Under fire for his handling of these matters, Yezhov quickly jumped on the bandwagon and reversed everything he had been saying for a year:

> I must tell you that no one has shown any attentiveness to the expellees. Some district committee secretary expels someone from the party and considers his role in the matter finished. What happens to this person, where he'll end up, will he find work or won't he—this concerns absolutely no one. . . . As you can see, it is vigilance turned upside down. Of course, that kind of vigilance isn't worth a farthing. . . . Naturally, this has nothing to do with vigilance. [Voices: That's right!] It is not vigilance but nonsense. It is nothing but a case of bureaucrats protecting themselves, so that no one will say that they are not vigilant.[56]

Yezhov's limitless capacity for hard work meant that he was practically everywhere at once in 1935. He was a member of the Orgburo, a secretary of the Central Committee, and party overseer of the NKVD. He headed the Party Control Commission and ran a large-scale national party purge. He spoke to meetings of chauffeurs and Central Committee members. He ran several Central Committee departments and served on countless ad hoc Politburo commissions. By the end of 1935 nobody had more official party positions than Yezhov, and, it is fair to say, nobody had more influence on party operations save Stalin.

Still, 1935 was not a shining year for Yezhov's career and his prominence was matched by a string of embarrassing failures. Twice, in January after the Kirov assassination and again in June, he had pointedly failed to prove his theory that Zinoviev, Kamenev, and Trotsky were the direct organizers of the Kirov assassination. Stalin refused to proceed on the slim evidence Yezhov had produced.

Yezhov's 1935 proverka, although he portrayed it as a great success, was a dismal failure. It took three times as long as planned and in the end had to be repeated in the guise of an Exchange of Party Documents.[57] The vague instructions of the proverka meant conflict and confusion among party committees, the NKVD, and local procurators, all of which Yezhov had to referee. There are no signs that he was more than temporarily successful at this, but it did give him the opportunity to take a few more slaps at Yagoda's NKVD.

Conflicting instructions also meant that the local and regional party leaders had considerable leeway in interpreting the screening (and defining the victims) in ways that suited them more than they suited Moscow. The resulting categories of those expelled showed that despite Yezhov's constant urgings to go after oppositionists, most of the victims were rank-and-file people with minor offences whom the local party people found safe to eject. Stalin was annoyed at the mix of oppositionists and average members in Yezhov's operation, and said so.

This central/regional tug of war also meant that the fallout from the proverka—mass appeals flooding into Moscow—clogged the party bureaucracy and created large numbers of discontented former members, both of which bothered Stalin.

Despite Yezhov's failure to convict Zinoviev and Kamenev and the dubious proverka that he ran, his stock remained high because of the other major effort he led in 1936. A new investigation of the Kirov assassination and other oppositionist conspiracies had come to the top of Stalin's agenda. At the beginning of 1936 Stalin approved an effort by

Yezhov to reopen the Kirov murder investigation and to broaden the investigation to include virtually all Trotskyists and Zinovievists. This put him in Yagoda's office and on his back to an even greater extent before; ultimately, this assignment would catapult Yezhov into the NKVD leadership by autumn.

# NINE

# Angling for the Job

We should shoot a pretty large number. Personally I think
that this must be done in order to finally finish with this
filth. It is understood that no trials will be necessary.
Everything can be done in a simplified process.

N. I. YEZHOV

Even before Yezhov assumed the NKVD leadership in the fall of 1936,
he had become one of the most powerful persons in the USSR. Most of
his main activities in 1936, as we shall see, were related to the growing
campaign of repression against former dissidents: followers of Trotsky,
Zinoviev, Kamenev, and Bukharin.[1] Since most of his activities related
to matters within the sphere of NKVD security, they gave him occasion, either implicitly or explicitly, constantly to snipe at Yagoda's leadership of the police.

No opportunity to trip up Yagoda escaped his notice. For example,
Yezhov kept files on suspicious "unusual events" that the wary Stalinists
thought might be threatening. This file contained investigations of po-
tentially suspicious airplane crashes, automobile accidents, and even
muggings. A Soviet pilot had misnavigated and accidentally strayed

into Latvian air space. In the Azov–Black Sea region, a collective farmer had discovered the theft of some bread and had been murdered for his trouble. A party member had been killed while walking along the railroad: the investigation continued. (This "terrorist act" had been forwarded to Yezhov by the NKVD.) A schoolteacher had committed suicide after pressure from a corrupt local government chief. Another schoolteacher had committed counterrevolutionary acts by getting her students to write subversive rhymes, including the politically dangerous "The steamship goes, water through the wheels, we will feed the young Communists to the fish!" The son of a regional soviet chief was playing with guns and shot a playmate. (It turned out that elite children of party officials often took their fathers' pistols into the woods for target practice.) Anonymous leaflets were scattered about in Gorky Park in Moscow.[2]

The attention senior Soviet leaders paid to such random events is a reflection of their constant anxiety about even the smallest matters.[3] Moreover, the Stalinists were inclined to attach sinister political meanings to everyday events. A farmer had murdered his children, claiming that he had no means to feed them. When an investigation showed that he did have food, the conclusion was that the affair had antiregime "political meaning." In another case, the sloppy police investigation of a fire on a farm "did not uncover the possible counterrevolutionary role of religious believers and sectarians."[4] According to a Politburo resolution, an apartment fire at Kaganovich's residence was "to be regarded not as an accident but as having been organized by enemies." The NKVD was ordered to investigate along those lines.[5]

Yezhov's file on "unusual events" reflected not only the usual extreme Stalinist suspicion. On his own initiative, Yezhov was checking up on Yagoda, looking for events that Yagoda might fail to investigate. He also saved particularly embarrassing material on Yagoda's deputies. In October 1935 NKVD Deputy Commissar Agranov (with whom Yezhov had worked on the Kirov investigation) had let his wife drive his car. She had crashed into a taxi, killing the occupants. Agranov's NKVD colleagues, department heads, and Yagoda intimates Pauker and Volovich quickly repaired his car, found a poor chauffeur to accuse, and covered up the incident. Yezhov put this in his file.[6]

In addition to his multilevel campaign against Yagoda, Yezhov still had time to tend to other matters as well. His capacity for work meant that he had other portfolios as well, and continued close participation and supervision in many other spheres, ranging from high-level dispute resolution to KPK disciplinary activities to approving travel abroad to investigating the Communist International. He supervised a variety of schools and educational administrations, continued to oversee Soviet aviation, helped organize a National Committee to Struggle for Peace, ruled on efforts to restore Stalin's birthplace in Georgia, and even worked on rules for buying train tickets and distributing automobiles to party committees.[7] Meanwhile, as head of ORPO he worked as chief editor of the party journal *Partiinoe stroitel'stvo*.[8]

Yezhov also continued his work with personnel, but at a higher level. Although G. M. Malenkov replaced him as head of ORPO early in 1936, his positions as CC secretary and Orgburo member meant that he actively worked as personnel referee at high levels, resolving disputes at the level of CC members. In July 1936 he intervened in and resolved a dispute between CC member and Voronezh region First Secretary Riabinin and Commissar of Heavy Industry Sergo Ordzhonikidze. It seems that Ordzhonikidze had removed one Shablygin as director of the Voronezh Radio Factory and replaced him with one Nude without consulting Riabinin's provincial party leadership. Riabinin pointed out that Nude had lost his previous job at a Moscow factory for being "unfit" and claimed that Ordzhonikidze's deputies were always sending unqualified specialists who then intrigued against director Shablygin. Clearly, Shablygin was part of Riabinin's circle in Voronezh, and the First Secretary had leapt to his defense.

Such disputes between a CC member and a People's Commissar could be handled only at the highest level, and short of Stalin there was now no senior leader higher than Yezhov. Yezhov began by soliciting briefs from the CC Industrial Department and Ordzhonikidze's departments. Of course, Ordzhonikidze's deputies claimed that Shablygin had been a poor factory director and asserted their right to remove him without anyone's agreement or permission. The Industrial Department, however, supported Riabinin, considering his protest to be "correct." They said that the newly appointed director Nude was in fact "worthless" and that the Heavy Industry administration had smeared outgoing director Shablygin in order to hide its own mismanagement. Yezhov decided in favor of Riabinin, inviting him and Shablygin to an Orgburo meeting and copying the decision to Ordzhonikidze.[9]

Similarly, in Smolensk, CC member and First Secretary I. P. Rumiantsev wrote to Yezhov on 27 August 1936 complaining about one Loginov, a Moscow plenipotentiary for harvest matters. Rumiantsev said that Loginov was insulting and, "under the guise of Bolshevik directness," discredited the regional party committee. Yezhov wrote across Rumiantsev's letter, "Have to send someone else to Smolensk and send Loginov to another region."[10]

The origins of Yezhov's savage 1937–38 "mass operations" against foreigners and Soviet citizens of foreign extraction go back several years. As we have seen, Hitler's rise to power in early 1933 had led to increasing numbers of foreign Communists fleeing to the USSR for asylum from Fascist regimes. And more broadly, Soviet concern about foreign security and threats increased in the 1930s, eventually to a full-blown spy mania in 1937–38. Yezhov was to play a key role in these xenophobic terror operations, but long before that he had concerned himself with foreign connections, and as secretary of the CC, already by 1934–35 he was charged with overall supervision of such things.

For example, he had authority to approve or disapprove foreign travel by Soviet citizens and delegations. We have numerous examples of how seriously the Soviet leadership took these matters. In March 1936 N. I. Bukharin was sent to Paris to arrange the purchase of some of Marx's manuscripts. Writing to Yezhov through Soviet Foreign Minister Litvinov, Bukharin asked for permission for his new wife, Larina, to join him there. Yezhov benevolently wrote across the top of Bukharin's letter, "For my personal files. Send the wife."[11]

In July 1935 French Communists wrote to Yezhov asking permission for a Soviet sport delegation to visit Paris in August. They complained that they had written before but had received no answer. Such a matter would be routine in most countries and resolved at a much lower level, but in the Soviet Union of the 1930s it was a security question for the highest authorities. Across the top of the letter, Yezhov scrawled, "Put the question to the Orgburo." Yezhov also directed a similar request from Sweden to the Orgburo.[12]

The highest leadership of the country occupied itself with the details of delegations traveling abroad. A Soviet delegation was to visit RCA Corporation in New York in 1936 pursuant to a formal agreement on technical assistance. Stalin was personally interested in the precise composition of the delegation, and Yezhov, as secretary of the CC, was expected to interview and vet each one. Late in 1935 Yezhov reported to Stalin on how the Soviet delegation members had been screened and selected, pointing out that each member had undergone a "strict checking" of party membership history, education, and occupation. His report was accompanied by detailed lists and charts of the delegation composition.[13]

Before the delegation's departure for New York, Yezhov, who himself had been abroad only for short vacations, lectured its members on how to conduct themselves abroad.[14] They were to be constantly vigilant against attempts by devious capitalists to subvert their loyalty or recruit them as foreign spies. They were to exhibit Soviet patriotism but not brag; be respectful of Western technological progress but not fawn over it. They were to dress properly, but not overdress. Yezhov solemnly advised them to follow Western customs by bathing more often than they did at home.[15]

As early as 1934 Yezhov had been involved in checking the activities of Soviet citizens working abroad. On 26 February of that year, a letter reached him about purportedly suspicious comments made by ambassador to England Ivan Maisky, who had praised the moderate socialist Sydney Webb. (Yezhov took no action.) Other reports on the conduct of Soviet diplomatic personnel abroad routinely crossed his desk over the next two years.[16] By 1936 Yezhov's position as CC secretary authorized him to make unilateral decisions on such matters. On 25 January of that year, Soviet ambassador to the United States Troianovsky wrote to Yezhov about one V. V. Gombard, who had been arrested back in 1930. Troianovsky informed Yezhov that Gombard's brother in the United States "had provided us several useful services" and asked Yezhov to look into the matter. Yezhov ordered the release of the imprisoned Gombard brother, who then successfully appealed to Yezhov to help him find an apartment.[17]

As we have seen Yezhov played a leading role in checking on the backgrounds of foreign Communists in the USSR. His recommendations in 1934 for more careful verification of these immigrants had not been implemented by MOPR and the Comintern, and late in 1935 the Politburo stopped free entry to the USSR from Poland and invalidated entry permits issued by these organizations for Polish Communists entering the USSR. Henceforth these immigrants would have to receive permits directly from Yezhov in his capacity as secretary of the Central Committee.[18]

On 4 January 1936 Comintern Secretary Dmitri Manuilsky wrote to Yezhov warning about spies entering the USSR under cover of foreign Communist Party membership. Despite Yezhov's earlier efforts, Communists from Poland, Finland, Latvia, Lithuania, and Estonia had found it easy to enter the USSR through a simplified procedure known as the "green corridor." Manuilsky wrote that this mass influx must stop and that applicants for entry should be considered on a case-by-case basis; "only people we know" through the Comintern or fraternal party leadership should be admitted. In good Soviet bureaucratic style, Manuilsky deflected major blame from his Comintern onto MOPR, whose "current leadership" he advised changing. In the margin of Manuisky's letter, Yezhov noted, "We need to call a conference."[19]

A month later, after soliciting memos from the NKVD on the problem, Yezhov got an earful. On 11 February the NKVD reported that there were 9,600 registered political émigrés in the USSR, but because MOPR kept such bad records, the actual number was probably more than 15,000. Since 1931 the NKVD had arrested more than 2,000 émigrés for espionage. One example was a German named Guber, who had entered the USSR through Inturist with MOPR sponsorship but who "turned out to be a Gestapo agent."[20]

A week later Yezhov wrote to Stalin and enclosed a suggested draft resolution for the Central Committee. As usual, he did not miss the chance to smear Yagoda and his NKVD for negligence. Already the week before he had sent Stalin a memo on the arrest of the Omsk NKVD counterintelligence chief, a Yagoda appointee, for being a Polish agent and had raised the suspicion that the exposed spy had friends higher up in Yagoda's NKVD.[21] Yezhov's subsequent letter said that it was pathetically easy for foreign powers to use political émigrés for espionage and that the NKVD had "let this slip out of their hands." MOPR was no better; since 1927 the CC had let MOPR handle these matters, but they had conducted no verification to speak of. Adopting the NKVD estimate of fifteen thousand political émigrés in the USSR, Yezhov claimed that MOPR knew about only fifty-five hundred of them. Something needed to be done, he wrote.[22]

Based on Yezhov's draft, the CC ordered the liquidation of MOPR's entrance commission. It ordered the NKVD to adopt a completely revised procedure to check émigrés, putting it in the hands of NKVD chief of border guards M. Frinovsky.[23] All political émigrés in the USSR were to be reregistered within three months, and procedures for entrance were drastically tightened: the foreign affairs ministry could no longer give visas to such persons, nor could cultural organizations with international ties; the number of schools for foreigners was to be sharply reduced; finally, a special commission consisting of Yezhov, Manuilsky, and NKVD counterintelligence operative M. I. Gai was to review political émigrés, especially in MOPR, and purge them of "harmful people." The Politburo approved Yezhov's recommendations within a week.[24]

Yezhov's new commission met for the first time on 15 March 1936 and every few weeks until June. At that time, Gai reported that they had found "compromising material" on 39 percent of those checked (Table 9.1). These proportions closely mirror the nationalities targeted in the notorious "mass operations" of the following year.[25]

TABLE 9.1

**Verification of political émigrés, March–June 1936**

|  | Checked | Compromising material found | % |
|---|---|---|---|
| Latvians | 73 | 67 | 92 |
| Koreans | 42 | 25 | 60 |
| Germans | 811 | 414 | 51 |
| Finns | 145 | 58 | 40 |
| Poles | 1,289 | 489 | 38 |
| Bulgarians | 673 | 236 | 35 |
| Estonians | 317 | 96 | 30 |
| Hungarians | 603 | 174 | 29 |
| Austrians | 576 | 142 | 25 |
| Americans | 52 | 9 | 17 |
| Czechs | 88 | 10 | 11 |
| Totals | 4,669 | 1,720 | 37 |

*Source:* Gai spravka to Yezhov, RGASPI, f. 671, op. 1, d. 73, l. 96.

The commission got tougher as time went on, in keeping with the rising political temperature of the hunt for enemies in mid-1936. In June it considered 368 people, of whom it proposed to punish 83 percent: to arrest 53 and deport 238, with an additional 13 to be exiled "to the periphery."[26] During June and July the commission considered the cases of 515 Polish émigrés. Nearly all were to be arrested, except for the students who were to be deported, even if there were no incriminating materials on them![27] The xenophobia that was to reach lethal levels in 1937 was beginning, and Yezhov was instrumental in raising the temperature.

As was often the case in Soviet politics, any campaign or initiative was accompanied by widespread blame shifting. In the present case, Comintern leaders Manuilsky and Georgi Dmitrov also launched an attack on Elena Stasova, the head of MOPR. We have seen that Manuilsky's January 1936 letter blamed MOPR for allowing spies into the USSR. On 8 June 1936 he renewed his attack in a joint letter with Dmitrov to Yezhov, advocating the total reorganization of MOPR.

They attacked Stasova personally, suggesting that she be removed because she was incapable and unwilling to do what was necessary.[28]

Yezhov's most famous activities in 1936 were his preparations of cases against major figures of the former anti-Stalin oppositions. We saw previously how he had supervised the investigation of the Kirov assassination, searching for any trails that might lead to oppositionist conspiracy. We also saw how he made a strong if ultimately unsuccessful case before the Central Committee in June 1935 for Zinoviev's and Kamenev's direct participation, with Trotsky's inspiration, in organizing the assassination.

Although Stalin had been unconvinced by Yezhov's evidence and had not followed up directly against Zinoviev and Kamenev, in the summer of 1936 he authorized Yezhov to push new investigations of lower-level oppositionists. This mandate not only involved Yezhov more deeply in investigations but gave him new opportunities to discredit Yagoda. Yezhov invited NKVD Deputy Commissar Agranov (with whom he had worked on the Kirov investigation and who was known not to be part of Yagoda's inner circle) to a private meeting at Yezhov's dacha. Yezhov told Agranov that the Central Committee — implying Stalin — was suspicious that not everything about oppositionist conspiracies had been uncovered at the time of the Kirov investigation. Agranov was ordered to conduct an "operation" against Trotskyists and Zinovievists in Moscow. But Yagoda and his deputy Molchanov in the NKVD Secret Political Department were unwilling to conduct such "operations," and apparently nothing happened. Yagoda even told his deputies that Yezhov did not speak for the CC and implied that he was acting personally.[29]

Did Stalin actually authorize Yezhov to go behind Yagoda's back and give Agranov orders? Stalin and Agranov had known each other for years, and if the dictator really wanted Agranov to act, it would have been a simple matter to call him in.[30] Stalin frequently involved himself in NKVD operations and personnel decisions, and such interventions were not understood to usurp Yagoda's authority. To work through Yezhov to contact Agranov would appear to be the long way around.

Yezhov was constantly working to undermine and embarrass Yagoda and may well have taken the initiative with Agranov. Yezhov as Central

Committee secretary also had the right to say what "the Central Committee" thought, whatever Yagoda might say. Sending Agranov off on a mission against oppositionists would strengthen the case Yezhov had made at the Yenukidze meeting if testimony could be produced from those arrested. And getting Agranov to act without his boss's knowledge or permission would have been an ideal strategy against Yagoda. It would not only undermine his authority in general but also begin to pry one of his deputies away from him, enlisting him as a Yezhov client and weakening Yagoda's control over his bureaucratic fief.

Yagoda had long resented Yezhov's meddling in NKVD affairs. He had also dragged his feet, at least from Yezhov's point of view, in moving against the opposition. Later Yagoda and Molchanov were accused of direct participation in the oppositionists' terrorist plans, and their reluctance was seen as protecting their fellow conspirators. In reality, though, Yagoda had good bureaucratic reasons for limiting investigations. If he conducted the kind of serious sweeps and interrogations that Yezhov wanted, NKVD investigators overseen by Yezhov would certainly produce whatever confessions might be required to posit or fabricate a vast and dangerous conspiracy. Such a scenario would cast doubt on Yagoda's previous leadership: how could the NKVD have been so sloppy and incompetent in previous years to have let this conspiracy go undetected? A year later, when Yagoda himself was under arrest and interrogation, he refused to admit that he had been a conspirator but explained that his limited investigations against the opposition had been a familiar Soviet practice to protect the reputation of his *vedomstvo* (bureaucratic organization).[31]

In this light, Yezhov's co-option of Agranov and his pressure for sterner investigations of oppositionists (at Stalin's behest or not) was not only about persecuting dissidents. In fact, Yezhov's moves can be seen as parts of the personal and bureaucratic struggle between Yezhov and Yagoda, with the oppositionists as pawns in that game. At any rate, Agranov did nothing. Perhaps he was blocked by Yagoda and Molchanov.[32] Perhaps he was chary of becoming a pawn in the Yezhov-Yagoda game. Perhaps he was afraid of his NKVD boss's retaliation.

Having failed again, in the second half of 1935 Yezhov turned his attention, as we have seen, to running the proverka of party documents. Here too he tried to steer things in the direction of incriminating the oppositionists, and here too he met resistance, this time from the regional party secretaries. But with the completion of the proverka at the beginning of 1936, he returned full-time to his "supervision" of the NKVD, pushing it in the direction of persecuting the opposition and embarrassing Yagoda in the process.

Sometime in the first days of 1936, Yezhov had received a mandate from Stalin to reopen the Kirov assassination investigation. He later said that for Stalin something "did not seem right" about that investigation, and Yezhov was charged with taking a new look.[33] This did not mean that Stalin intended to replace Yagoda, or that he was grooming Yezhov for the job. Stalin had not criticized Yagoda openly, nor had he supported Yezhov at CC plena when he did. It is more likely that the Kirov and Yenukidze affairs made Stalin wonder about the competence (or enthusiasm) of Yagoda's NKVD. Yagoda ran a tight ship, and his organization was compartmentalized and secret. It was therefore not so easy even for Stalin to know exactly what was going on there; Yezhov's early 1935 report on how informers were deployed by the NKVD provided information that was new to Stalin. Attaching a diligent bulldog like Yezhov to inquire into and oversee NKVD affairs was as likely to be an attempt to gather information as part of a plan to replace Yagoda. In any event, arrests of former Trotskyist and Zinovievist oppositionists now began in earnest. They, along with some oppositionists already serving prison or camp terms, were interrogated anew.

Yagoda and his deputies had not been completely lax in investigating oppositionist and other conspiracies. Throughout 1935 they had sent Yezhov reports of investigations of their arrests of various "counter-revolutionary organizations" around the country.[34] Sometime in early 1936 they produced a compilation ("Svodka No. 1 of Investigatory Materials on the Case of the Trotskyist Terrorist Organization of V. P. Olberg, I. K. Fedotov and others"). But in these reports, they steered away from any discussion of assassination and limited themselves to listing membership in various dissident organizations, prison networks, mutual aid groups, and so forth.[35]

Yezhov wanted more. His trail of investigations began with the arrest on 5 January 1936 of V. P. Olberg, who within a month confessed to being a Trotskyist agent dispatched to the USSR by Trotsky to organize the assassination of Stalin. His wife testified that Olberg had received money and false passports from Trotsky's son Sedov and other Trotskyists in Paris and Prague. The Olbergs provided names of alleged co-conspirators, who were in turn arrested. By the end of March, 508 former oppositionists were under arrest.[36] Yagoda forwarded the transcripts of all the interrogations to Stalin, Molotov, and Yezhov. Yezhov put them in his growing "file on Trotskyists."[37]

By February 1936 Yagoda realized that he had better act quickly to protect his organization and get on the new oppositionist-as-terrorist bandwagon. On 9 February his deputy G. E. Prokofev wrote to local NKVD organizations that there was evidence of activation of Trotskyist-Zinovievist underground cells with terrorist intentions. "Our task is the complete and total liquidation of the Trotskyist-Zinovievist underground."[38] Two weeks later, Prokofev reported directly to Stalin, announcing the discovery of a Trotskyist "archive" during the search of a Trotskyist's apartment. Across the top of Prokofev's letter, Stalin wrote "To Molotov and Yezhov. I propose transferring the whole Trotskyist archive and other Trotsky documents to Comrade Yezhov for analysis and reporting to the Politburo, and to conduct NKVD interrogations together with Comrade Yezhov. Stalin." Yezhov filed the Prokofev report into his Trotskyist file.[39] By the end of March a newly vigilant Yagoda was suggesting to Stalin that all Trotskyists participating in "terrorist acts" of any kind be summarily convicted and shot.[40]

Building on a growing network of confessions, on 19 June 1936 Yagoda and USSR Procurator A. Ya. Vyshinsky proposed the trial and execution of eighty-two members of the Trotskyist "terrorist organization." Their list was limited to Trotskyists, but they included in a cover letter the possibility of including Zinoviev and Kamenev, even though they had not confessed.[41] By limiting the scenario to Trotskyists, Yagoda could show that the center of the conspiracy was abroad, where Trotsky lived, rather than in the USSR, where the Zinovievists were. By implication, his failure to prosecute distant Trotskyists would not be as damning as his failure to move against Zinovievists in the country itself. In this light, it is not a surprise that Yezhov wanted to include Zinovievists in the dock as well. Yagoda was afraid that including Zinovievists in the dock would reflect badly on his own investigation, which he had limited to Trotskyists, and he rejected the Zinovievist "evidence," writing "nonsense," "rubbish," and "impossible" across the top of the papers.

Stalin sided with Yezhov, whom he empowered to order Yagoda to prepare a joint Trotskyist-Zinovievist scenario.[42] This required securing confessions from Zinovievists and from Zinoviev and Kamenev themselves. In June and July, NKVD interrogators worked hard to break Zinoviev and Kamenev, under Yezhov's watchful eye. By 23 July, Kamenev was admitting membership in a counterrevolutionary center that planned terror, but he denied being one of the organizers; he implicated Zinoviev as being closer to the matter. Three days later Zinoviev was confronted by one of his followers, Karev, who directly accused him. Zinoviev asked that the interrogation be stopped because he wanted to make a statement that, in the event, amounted to a full confession of organizing assassination and terror.[43] Shortly thereafter, he submitted to his interrogators a 540-page manuscript he had written in prison. In "A Deserved Sentence" he wrote,

> There is no question about it. . . . It is a fact. Whoever plays with the idea of "opposition" to the socialist state plays with the idea of counterrevolutionary terror. . . . Before each who finds himself in my position this question stands in sharp relief. If tomorrow war comes — it stands yet a million times sharper and bigger. And for myself this question in prison for a long time is irreversibly decided. Rise from the dead! Be born again as a Bolshevik! Finish your human days conscious of your guilt before the party! Do everything in order to erase this guilt.[44]

Zinoviev's confession supported Yezhov's long-term contention that Trotsky, Zinoviev, and Kamenev were associated in a combined monstrous plot of terror and assassination to overthrow the Soviet leadership. Less than a week later, Yezhov drafted a secret letter to all party organizations about the upcoming trial, which now was to be a smaller affair of sixteen defendants drawn from both Trotskyists and Zinovievists. Stalin put Yezhov in charge of organizing the trial and supervising press coverage. This included issuing press bulletins, coordinating daily coverage in *Pravda* and *Izvestiia,* and arranging for passes to foreign correspondents to cover the trial.[45]

Stalin paid close attention to how the trial was presented and covered, and on at least one occasion was not satisfied with the press coverage Yezhov supervised. On 6 September 1936 he wrote to Kaganovich and Molotov that a *Pravda* article about the trial was "wrong." *Pravda* had made the conspiracy sound too personal, a matter of one group of politicians against the other. Rather, it was important to assert that the oppositionists did have a political platform — the restoration of capitalism — but were afraid to speak of it. "It was necessary to say that he who struggles against the leaders of the party and government of the USSR also struggles for the defeat of socialism and the restoration of capitalism."[46] Stalin made a similar point to Comintern leader Georgi Dmitrov: "Workers think that everything is happening because of a fight between me and Trotsky, from the bad character of Stalin. It is necessary to point out that these people fought against Lenin, against the party during Lenin's lifetime."[47]

Despite Stalin's rebuke, Yezhov had won a major victory: the current official formulation was identical to the line he had defended more than a year ago at the Yenukidze accusation meeting but which had not been accepted at that time. As a bonus, Yagoda appeared to have been dragging his feet. As Yezhov wrote in the July 1936 letter to party organizations:

On the basis of new materials gathered by the NKVD in 1936, it can be considered an established fact that Zinoviev and Kamenev were not only the fomenters of terrorist activity against the leaders of our party and government but also the authors of direct instructions regarding both the murder of S. M. Kirov as well as preparations for attempts on the lives of other leaders of our party and, first and foremost, on the life of Comrade Stalin. . . .

Similarly, it can be considered an established fact that Zinovievists carried out their terroristic practices in a solid bloc with Trotsky and Trotskyists. . . .

From abroad, Trotsky, who was directing the activities of the all-Union, united Trotskyist-Zinovievist center, has used every means at his disposal, especially after the arrest of Kamenev and Zinoviev, to speed up the murder of Comrades Stalin and Voroshilov. He has been systematically sending directives and practical instructions through his agents concerning the organizing of the murder. . . .

Now, when it has been proven that the Trotskyist-Zinovievist monsters unite in their struggle against Soviet power all of the most embittered and sworn enemies of the workers of our country — spies, provocateurs, saboteurs, White Guards, kulaks, and so on, when all distinctions between these elements, on the one hand, and the Trotskyists and Zinovievists, on the other hand, have been effaced — all party organizations, all party members must come to understand that the vigilance of Communists is necessary in every area and in every situation.[48]

Experienced readers of party documents surely noticed Yezhov's implicit swipe at the NKVD. If the conspiracy dated from 1932, why had the NKVD uncovered it only four years later?[49]

Yezhov was also able to emphasize the dilatory negligence of Yagoda and his police through another trail of arrests and interrogations in 1936. Back in 1934 one Kotsiubinsky, an official of the Ukrainian Marx-Lenin Institute, had been arrested along with his associates and interrogated for alleged participation in Trotskyist circles. At that time, the evidence the NKVD produced against him and his friends was inconclusive, and he was allowed to continue in his job.[50] With Yezhov's new round of interrogations in 1936, the same people were reinterrogated. In February 1936 one Rappoport-Darin directly implicated Kotsiubinsky as a conspirator, and D. B. Naumov-Lekakh, another member of Kotsiubinsky's circle, led interrogators to N. V. Golubenko. Golubenko told Yezhov's men that G. L. Piatakov, a deputy commissar of heavy industry, had said in 1932 that it was necessary to kill Stalin.[51] Piatakov, a former Trotskyist but in 1936 the trusted deputy of Heavy Industry Commissar Sergo Ordzhonikidze, was said to have been the leader of a cell of Trotskyist terrorists in Ukraine.[52]

In Ukraine in spring and summer 1936, Trotskyists were being arrested and interrogated by V. A. Balitsky, NKVD chief for Ukraine. As he had done with Agranov, Yezhov pried Balitsky away from Yagoda and established a direct relationship with him outside the NKVD chain of command. At the beginning, Balitsky was sending records of his interrogations to Yagoda, who was supposed to forward them to Yezhov. But at some point, Yezhov stopped getting the copies and complained to Balitsky. Balitsky replied, "I've checked all the protocols of interrogations about which you chewed me out. All protocols have been sent to NKVD center; they decide who to send them to. If you have not received certain protocols, it can be explained only by the fact that someone in the central [NKVD] apparat goofed, or didn't consider it necessary to send them to the CC [Yezhov]." Balitsky was no fool: after this interchange, he began to send the interrogation protocols directly to Yezhov, signing his reports "I send you greetings! Balitsky."[53]

The trail to Piatakov eventually led to the second Moscow show trial in January 1937, when Piatakov, K. Radek, and fifteen other prominent Soviet leaders were accused of treason.[54] Now, though, in the summer and fall of 1936, Yezhov used his new friend Balitsky's materials in his reports to Stalin that "recent protocols" and "new materials" pointed directly to a conspiracy led by Piatakov and other current members of the industrial bureaucracy.[55] Once again, Yezhov implied that Yagoda's NKVD had been asleep at the switch for years.

At the August 1936 trial, some of the defendants had mentioned the names of the former rightist dissidents Nikolai Bukharin and Aleksei

Rykov, and prosecutor Vyshinsky announced the opening of an investigation of them.[56] The supposed links between the now "unmasked" Zinoviev-Trotsky conspiracy and the former rightists were the former rightists Mikhail Tomsky and G. Sokolnikov. The next day, Tomsky committed suicide.[57] Yezhov was put in charge of investigating the suicide and its circumstances, which included a suicide letter that Tomsky had left with his wife.

Tomsky's suicide letter gave Yezhov a new and powerful weapon in his struggle against Yagoda. It not only opened the door to further investigations of rightists but circumstantially identified Yagoda himself as a former secret collaborator of the right opposition. Yezhov decided to write an unsolicited letter to Stalin.

As a skilled Bolshevik official, Yezhov played his cards carefully. He did not run to Stalin denouncing Yagoda but instead pretended to be careful and circumspect while at the same time casting doubt on the NKVD chief. Because this letter represents the culmination of Yezhov's campaign against Yagoda, it is worth quoting at length. Moreover, because both the rough draft and final version of the letter survive, we have a rare opportunity to compare the texts and to see what might have gone through Yezhov's head as he tried to handle his boss.

In the final version he sent to Stalin, Yezhov cast suspicion on Yagoda by suggesting that the NKVD chief knew he was going to be named in Tomsky's suicide letter. But in the next sentence, he was scrupulously neutral about evaluating that accusation:

> [Tomsky's widow] named Yagoda. According to her, Tomsky asked her to tell you that Comrade Yagoda played an active role in the leading troika [Bukharin, Rykov, Tomsky] of the rightists and regularly passed them materials on the situation in the Central Committee. . . . This communication strangely coincides with Yagoda's own suggestion. Even before I arrived at Tomsky's, Yagoda in conversation with Agranov . . . expressed the suggestion that Tomsky named him because he [Yagoda] had visited Tomsky several times.

Is this Tomsky's counterrevolutionary kick from the grave or a real fact? I don't know. I personally think that Tomsky chose a peculiar way to revenge himself [on Yagoda], counting on the plausibility [of the story]: dead men don't lie.[58]

Yezhov's letter to Stalin was thus noncommittal, even doubtful about Yagoda's guilt, although his even raising the issue was obliquely damning to Yagoda. In his first draft Yezhov had gone further and provided his own personal theory of Yagoda's guilt. Yezhov had written in his rough draft: *"Personally I think that [Yagoda] undoubtedly had friendly relations with several of the rightists. When he saw which way things were going, he broke with them but maintained some kind of connections."*[59]

Upon reflection, Yezhov probably understood that Stalin did not care about Yagoda's internal struggles or motivations, much less a subordinate's self-interested speculation on them. The point was that Yagoda had "connections" (*sviazi*) with the rightists and had hidden this from Stalin. That was guilt enough, and party leaders had been punished for less. From Yezhov's point of view, therefore, the useful point had already been made by Tomsky himself. Nothing was to be gained by belaboring the point. It would also have been presumptuous of Yezhov to press it with what might seem to be an openly ambitious attack on Yagoda. So he removed these lines from the final draft to Stalin and took the high road by seeming to give Comrade Yagoda the benefit of the doubt. Yagoda was already sufficiently tarred, and Yezhov could afford to look clean and fair.

In the final letter, Yezhov went on to tell Stalin that there might be reason to take another look at the possible guilt of the rightists, including V. V. Shmidt, an Old Bolshevik since 1905, who had briefly sided with the rightists in the late 1920s: "In light of recent testimony from previously arrested people, the role of the rightists has to be seen differently. . . . I think that earlier we did not get to the bottom of it. . . . In any case, there is every reason to suppose that we will uncover much that is new and will look anew at the rightists and in particular Rykov, Bukharin, Uglanov, Shmidt, and others."

But in his rough draft, Yezhov once again had gone much further, again proposing his own theory and suggesting harsh action:

> *The Trotskyists and Zinovievists were so discredited that the rightists were afraid to ally with them.*[60] *I think that the rightists knew about the existence of the Trotskyist-Zinovievist bloc, knew about terror, informed each other, and watched from the sidelines, thinking that if the Trotskyists were successful in their terrorist activity, they could use the results without discrediting their own organization. Accordingly, they doubtless had their own rightist organization which also obviously stood for terror. . . . I now request that the chekists [NKVD] gather together for me the materials on the rightists and in particular on certain groups of them in order to again carefully examine the rightist line.*
>
> *Independently of the results of this work, the rightists are so compromised that to leave them unpunished is impossible. Now practically all party organizations are bombarding the Central Committee and the press with questions about what measures to take against the rightists. The most minimal punishment, which is politically completely justified, is in my view expulsion from the Central Committee and exile to work in far away regions. To leave things the way they are is impossible. But for this it will be necessary to have your firm order.*

Once again, though, Yezhov decided that this was not the right way to deal with Stalin. Stalin could draw his own conclusions, and Yezhov must have sensed that the dictator was wavering on how far or fast to move against Bukharin, Rykov, and the other leading rightists.[61] Moreover, in the draft letter, Yezhov would have been proposing punishments and ambitiously asking Stalin to put him in charge of a full-blown repression of the rightists. Bukharin and Rykov were still big fish, and it was not Yezhov's place to suggest their fates. As with undermining Yagoda, Yezhov had planted the seed with Stalin: there were still possible conspiracies still to be uncovered. "Personally" expressing his theories and opinions to Stalin was immodest and not useful. Thus fear of presumption and explicit ambition made Yezhov delete these two paragraphs.

In his final letter to Stalin, Yezhov went on to propose harsh punishments for many of those previously arrested. After reexamining "all lists of those arrested in current matters and all punished in the Kirov and other matters," Yezhov recommended mass secret executions and punishments of former oppositionists. He divided them into five categories:

The first category, to shoot. Here go all immediate participants in terrorist groups, provocateurs, double agents and the most important active organizers of terror.

The second category, ten years in prison plus ten years in exile. Here go the less active participants in terrorist groups, people knowing of terrorist activities and those helping terrorists.

The third category, eight years in prison plus five years exile.

The fourth category, five years in prison plus five years exile.

And the fifth category, to send to the NKVD Special Conference, which has the right to specify punishments up to five years.

Once again, though, his first draft had been much more strident. To the recommendations above, he had originally added: "*We should shoot a pretty large number. Personally I think that this must be done in order to finally finish with this filth. It is understood that no trials will be necessary. Everything can be done in a simplified process according to the Law of 1 December 1934 without formal court sittings.*"

In his draft he also recommended the immediate arrest and secret execution of Radek and Piatakov, and while noting that this would be noticed abroad and could result in bad publicity, "nevertheless, we have to do it." Upon reflection, Yezhov surely again decided that he was being presumptuous in telling Stalin what to do with senior colleagues. Again he pulled back and deleted these sections.[62]

Finally, in his letter to Stalin, Yezhov could not resist returning to the matter of Yagoda and the NKVD:

On the matter of clarifying the connections of Trotskyists with the ChK [NKVD], at the moment nothing concrete has turned up. I have collected quite extensive materials, but they only show that there were signals of the Trotskyist-Zinovievist activities in 1933 and 1934. All this, however, went barely noticed. . . .

I very much want to tell you about several inadequacies in the work of the NKVD which cannot long be tolerated. Without your intervention in this matter, nothing will come of it.

The corresponding part of his rough draft was, like the above deleted sections, much more direct. More than that, it sounded like a personal play for Yagoda's job. In the first draft, Yezhov had written:

*There have been uncovered so many inadequacies that it is impossible to tolerate them any more. I have held back on this until now* [!] *because the basic emphasis has been on the destruction of the Trotskyists and Zinovievists. Now, it seems to me, it is necessary to reach some kind of conclusion on all these affairs to rebuild the work of the NKVD itself.*

*It is all the more necessary that among the top leadership of the NKVD one sees a mood of self-congratulation, tranquility, and bragging. Instead of drawing conclusions from the Trotskyist business and criticizing and correcting their own deficiencies, people dream now only of medals for exposing that business. It is hard to believe that those people do not understand that in the final analysis, it is not the merit of the NKVD to have uncovered a five-year-old conspiracy that hundreds of people knew about.*

Yezhov managed to control himself again; he deleted this part too. With such an approach—with his claim that in Yagoda's NKVD there were "so many inadequacies that it is impossible to tolerate them any more"—Yezhov would have exceeded the limits of self-effacing Bolshevik tact. Although ostensibly a routine advisory from one senior party leader to another about the poor performance of a state agency, Yezhov's language was too strong, and he knew it. Combined with the suspicion of Trotskyist infiltration of the secret police and the ever-darkening shade Yezhov was casting on Yagoda, a set of "intolerable

k

shortcomings" left only one conclusion: Yagoda had to go. There was really only one plausible candidate to take his place, Nikolai Yezhov, but it would have been too direct to say so.

Yezhov's agenda in writing the letter is clear. He wanted to finally undermine Yagoda in order to get his job. He wanted summary shootings of Trotskyists already under arrest, and he sought a license to move against the rightists. The question was how to get what he wanted.

In his rough draft, he had taken the direct approach. "Personally," he spelled out a theory of Yagoda's unquestioned criminal association with the rightists. He accused those rightists of having a terrorist organization and claimed that there was an uproar in the party demanding punishment of them. "Personally," he demanded that the NKVD turn over all its materials to him on the rightists and even proposed the level of punishment they should get. He proposed summary shootings of "a pretty large number" of those already arrested without trial. He told Stalin that to tolerate the NKVD's incompetence was now "impossible," that Yezhov had patiently restrained himself in criticizing that incompetence, but that now, "it seems to me," something had to be done.

Upon reflection, however, Yezhov knew how to handle the boss tactfully. He realized that it was unseemly for a subordinate to present Stalin with personal unsolicited opinions, theories, demands, and proposed policies and punishments. He removed those opinions, the shrill attacks on Yagoda and his NKVD, and his various theories about Yagoda and the rightists. Without offering opinions, conclusions, or recommendations, he pretended to be neutral on Yagoda's association with the oppositionists. He rather blandly suggested that some further investigation of the rightists might be in order. He did not call them names, did not suggest how many should be shot, and did not suggest doing it without trial. Finally, he sounded an alarm about the deficiencies within the NKVD, but removed the crisis language that would appear to force the issue. Even with his tactful, toned-down text, he was a bit worried about how Stalin might react, so he closed the actual letter he sent to the dictator with: "Comrade Stalin, I hesitated about whether it was right to write about such things in a letter. If I did wrong, [you will] curse me."

We do not know whether Stalin cursed him, or indeed how he reacted to Yezhov's letter. We do know, however, that Yezhov was given permission to expand the investigation of rightist "terrorism." Stalin approved summary shootings of arrested Trotskyists (although not yet mass executions without trial). We do not know whether Stalin had planned all these things in any case. We do know, however, that in terms of his letter Yezhov knew exactly how to ask, and he got what he wanted.

The content and tone of Yezhov's letter to Stalin allow us to speculate a bit about Stalin's intentions at this point, as well as about his relationship with Yezhov. Hypothetically, Stalin could already have decided to remove Yagoda, and on an escalation of harsh repression of the opposition. In this scenario Stalin would encourage his creature Yezhov to make the severe proposals, allowing the dictator to appear to be a neutral decision maker and to avoid blame if something went wrong. This was a common Stalin tactic over the years.[63]

If that was his intention here, however, Stalin would have been better served by, and could easily have solicited, the strident language and demands of Yezhov's rough draft. Stalin could then have taken Yezhov's "proposals" to the Politburo for consideration, presenting them to the party leadership as having originated with someone else. The Politburo would certainly have approved, and if problems or embarrassments ensued later, Yezhov would have been the convenient scapegoat and, in light of his "personal" opinions in the letter, an obviously ambitious one at that.

Instead, Yezhov sent Stalin a relatively restrained letter that ended with a timid apology. Absent specific proposals and personal opinions, as a discursive strategy the letter left everything to Stalin's discretion. If Stalin planned to use Yezhov as his stalking horse, this letter was not the most useful possible document; it was not the work of a robot acting under orders. From this, one might draw two conclusions. First, Stalin did not have a specific agenda, and the letter was not a put-up job:

Stalin may not have decided what he wanted to do and in any event had not told his servant. Yezhov's letter was exactly what it seemed to be: a modest series of reports on the current situation that originated with Yezhov, not Stalin.

Second, Yezhov was a skilled bureaucratic player who understood blame shifting as a Soviet way of life. He deliberately avoided personal opinions and specific proposals that could leave him exposed later. Of course, Stalin made the final decisions anyway and could in any event blame Yezhov. But with this letter, Yezhov made that a bit more difficult. He was conducting a subtle, self-protective discursive manipulation, using language to dance with the boss as all subalterns do with all masters, even though the boss seemed to call the tune. He was not making policy, but by packaging and presenting the issues as he did, he was certainly influencing it. Yezhov could not escape Stalin's power, but he could maneuver within it. He was not new to Stalinist personalized politics, nor was he stupid. He may have seemed to be a servant, but he deployed the same weapons of the weak that all servants command.

All Yagoda needed now was a push. It might at first glance seem strange that Stalin had tolerated Yagoda as long as he did. After all, he had been under a cloud more than a year and a half, since the Kirov killing in early 1934. One answer might have to do with the technical police skills required to run the NKVD; it was considered a place for professional policemen. Years later Molotov emphasized the shortage of such technical professionals. Speaking of Yagoda, he said, "We had to work with reptiles like that, but there were no others. No one!"[64] Party leaders like Stalin, Molotov, and Kaganovich had no experience running a specialized investigative organization. Replacing a professional like Yagoda could lead to disruptions and inefficiencies in the secret police unless advance preparations were made. The NKVD, like other Soviet institutions, was organized according to a patronage system. When a boss was removed, all his clients and appointees were removed as a matter of course, and it may well be that Yagoda could not be fired until Yezhov had pried away senior NKVD leaders from their boss and patron.

Replacing the head of the NKVD was therefore a serious step, and one that Stalin did not take lightly. By September 1936 Yagoda was discredited and the work of his agency was considered deficient. But there was still no directly incriminating evidence against Yagoda himself. Yezhov had to supply that in order to tip the balance.

Back in March 1935 the chief of the Voronezh NKVD, S. S. Dukelsky, had written to his boss Yagoda about poor operational work and administrative confusion in the NKVD. In 1936 Yezhov had discovered Dukelsky (or vice versa), and Dukelsky wrote to Yezhov on 13 July with an amazing story.

According to his letter, at the beginning of 1933 Moscow NKVD agent Zafran had informed NKVD central about a group of Trotskyists that included one Dreitser, who would become one of the defendants at the August 1936 trial. Yagoda's NKVD had refused to arrest Dreitser and had instead arrested the informant Zafran, who was sentenced to five years in a camp.[65] After the Kirov assassination, Zafran escaped from camp and returned to Moscow and told his story. Yagoda's NKVD arrested him again, but KPK leader M. F. Shkiriatov secured his release. Then, in 1936, Zafran was arrested again, and this time his file was sent by the Yagoda team to the military tribunal with a recommendation for a death sentence.

Yezhov sat on the Dukelsky revelations for two months. But now, when the time was right, Yezhov sent a handwritten memo to Stalin on 12 September about the Dukelsky revelations. The clear implication was that Yagoda and/or his men were dirty: they had silenced and tried to kill Zafran to favor the convicted Trotskyist Dreitser. If this was true, that would make Yagoda complicit in Trotskyist conspiracy as a protector. The next day, Yagoda fired Dukelsky from his Voronezh job for going to Yezhov out of the chain of command with his revelations about Zafran, and the same day Dukelsky appealed to Yezhov and asked to be transferred to nonoperational NKVD work. Yezhov called a conference on the matter, writing that all this deserved serious review.[66]

We do not know whether Zafran was in fact executed, but we know the fate of the whistleblower. Yezhov reversed Yagoda's order to fire

Dukelsky, who kept his job in Voronezh.[67] The Dukelsky letter was only the last nail in Yagoda's professional coffin. But it was not unimportant: it suggested to Stalin that Yagoda's team was not only incompetent but possibly complicit in the Trotskyist treason. Later, when Yagoda's chief assistant Molchanov was arrested for protecting traitors, the Zafran affair played a prominent role in his interrogation.[68]

Less than two weeks later, Stalin dropped the other shoe. While on vacation, he telegraphed the Politburo, removing Yagoda and appointing Yezhov to head the NKVD. Stalin's telegram, which he drafted by hand at his Sochi vacation location, blamed Yagoda for not uncovering the Trotskyist treason sooner: "The NKVD is four years behind in this matter," a fact Stalin said was recognized by all party workers and a majority of the NKVD officers. Yagoda was shifted to be People's Commissar of Communications, from which post former rightist Rykov was now ejected: "No need to explain this, it is clear." The telegram noted that Yezhov had [doubtless!] agreed to the appointment. He retained his position as head of KPK, although he was to devote 90 percent of his time to the NKVD, and "it is understood" that Yezhov would remain a secretary of the Central Committee.[69]

Yagoda was distressed; Kaganovich wrote to Ordzhonikidze that Yagoda "took his transfer quite painfully."[70] Stalin tried to soothe Yagoda's ruffled feathers, writing to him, "The Commissariat of Communications is a very important business. It is a defense commissariat. I do not doubt that you will know how to put this organization on its feet. I very much ask that you agree to work as Commissar of Communications [narkomsviaz]. Without a good narkomsviaz, we will feel ourselves without hands. It is impossible to leave it in its current condition. We have to put it on its feet quickly."[71] Yagoda agreed to take the job.

Yezhov's appointment represented the first time a senior party official, a secretary of the Central Committee instead of a professional policeman, had headed the police since the time of Feliks Dzerzhinsky in the early 1920s. Some thought that a "party atmosphere" would be a refreshing improvement at the NKVD.[72] Indeed, Yezhov quickly began to recruit new NKVD staff from party schools.[73]

Yagoda had been widely unpopular. He had a reputation for being a corrupt patronage boss who controlled his subordinates through pressure and even blackmail. He was said to have had his circle of favored clients; other NKVD officials could expect few favors or promotions. One senior NKVD official outside Yagoda's circle hoped that Yezhov would "overcome the unhealthy atmosphere and careerist, degenerate, and falsifying tendencies" that had characterized Yagoda's work.[74] Even former oppositionists like Bukharin "got along very well" with Yezhov, considered him an "honest person," and welcomed the appointment.[75]

L. M. Kaganovich wrote from the Politburo in Moscow to his friend Sergo Ordzhonikidze with the news: "The latest news from here concerns the appointment of Yezhov. . . . Surely, things will go smoothly with Yezhov at the helm."[76]

# Conclusion

Much of the literature on the terror of the 1930s focuses on the question of responsibility. Post-Soviet historical writing, a clear descendent of Soviet polemic, still seeks categorically to fix responsibility on bad persons and bad systems. Thus the most authoritative study of Yezhov's time at the NKVD tells us that "Stalin himself bore full responsibility for the purge as well as for its excesses." Even within the dubious historical methodology of limiting analysis to responsibility, is it possible that any single person bore "full" responsibility for anything? No one else was culpable? Only Stalin bears responsibility? Just as simplistically, we are told that Yezhov "was above all a product of Stalin's totalitarianism, terrorist, and bureaucratic system."[1] In this approach, certain persons have to bear "full" responsibility and their "crimes" are products of a "terrorist system" that is discredited today.

There has never been any doubt that Stalin was "responsible" for the terror. But how are we to understand "responsibility"? As the term is usually employed, it carries a moral charge of guilt and blame. In a moral sense, of course Stalin was responsible. He was also responsible in a phenomenological sense in terms of agency. It is highly unlikely that the terror would have taken place without him.

Understood either as blame or as agency, such a broad term does not tell us very much about what happened, how it happened, or even why it happened. Responsibility is a concept with limited analytical value, difficult to fix and largely dependent on context. For example, if Ivan Ivanovich is arrested and shot in a mass operation in 1937, who is responsible? Stalin, for approving the mass operations with victims by provincial quota? Yes. Regional party secretaries for pressing for mass operations in the first place? Yes. Yezhov, for organizing and carrying them out? Yes. The low-level NKVD officer who determined who went on the list and selected Ivan Ivanovich? Yes. In our broad historiographical tradition, Stalin is "fully responsible." But for a victim, the question of whether he lived or died was in the hands of the NKVD official on the spot. So for Ivan Ivanovich, that local policeman was most responsible—even "fully responsible"—for his death.

The terror was so massive, so horrible, that our minds grasp it only with difficulty. As Catherine Merridale has written, many ordinary Russians today can deal with it only in terms of the individual stories of friends and family members.[2] Some attempt an empirical historical approach, seeking causes in Stalin's psychology, the inherent ideological evil of Marxism, or notions of Russian character. Others, overwhelmed by the suffering of the countless victims, abandon any attempt at analysis and fall back into a kind of unempirical contemplation of overwhelming evil. All of these attempts at understanding have one thing in common: a search for a single more or less simple way to understand something that in its horror and scale seems to defy understanding. This difficulty also characterizes our attempts to understand the Yezhovs of the world.

Our study has focused on three related questions, each with a biographical and historical component.

The first questions we posed at the outset of this study—Was Yezhov just Stalin's tool? What was the scope for power for politicians working under a dictator?—turn out to be complicated. Traditionally, in the literature, Stalin chose Yezhov because he was obedient and because he so worshiped the dictator that he was willing to do anything.[3] Yezhov as obedient tool is an easy way to answer another of our questions: why was he willing to carry out monstrous tasks for his malevolent master? Yezhov was obedient to Stalin, but so was everyone else in the country, in varying quality and degree. As in any hierarchical organization, the successful executive obeys orders, or at least has the skill to make it seem that he is doing so. So much more for the Stalinist leadership: every member of the Politburo and Central Committee was obedient, and several of them were older and more experienced than Yezhov. That he was obedient, therefore, does not explain Yezhov's rise to the NKVD. We still wonder why Stalin chose Yezhov and not someone else.

A more serious inquiry would worry less about categorical obedience and would rather look at the individual and group interests of the various officials at different levels and try to see how they deployed the power and resources available to them for various purposes. Obedience, however defined, is about power or the lack of it. In the Soviet system, as in all systems, everyone from bottom to top had some measure of power and acted with some measure of obedience. From Stalin down to the lowly collective farm chairman, everyone tried to maximize power and protect himself (and his friends) within his sphere.

The concept of obedience needs to be nuanced. The scope of real, imagined, or feigned behaviors coming under the rubric of obedience is wide. They can range from slavish compliance to conformity based on sincere conviction, to willing or unwilling compliance, to various forms of covert resistance. Even resistance can be active or passive, total or partial, and each of these resistance modes and behaviors contains some mix of defiance and compliance. People can take actions or not take them. They can influence those around them in subtle and not so subtle ways. They can work, work badly, or avoid work altogether. They can cooperate with their bosses, sabotage them, or pretend to do either. As recent studies on social history and subjectivity in Soviet history have shown, even ordinary people could choose to resist the regime, accommodate themselves to it, or believe in it wholeheartedly. Nobody was a faceless product; everyone made choices that influenced his life and his surroundings.[4]

Recent biographies of other Stalinist Politburo members suggest the complexities of the relationship between the dictator and his lieutenants.[5] As Khrushchev reminded us, Stalin had immediate life-and-death power over his lieutenants, who when leaving Stalin's office never knew whether they would be taken straight to prison. On the other hand, they managed their careers, agendas, and intrigues within the considerable fields of politics available to them.

These lieutenants were certainly not independent politicians. Yezhov, like all of Stalin's lieutenants, never became an "independent" maker of grand policy. (It is not clear, of course, how independent any minister in a Western parliamentary system could be in making policy.) But policy can also be made in the course of implementing strategic decisions taken by others. Real political power is not always about having the final say in those lofty decisions. Stalin's lieutenants, including Yezhov, were powerful men and, within their spheres, independent politicians in real ways that mattered. Each of them headed his own network of patronage and was a master in his own bureaucratic house.[6] Stalin entrusted large areas of implementation to his lieutenants, and held them accountable for the results. Implementation is also a form of power, and even of policy making. Along with mortal accountability before Stalin came vast authority and leeway in carrying out policy.

If nothing else, Stalin's lieutenants wielded considerable power as framers of questions. Information is power, and they were Stalin's main sources of information on their spheres. Matters coming to Stalin for his personal decision or approval usually arrived as recommendations from below. In matters of personnel appointment, for example, his lieutenants usually offered the dictator a proposed candidate for a post, and sometimes Stalin refused the choice and appointed another candidate altogether. But most often a single nomination came to Stalin, and most often he approved the recommendation. Stalin frequently referred questions that had reached him down to his lieutenants for decision. His notation "kak byt'?" [what to do?] is frequently found on archival documents that Stalin directed to his associates for their decision on important matters.[7]

In a simple and simplistic way, Stalin's lieutenants were all obedient tools. But in real life, and in ways that counted, they were also powerful semi-independent politicians with their own hands on levers of power. They generally picked their own personnel. They battled with one another over budgets and lines of turf authority. In such fights, Stalin was at pains to moderate and act as referee.[8] Senior Stalinist leaders were not slaves, nor was their power reduced as Stalin's increased.[9] They were extremely powerful men whose authority grew along with Stalin's.

Although we have biographies of bureaucratic operators like Molotov and Zhdanov, Yezhov has remained an exception. Perhaps the horrible nature of his work has reinforced the flat picture of him as a mere slave and robot. However, living up to this primitive image would be impossible in any bureaucracy, because management of large administrations and implementation of policy requires judgment, initiative, choices, and strategies.

The authors of an authoritative study of Yezhov at the NKVD rightly remind us that "Yezhov could not consult Stalin on every detail, and his role as Stalin's instrument had to involve a certain amount of autonomy."[10] Unfortunately, we do not know what kinds of "details" Stalin did or did not know, and therefore we cannot measure that autonomy. We do not know how far down the hierarchy one had to be to have one's arrest approved or ordered by Stalin. Similarly, we do not know what kinds of party members could be arrested by Yezhov's subordinates without his order or permission.

It has become a truism in Soviet history that as they came down the chain of command, orders—including Stalin's—were routinely modified at various levels and even ignored when it suited the purpose of the official receiving them. The degree of modification depended on many things, from the costs and benefits of enforcing the order to the calculation of getting caught to the likelihood of being protected by a patron if you were caught. We now understand the system as a network of Stalins, each of whom was both subordinate and boss. One was strict and forceful with subordinates, but with the boss one deployed appropriately subservient language, real or feigned respect, pledges of loyalty and other weapons of the weak. The lines between obedience and initiative, independence and disobedience are difficult to establish in any organization.

Because both Stalin and Yezhov functioned within this system, there is little reason to believe that their relationship was any different. Yezhov wrote to Stalin asking for instructions, orders, and rulings on various questions. He used the same fawning, obsequious tone that subordinates had used with their bosses throughout Russian history. In the same tradition, Stalin wrote to Yezhov, sometimes fondly and sometimes curtly, giving instructions and orders, which Yezhov carried out. Of course, language can be used to dissimulate, deploy power (great and small), or worship, and on the basis of these texts alone, it is impossible to say much about their actual relationship.

There is no question that Stalin supervised the terror, but there is much we still do not know about how that process worked. We know that Yezhov submitted lists of proposed arrests to Stalin, who approved them while sometimes adding or subtracting names. We have not found any lists of arrests that Stalin wrote and gave to Yezhov, but such information could have been conveyed orally by the careful dictator. Although we know that Yezhov met Stalin in his office more frequently than anyone except Molotov, we do not know the kinds of face-to-face explicit and implicit understandings that existed between the two. And we know nothing of their telephone conversations.

Although Yezhov was certainly never an independent player in the top leadership, he knew how to influence The Boss and to pursue agendas that were not necessarily identical to Stalin's. It is perhaps significant that at the time of Yezhov's fall, Stalin accused him of withholding information and demanded that he reveal the contents of his "secret archive," which contained names of officials whom Yezhov had not arrested and therefore was protecting.[11]

The second set of questions we posed had to do with career paths. How did Yezhov climb the ladder? How did one rise and prosper in Stalinist administration?

In addition to Yezhov's supposedly servile nature, a second common answer to our questions is that Stalin prepared Yezhov, selecting and promoting him as an obedient and unquestioning robot, nurtured and prepared for his role as master purger.[12] One often reads that Yezhov was deliberately brought to Moscow and put to work studying the party's composition so that he could later orchestrate a long-planned purge of the ranks.

However, the idea that Stalin planned the terror for a long time is highly speculative and is in fact contradicted by a substantial body of evidence. There are many signs before late 1936 that terror was not on Stalin's mind. Twists and turns of policy, crackdowns followed by real liberalization, inexplicable and contradictory changes in public statements, personnel shuffles and reshuffles throughout the 1930s do not suggest a plan for terror. They rather seem to indicate indecision, false starts, contradictions, and short-term improvisation as Stalin's mode of operation.[13] Yezhov's unpublished book, "From Fractionalism to Open Counterrevolution," exists in several versions and rewrites that run from early 1935 to the fall of 1937. From version to version, year to year, the story of the "Fascist conspiracy" against the USSR changed, and the final 1937 versions contradicted 1935 ones. For example, in the first 1935 draft, Zinoviev and Kamenev are "finally" accused of having only morally abetted the assassination of Kirov, but in later versions, when the official line changed, this was replaced with statements on their direct guilt in organizing "terrorist acts."[14] The fabricated 1937 terror conspiracy was obviously not planned or foreseen in Yezhov's 1935 writing, which Stalin approved.

Moreover, Yezhov's rise through the ranks is easily explained without imagining him as having been cultivated and brought along by someone. Although his career was meteoric, it was not atypical and illustrates the chain of general experiences necessary for work at the top of the Stalin apparatus. This was a time of meteoric careers and rapid advance for an entire cohort of "new Bolsheviks." The rapid promotions of Andrei Zhdanov, Georgy Malenkov, Nikita Khrushchev, and hundreds of thousands of lesser party members followed trajectories as steep as Yezhov's. Even for someone without powerful patrons, a desperate shortage of administrative talent in the early Soviet regime propelled skilled and loyal young administrators—cultivated or not—up the ladder as the scope of the regime's activities dramatically expanded. There are no sources indicating that before the early thirties Stalin or anyone else advanced Yezhov's career in any unusual way. His early career was not the result of the manipulations of his superiors. He needed no patrons to move up, and in fact sometimes maneuvered his career in spite of them.

Yezhov was simply good at what he did, and this brought him promotions, as the same set of qualities would in any organization. He took an active hand in his own career. In 1935–36, he skillfully angled for the NKVD leadership position, playing to Stalin's suspicions and actively but tactfully undermining Yagoda's police leadership. Stalin certainly approved all of Yezhov's promotions, but Yezhov's own abilities are sufficient to explain his rise.

His rise can also be partly explained by personal qualities, which bring us closer to plausible reasons for his ascent. Many Old Bolshevik professional revolutionaries disdained administrative work, partly because of their glorious revolutionary self-images and partly because of the antibureaucratic voluntarism of their revolutionary generation. But younger Bolsheviks like Yezhov fit more comfortably into an apparatus and excelled at such work. They were willing to take on any assignment, however mundane, and complete it thoroughly and on time not only because they were obedient but because they were conscientious. They were energetic, "can-do" types who worked day and night to finish a job. Every document we have from Yezhov's bosses over the years testifies to his capability and capacity for hard work. All his performance reports are full of words and phrases like "good organizer," "conscientious," "energetic," "works independently," and "good at practical work." This assessment is so consistent over the years as to be conclusive: Yezhov was a hard worker. Stalin had to force Yezhov to take vacations, and on at least one occasion it took a Politburo resolution to keep him from coming back early.[15]

Yezhov's drive and energy were not unique in Stalin's entourage. All those who became Stalin's close collaborators were hard workers. Molotov and Kaganovich were legendary for taking on any task, for putting out any fire, and for using tough methods to solve administrative problems. A recent biography of Andrei Zhdanov also stresses his capacity for work and for successful completion of assignments. Stalin shunned lazy officials, and nobody made it near the top unless he was a workaholic.[16] Hard work is therefore another explanation of Yezhov's rise to the NKVD, as well as a general marker for success in the Stalinist system.

Yezhov also had an attractive personal modesty, a quality esteemed among Bolsheviks in Stalin's times. Upon taking office in 1936, he was bombarded by requests for biographical information.[17] Publishers of encyclopedias, pamphlets, and peasant calendars asked him for a biography. Famous historians, such as the prominent I. I. Mints, went to work researching learned biographies.[18] Novelists, including the Socialist Realist writer Alexander Fadeev, began to write colorful accounts of his life.[19] Yezhov generally replied to such requests for information with a note that he was too busy to provide information. It would have violated his modesty to take much of an interest in his evolving hagiography, and he was at pains to tone down the worshipful prose that began to surround him.

According to the poet Dzhambul, "When the October [revolution] dawn began to shine, with courage in his eyes he stormed the Palace."[20] Fadeev and others had Yezhov as the primary organizer of the Vitebsk workers' militia, more or less single-handedly turning Vitebsk into a "Bolshevik fortress." But Yezhov described his 1917 activities humbly, writing only that he organized radical cells in factory shops where he worked, helped distribute leaflets in kiosks, and worked for radical candidates in local elections.

Similarly, Fadeev wrote that during the Civil War, Yezhov was a military commissar who displayed a "natural heroism" at the front, facing Kolchak's White Army. Wounded in a crucial attack, he was carried from the battlefield severely injured. Unable to remain inactive, he soon left the hospital and found political work in another unit. Once again, Dzhambul carried the glorification furthest:

> I remember this. In the purple sunsets
> I saw Comrade Yezhov through the smoke.
> With his sword held high, dressed in the greatcoat
> Of the people, he led the attack. . . .
> Hardened in battle was brave Yezhov.

This was all far too much for the unassuming Yezhov. In his first revision of his official 1936 *Pravda* biography, he crossed out words about his having served "at the front" against Kolchak's White Army. In his second revision, he further scratched out words suggesting that he had served "against Kolchak and in important detachments on the eastern front," as well as a line suggesting that he had been commissar of a division.[21] He was at pains to write in another autobiographical statement that he had not seen combat.

Yezhov's personal life also reflected a modesty that not all Bolshevik officials managed to maintain. Stalin himself lived simply, usually in one room with a sofa and a table for work. After the former NKVD chief Yagoda's arrest, an audit showed that he had used state funds to build himself a palatial dacha. In 1936 alone Yagoda spent more than a million rubles on maintaining apartments, dachas, and rest homes that his family used.[22] Stalin went through the roof; he drafted a Politburo resolution condemning such "dacha palaces" and ordering sharp restrictions on their size. Officials should live modestly, he insisted.

Yezhov did. At the time of one's arrest, the NKVD made an inventory of the detainee's possessions, and a comparison between those of Yagoda and of Yezhov is instructive. The inventory of Yagoda's goods ran to 130 categories and several thousand items, including more than 25 men's overcoats, 42 pairs of boots, 32 soldier's blouses, 22 women's coats and 50 women's dresses, 22 men's suits of European tailoring, 31 pairs of foreign made women's shoes, 91 women's foreign-made berets, 130 pairs of silk stockings, 37 pairs of foreign-made gloves, 95 bottles of

French perfume, 1,008 antique dishes, and 73 foreign-made fishing rods. Investigators must have been especially impressed with Yagoda's collection of 3,904 pornographic pictures and 11 pornographic films.[23]

Yezhov, at the height of his fame, had a single overcoat, 9 pairs of old boots, 13 soldier's blouses, 48 simple shirts, 34 figurines, and several empty and partially empty vodka bottles.[24] He dressed simply, in military-issue pants and blouse, and his boots were worn and rough. Years later Dmitri Shepilov remembered Yezhov as "a totally ignorant man" in matters of culture and theory and was horrified that "he spit straight on the luxurious carpet."[25] One doubts that Stalin or his generation found Yezhov's coarse worker's behavior as distasteful as did Shepilov. Stalin put great store in class and by all accounts could not tolerate stuffed shirts, pretentious intellectuals, or "bourgeois" seekers of wealth. Yezhov was none of those.

Stalin also trusted Yezhov's judgment. Yezhov's archive is full of notes and memos from Stalin (and his lieutenants) redirected to Yezhov with handwritten marginal notes like "Comrade Yezhov! Your opinion?" or "to Comrade Yezhov. What's this all about?—I. S. [Stalin]" or "Comrade Yezhov, what to do about this?"[26] When Bukharin, the editor of *Izvestiia,* was having personnel troubles, Stalin wrote to Yezhov, "Please talk to Bukharin and straighten this out."[27] Stalin was also personally concerned about Yezhov's health, which had never been good. At various times Yezhov had been treated for tuberculosis, anemia, malnutrition, angina, sciatica, exhaustion, and colitis.[28] In the fall of 1935, Stalin wrote to Yezhov, "The main thing now is that you hurry off on vacation to one of the Soviet resorts or abroad, as you like or as the doctors recommend. If you don't, I'll make a big fuss."[29] During Yezhov's enforced vacations, Stalin checked to make sure he was actually resting.[30]

Yezhov's career also certainly benefited from an attractive résumé and broad experience. As a former Putilov factory worker, Red Guard organizer, and Civil War commissar, he had the right social and political pedigree. His experience in regional party organizations and in the non-Russian nationality areas in the 1920s also stood him in good stead; Stalin himself had been an expert in nationality policy. Yezhov's experience in the Commissariat of Agriculture and the Industrial Department of the Central Committee had given him experience in the two key areas of Stalinist economy.

Each of Yezhov's positions, as we have seen, was not simply a formal office in the bureaucratic hierarchy. In practice, each assignment carried with it the ability to short-circuit the bureaucracy and appeal to high-ranking persons. Authority attached to persons and patrons, not to institutions. The Stalinists instinctively grasped the unreality of institutions and the personal practices behind them. Their habit of creating a new institution for each new task, the chronic overlapping of functions between agencies, and the bewildering array of large and small agencies devoted to the same task were hallmarks of Bolshevik institutional nihilism. What counted was the personal power of the person leading an agency. Of all the committees, temporary and permanent commissions, commissariats, and the like devoted to a given policy area, the one headed by an authoritative person was the one that called the tune.

This was a system of personalized politics rather than of rational institutions. Institutions in the Bolshevik system had always been weak.[31] The Bolsheviks' own backgrounds as professional revolutionaries at odds with tsarist institutions had left them with no love for formal organizations. After the Revolution, as radical voluntarists out to change the world, they naturally distrusted rule-bound bureaucracies that were by nature conservative. Trotsky's famous remark upon being appointed foreign commissar in 1917 could apply to any Bolshevik's attitude toward institutions: "We will publish the secret treaties and close up shop." When it came to the state, many Bolsheviks' views bordered on anarchism, especially in the early days after the Revolution.

The Bolsheviks were simultaneously state builders and institutional nihilists. On the one hand, beginning in the 1930s there were obvious efforts to strengthen the state. Class-discriminatory practices in education, legality, and employment were abandoned in favor of a unitary concept of citizenship to be enshrined in the 1936 Constitution. There was a new emphasis on rule-bound procedures and a new discourse about the state.

But a strong tendency toward voluntarism remained, side by side and in contradiction to statism.[32] It reflected a prerevolutionary distrust of bureaucracy and bureaucracies, along with a fortress-storming campaign mentality and an equally strong reliance on cadres, personalities, and "our people" rather than rules. The governmental system was an irrational hodgepodge of overlapping institutions and jurisdictions with unclear mandates and constantly changing normative rules. Whenever a new policy had to be implemented, a new commission, committee, or ministry was casually created even if one was already available. What was important was not paperwork or the competencies of institutions but finding "our" people to staff the institutions and carry out policy. Yezhov expressed this typical Bolshevik attitude when he told his subordinates: "Writing a paper will not do any good. We will have to send some of our people there to straighten it out."[33]

Real political power was also reflected in the right to referee and resolve disputes between and among personalities. In a personalized system of politics, where formal rules and procedures do not matter so much as persons, bureaucratic relationships often resolve themselves into personal ones. Disputes ostensibly about budgets, personnel, and even policy were resolved and adjudicated in personal terms. Participants in both sides of a given conflict called in favors and appealed to protectors and allies, and the conflict was generally settled by decision of a superior referee. Much of the day-to-day business of any Stalinist official, at any level, was taken up with resolving such disputes coming up from below. Indeed, in a confused bureaucratic structure of overlapping institutions with unclear authority, one's real power and position had to do with the level of dispute one could referee.

Yezhov was good at this. At Orgraspred he settled arguments between party committees that competed for personnel. At the Commissariat of Agriculture, he used his accumulated experiences and personal contacts to fight others for valuable personnel and staff a new agency. In the Orgburo and the Secretariat, he was able to resolve disputes between Central Committee members and commissars. His résumé experience, therefore, was not only about offices and agencies. It was about his ever growing skill to deal with people: to know who they were, what were their interests and goals, and what kind of compromises might be possible. The system was about people, not flow charts. It was his skills with people that fueled his rise.

In this light, it should not be surprising that we conclude that the key factor in Yezhov's NKVD appointment—and his general success in the Soviet system—was his long-term experience with personnel assignment. He had been continuously working in cadre selection since 1924. Nobody in the leadership could match these twelve years of experience. Yezhov mastered the fundamental practice of Bolshevism: party personnel.

When in a famous speech in 1935 Stalin said, "Personnel policy is the most important thing," he was expressing a profound Bolshevik belief. Yezhov himself put it another way when he told his subordinates, "The party leads by appointing people. . . . This is the political expression of party leadership in its organizational form."[34] For the Stalinists, personnel policy was not only important; it was the very heart of their system. The key was to separate "our people" from "alien elements." If matters could be arranged so that the right people were put in charge, then it really didn't matter what institution they were in charge of. Personnel were to be selected according to political reliability, loyalty, and (with luck) "businesslike qualifications."[35]

A vital part of Yezhov's experience, and something at which Stalin himself had excelled, was detailed knowledge of who was in the party. In the early 1920s, when Stalin was actively involved in personnel selection, he had an amazing memory for who was who, who had done what, who had been where, and who had betrayed him. He knew everybody. From the mid-1920s, Yezhov had also come to know everybody who was anybody in the party. He spent long hours poring over card files and personnel dossiers. He had long experience matching jobs with appointees. He knew where to find candidates to mobilize for particular tasks and had the name of a qualified candidate at the tip of his tongue when he needed it. As he told his subordinates, "You must know each of your party workers personally. If I call you and wake you up any time of night, you have to be able to tell me where such and such a worker works, how he conducts himself, and so forth."[36]

When in 1936 Stalin was looking for someone to head the NKVD, Yezhov was the obvious candidate, not because he was "obedient" or because he had been cultivated. By that time, as the party's leading expert on cadres, Yezhov had more experience at the heart of the system than anyone else. He had the right résumé. He knew how to manage and run organizations. He had been overseeing the NKVD for two years and knew how that institution worked. But most important of all, he knew who was in the party. His experience in the three party screenings of the 1930s (1933, 1935, 1936), combined with his work in KPK investigating individual party members, only contributed to his years of experience in Orgraspred.

If the matter at hand was sorting out friend from foe, nobody was better qualified than Yezhov. In this sense, running the NKVD during the terror was a kind of mirror image of the kind of personnel selection that Yezhov had done for years. It is clear from interrogation protocols of arrested terror victims that the highest priority was to get the accused to name names. Again reflecting the personalized politics of the system, when it came to political crimes, the investigators were much more concerned about "with whom" than with "what" when they interrogated suspects. Arrests spread out in trees of personal connections, and a key goal of the terror in general was to uproot personal networks. Whenever a key official was arrested, his clients, appointees, and friends were also arrested. Yezhov already knew who was connected to whom, who had worked where with whom, who had some dirt in his past. He knew whom to suspect, whom to trust. He was perfect for the police job, and he brought with him to NKVD several assistants from his years in personnel selection.[37] His appointment was logically based on his qualifications, given the task at hand.

Out third question was about belief. Who could do these things; what did Yezhov believe? How did Stalinist Bolsheviks see the world in general?

We have often looked for simplistic answers having to do with omniscient and omnipotent dictators, malevolent long-range plans, willing one-dimensional dupes, and bad systems. It seems that we must use evil as an explanatory device, even in our research: only a monster, a devil, could do monstrous deeds, so we end up with one-dimensional fairy tales. Thus one explanation of Yezhov's behavior in the 1930s is based on the idea of a sudden personality change. Somehow the modest, friendly, and gallant fellow of the 1920s is said to have transformed himself at some point into a monster, perhaps having fallen under the spell of Stalin's personality.[38] Good was corrupted by evil.

The Stalin terror was unbelievably cruel and horrible. Millions of lives were snuffed out or needlessly destroyed. Husbands and wives were torn apart. Children were ripped from their parents and raised as orphans. Huge numbers of innocent people were shot in the head and thrown into pits. Even larger numbers wasted what remained of their lives behind barbed wire in desolate and cruel Gulag camps. But it does not follow from this that the purgers were red-eyed devils whose actions can be conveniently dealt with under labels like "insane" or "evil."[39] Confronted by the utterly ordinary Adolf Eichmann in the trial dock, Hannah Arendt suggested that terror was carried out by ordinary people rather than by hysterical monsters. They made choices about their interests and believed, in many cases, that what they were doing was simply their job. They remained pleasant, polite, normal people with families; they enjoyed music, outings in the country, and poetry.[40] The evil of the Eichmanns (and by implication of the Yezhovs) was horrible precisely because they were normal people.

They did not think that what they were doing was evil; they thought they were fighting evil. They thought that what they were doing was a nasty job that had to be done to ensure a happy future. To dismiss that as simple evil and to probe no further is to project particular values onto them and to explain their actions by our standards of morality. To do so also simplifies our analytical task to the point where no more research is really necessary: they were bad people and that's that. All we have to do is adduce more examples of just how evil they were and we are finished.

We must wonder what Yezhov thought he was doing. How did he

justify the cruel repression he conducted? Did the pleasant sociable fellow of the 1930s undergo a personality change? Of course, given the state of our sources we cannot answer this question conclusively. We do not have a Yezhov diary, and the few personal letters we have do not touch on justifications for the terror beyond official formulations. We can, however, make some observations and possible inferences based on his biography, social origins, and early experiences. In this light, we can see a continuity that obviates the need to posit a personality change or to impose on a person from another time our own liberal ideas of good and evil, right and wrong. Turning Yezhov into a flat, obedient robot who suffered a personality change from good to evil is not only implausible; it hides the cultural and historical context from which he emerged.

It is clear from everything Yezhov wrote and said, including his final statement before his own execution, that he sincerely believed in the existence of a monstrous oppositionist-Fascist conspiracy against the Soviet government.[41] No measure was too harsh in uprooting these alien traitors. He even believed that his own fall was engineered by still unmasked conspirators: he had failed to purge enough. Yezhov's beliefs on this, although reflecting the hysterical tenor of the times, are not without resonance in his own social and cultural origins and early life experiences.

According to the Bolshevik "algebra" of guilt, anyone who opposed the Bolsheviks was objectively and by definition opposing the Revolution, opposing socialism, and opposing human welfare, regardless of that person's subjective intent. All those who opposed collectivization, therefore, might as well be saboteurs because their opposition had the same effect as actual resistance. Those who knew of dissent or opposition and did not report it were themselves guilty of it. All those who opposed, or might oppose, the Stalin Revolution and General Line in the 1930s might as well be spies, because the objective effects of their stance were just as harmful as actual espionage.

Rebels are labeled as "bandits"; reluctant peasants become "kulaks"; dissenters become "Trotskyists." Any unauthorized political organization becomes ipso facto a "counterrevolutionary organization." Neither the identification nor the analogy was false for the Stalinists; these were not analogies but equations. The Stalinists said the same things to each other behind closed doors that they said to the public: in this regard their "hidden transcripts" differed little from their public ones. Bolsheviks saw the world through a prism that interpreted reality in a special way. The world was divided sharply and exclusively into friends and enemies, orthodox and heretical. Small political deviations were portrayed, and sincerely understood, as attacks by enemy forces.

The "enemies of the people" in 1937 were the "others." Yet this 1937 thinking was nothing new for Bolsheviks or indeed for Russian society. We have seen the brutal and brutalizing nature of the 1918–21 Civil War, in which the enemy "others" were treated with vicious cruelty. But even before that, concepts of "us" vs. "them" were embedded in Russian plebeian culture and practice.

Yezhov's earliest political experiences were those of a radicalized worker before and during the 1917 Revolution. Studies of worker discourse at that time, as we have seen, reveal a political world divided between enemies and friends, between "others" and "us." In 1917, even before the establishment of the Soviet regime and long before Stalin took power, workers were using the language of traitors, enemies, and betrayers. In language reminding us of 1937, they were saying that it was necessary to be "merciless with the enemies of the people." For these 1917 workers "true freedom necessitated silencing the voices of those who opposed the struggles and demands of workers, soldiers, and peasants."[42] This was Yezhov's early political education and socialization.

After 1917 these ideas were strengthened in the brutal Civil War and then translated into hard state practice. From the beginning of his career, Yezhov was known to his fellows as someone for whom class identity and struggle were everything. Writing in 1922 of his comrades in Kazan, Yezhov was proud that "they put their hopes on me thinking I can uphold the class line."[43] As workers and Bolsheviks saw it, cruel dictatorship against others was necessary to preserve a humane life for "us." "Our" democracy and happiness in fact depended on using dictatorship to deprive "them." In 1917 and in 1937, "the community must be unitary. Opposition and diversity is falsehood and therefore deserves no hearing. Government must be an expression and protector of this community based on a uniform commitment to truth."[44] In 1917 and in 1937, "a just government would not mediate among interests. . . . It was only the ill will of evil-doers that obstructed change. . . . All problems were caused by ill-intentioned people, by enemies of the people."[45] The sense of community in Russia was always in opposition to some other, usually malevolent group.[46] The worker idea of happy brotherhood was intimately related to protecting that community, at any cost, from "them."

Although it seems so from our liberal perspective, Yezhov's cruelty was not in contradiction with the specific ideas of humanity and community he shared with his fellows. For him and his contemporaries, there was no conflict between singing and dancing with "our" brother workers and then going out and torturing the enemy other. For the radical plebeians of Yezhov's time, the two traits affirmed and even depended on one another. The pleasant Yezhov of the 1920s and the hard killer of the 1930s were the same person.

# Notes

## Introduction

1. *Pravda,* 3 December 1937. I am grateful to Peter Wolfe for his translation.

2. Yezhov was arrested by his successor, L. P. Beria, on 10 April 1939. He was tried and executed on 4 February 1940. N. V. Petrov and K. V. Skorkin, eds., *Kto rukovodil NKVD, 1934–1941: Spravochnik* (Moscow: Zven'ia, 1999), 185.

3. Among other works, see Robert Conquest, *The Great Terror: A Reassessment* (New York: Oxford University Press, 1990), and Marc Jansen and Nikita Petrov, *Stalin's Loyal Executioner: People's Commissar Nikolai Ezhov, 1895–1940* (Stanford: Hoover Institution Press, 2002), the best study of Yezhov and the terror. Also see J. Arch Getty and Roberta Thompson Manning, eds., *Stalinist Terror: New Perspectives* (Cambridge: Cambridge University Press, 1993); J. Arch Getty and Oleg V. Naumov, *The Road to Terror: Stalin and the Self-Destruction of the Bolsheviks, 1932–1939* (New Haven: Yale University Press, 1999); O. V. Khlevniuk, "The Objectives of the Great Terror, 1937–1938," in *Soviet History, 1917–53: Essays in Honour of R. W. Davies,* ed. Julian Cooper, Maureen

Perrie, and E. A. Rees (London: Macmillan, 1995); O. V. Khlevniuk, "Les mechanismes de la 'Grande Terreur': des années 1937–1938 au Turkmenistan," *Cahiers du Monde Russe* 39, nos. 1–2 (1998); O. V. Khlevniuk, *1937-i: Stalin, NKVD i sovetskoe obshchestvo* (Moscow: Izd-vo "Respublika," 1992).

4. See, for example, Robert C. Tucker, *Stalin as Revolutionary* (New York: Norton, 1973), and Erik H. Erikson, *Young Man Luther: A Study in Psychoanalysis and History* (New York: Norton, 1962).

5. See B. B. Briukhanov and E. N. Shoshkov, *Opravdaniiu ne podlezhit. Ezhov i Ezhovshchina, 1936–1938* (St. Petersburg: Petrovskii Fond, 1998); Jansen and Petrov, *Stalin's Loyal Executioner;* V. A. Kovalev, *Dva stalinskikh narkoma* (Moscow: Izd-vo gruppa "Progress": "Univers," 1995); Aleksei Polianskii, *Ezhov: istoriia "zheleznogo" stalinskogo narkoma* (Moscow: ARIA-AiF, 2001).

6. The best study here is Graeme Gill, *The Origins of the Stalinist Political System* (Cambridge: Cambridge University Press, 1990).

7. The fullest popular biography is Polianskii, *Ezhov: istoriia*. Like other representatives of this genre, this book contains imagined conversations and no documentary or source references. The only serious scholarly study is Jansen and Petrov, *Stalin's Loyal Executioner.*

8. Jansen and Petrov, *Stalin's Loyal Executioner,* contains eight substantial chapters on Yezhov's police tenure and only one on the forty-one years of his life leading up to them.

9. Yezhov's archive is in Rossiiskii gosudarstvennyi arkhiv sotsial'no-politicheskoi istorii (hereafter RGASPI), f. 671, op. 1.

## 1. Epilogue as Prologue

1. Feliks Ivanovich Chuev, Vyacheslav Mikhaylovich Molotov, and Albert Resis, *Molotov Remembers: Inside Kremlin Politics, Conversations with Felix Chuev* (Chicago: I. R. Dee, 1993), 257.

2. A. M. Larina, *Nezabyvaemoe* (Moscow: APN, 1989), 269–70.

3. RGASPI, f. 85, op. 27, d. 93, ll. 12–13, Kaganovich to Ordzhonikidze. See also Vyacheslav Mikhaylovich Molotov and Feliks

Ivanovich Chuev, *Sto sorok besed s Molotovym: iz dnevnika F. Chueva* (Moscow: "Terra," 1991), 398, 406, 38.

4. Yezhov's role in preparations for this first show trial is reflected in his personal archive. See RGASPI, f. 671, op. 1, d. 189.

5. *Report of Court Proceedings; the Case of the Trotskyite-Zinovievite Terrorist Centre. Moscow, August 19–24, 1936, in re G. E. Zinoviev [and others]* (New York: Fertig, 1967).

6. Marc Jansen and Nikita Petrov, *Stalin's Loyal Executioner: People's Commissar Nikolai Ezhov, 1895–1940* (Stanford: Hoover Institution Press, 2002), 182.

7. *Izvestiia TsK KPSS,* no. 8 (1989), 100–115.

8. *Izvestiia TsK KPSS,* no. 5 (1989), 74.

9. RGASPI, f. 17, op. 2, d. 575, ll. 11–19, 40–45, 49–53, 57–60, 66–67. N. A. Uglanov, former First Secretary of the Moscow party organization in the late 1920s, had sided with rightists Bukharin and Rykov.

10. RGASPI, f. 17, op. 2, d. 576, ll. 67–70.

11. RGASPI, f. 17, op. 2, d. 575, ll. 11–19, 40–45, 49–53, 57–60, 66–67.

12. RGASPI, f. 671, op. 1, d. 52, ll. 190–94.

13. Boris Starkov, *Oni ne molchali* (Moscow: Politizdat, 1991), 217.

14. V. N. Khaustov, V. P. Naumov, and N. S. Plotnikova, eds., *Stalin i NKVD-NKGB-GUKR "Smersh," 1939-mart 1946* (Moscow: Fond "Demokratiia," 2006), 45–46.

15. The best analysis of the witch hunt in the Comintern is William Chase, *Enemies Within the Gates? The Comintern and the Stalinist Repression, 1934–1939* (New Haven: Yale University Press, 2001).

16. Ivo Banac, ed., *The Diary of Georgi Dimitrov, 1933–1949* (New Haven: Yale University Press, 2003), 36, 61.

17. Jansen and Petrov, *Stalin's Loyal Executioner,* 75–77.

18. Roger R. Reese, *Stalin's Reluctant Soldier: A Social History of the Red Army, 1925–1941* (Lawrence: University Press of Kansas, 1996), 134.

19. NKVD operational order no. 486, 15 August 1937. Tsentral'nyi arkhiv Federal'noi sluzhby bezopasnosti Rossiiiskoi Federatsii (hereafter TsA FSB), f. 100. op. 1, por. 1, l. 224–35.

20. Khaustov, Naumov, and Plotnikova, eds., *Stalin i NKVD-NKGB-GUKR "Smersh,"* 46; Jansen and Petrov, *Stalin's Loyal Executioner,* 200–201.

21. J. Arch Getty and Oleg V. Naumov, *The Road to Terror: Stalin and the Self-Destruction of the Bolsheviks, 1932–1939* (New Haven: Yale University Press, 1999), 474–77.

22. J. Arch Getty, "'Excesses Are Not Permitted': Mass Terror and Stalinist Governance in the Late 1930s," *Russian Review* 61, no. 1 (2002); M. Junge and R. Binner, *Kak terror stal 'bol'shim.' Sekretnyk prikaz No. 447 i tekhnologiia ego ispolneniia* (Moscow: AIRO, 2003).

23. Jansen and Petrov, *Stalin's Loyal Executioner,* 84.

24. Ibid., 83.

25. Terry Martin, "The Origins of Soviet Ethnic Cleansing," *Journal of Modern History* 70, no. 4 (1998).

26. V. N. Khaustov, V. P. Naumov, and N. S. Plotnikov, eds., *Lubianka. Stalin i Glavnoe Upravlenie Gosbezopasnosti NKVD, 1937–1938* (Moscow: Fond "Demokratiia," 2004), 302–21.

27. Jansen and Petrov, *Stalin's Loyal Executioner,* 96.

28. N. V. Petrov and A. B. Roginsky, "'Polskaia operatsiia' NKVD 1937–1938," in *Repressii protiv poliakov i pol'skikh grazhdan,* ed. A. E. Gur'ianov (Moscow: Zveniia, 1997), 33.

29. N. Okhotin and A. Roginskii, "Iz istorii 'nemetskoi operatsii' NKVD 1937–1938 g." in *Repressii protiv rossiiskikh nemstev: Nakazannyi narod,* ed. N. Okhotin and A. Roginskii (Moscow: Zveniia, 1999), 35–75.

30. Petrov and Roginsky, "'Polskaia operatsiia,'" 33.

31. NKVD operational order no. 693, 23 October 1937. TsA FSB, f. 100. op. 1, por. 1, ll. 239–42.

32. J. Arch Getty, Gabor T. Rittersporn, and V. N. Zemskov, "Victims of the Soviet Penal System in the Pre-War Years: A First Approach on the Basis of Archival Evidence," *American Historical Review* 98, no. 4 (1993).

33. Politburo decision "On Arrests, Procuratoral Supervision, and Conduct of Investigations," 17 November 1938, RGASPI, f. 17, op. 3, d. 1003, ll. 85–87.

34. Yezhov's file on Beria's "methods of work" is RGASPI, f. 671, op. 1, d. 264. His file on Stalin is a collection of postal receipts for money sent to Stalin in exile before the revolution, the time during which the rumor had been that Stalin was a tsarist police agent: RGASPI, f. 671, op. 1, d. 287.

35. Jansen and Petrov, *Stalin's Loyal Executioner,* 399.

36. RGASPI, f. 17, op. 3, d. 1003, ll. 82–84.

37. Yezhov mentioned the Liushkov defection as a key reason he should be removed at NKVD. RGASPI, f. 17, op. 3, d. 1003, ll. 82–84.

38. Unfortunately, some scholarly studies make serious use of these "confessions" as sources. See B. B. Briukhanov and E. N. Shoshkov, *Opravdaniiu ne podlezhit. Ezhov i Ezhovshchina, 1936–1938* (St. Petersburg: Petrovskii Fond, 1998), and Jansen and Petrov, *Stalin's Loyal Executioner.*

39. *Moskovskie novosti,* 30 January 1994.

## 2. The Making of a Bolshevik

1. Here and below, statistics on St. Petersburg's working class are taken from S. A. Smith, *Red Petrograd: Revolution in the Factories, 1917–1918* (Cambridge: Cambridge University Press, 1983), chapters 1 and 2. For more on the working class, see Victoria Bonnell, "Radical Politics and Organized Labor in Pre-revolutionary Moscow, 1905–1914," *Journal of Social History* 12, no. 2 (1978).

2. Robert B. McKean, *St. Petersburg Between the Revolutions: Workers and Revolutionaries, June 1907–February 1917* (New Haven: Yale University Press, 1990), 38.

3. See Heather Hogan, *Forging Revolution: Metalworkers, Managers, and the State in St. Petersburg, 1890–1914* (Bloomington: Indiana University Press, 1993); Eduard M. Dune, *Notes of a Red Guard,* trans. Diane P. Koenker and S. A. Smith (Urbana: University of Illinois Press, 1993); Charters Wynn, *Workers, Strikes, and Pogroms: The Donbass-Dnepr Bend in Late Imperial Russia, 1870–1905* (Princeton: Princeton University Press, 1992).

4. R. Zelnik, ed., *A Radical Worker in Tsarist Russia: The Autobiogra-*

*phy of Semen Ivanovich Kanatchikov* (Stanford: Stanford University Press, 1986), 96.

5. McKean, *St. Petersburg Between the Revolutions,* 38.

6. Quoted in Wynn, *Workers, Strikes, and Pogroms,* 119.

7. Ibid., 127.

8. V. A. Giliarovskii, *Moskva i moskvichi; ocherki staromoskovskogo byta* (Moscow: Moskovskii rabochii, 1955).

9. Quoted in Zelnik, *Radical Worker,* 99.

10. McKean, *St. Petersburg Between the Revolutions,* 57, 253, 259, 482.

11. In a questionnaire in the early 1920s, Yezhov claimed that he "could make himself understood in the Polish and Lithuanian languages." See "Yezhov Nikolai Ivanovich," in *Kto rukovodil NKVD, 1934– 1941: Spravochnik,* ed. N. V. Petrov and K. V. Skorkin (Moscow: Zven'ia, 1999), 185–86.

12. Fadeev's unpublished manuscript, "Nikolai Ivanovich Yezhov: Syn nuzhdy i bor'by" [Nikolai Ivanovich Yezhov: Son of necessity and struggle], is in RGASPI, f. 671, op. 1, d. 270, l. 70.

13. *"Kol'ki knizhinka."* Yezhov's recollections come from an autobiographical statement he wrote in 1921: "Kratkaia biografiia N. I. Yezhova" [Short (auto)biography of N. I. Yezhov], 1, RGASPI, uncatalogued documents. Much of the following account is taken from this statement, elements of which can be verified from other sources. Yezhov's short autobiography may be more dependable than subsequent accounts. It was written before Yezhov became a "leading party worker" and at a time before hagiography or self-promotion were common. It also contains personal references to comrades who knew Yezhov at various times and who could confirm his own account of his activities.

14. "Kratkaia biografiia," 1, and RGASPI, f. 671, op. 1, d. 270, l. 53.

15. See Leopold Haimson, "The Problem of Social Stability in Urban Russia, 1905–1914," *Slavic Review* 23, no. 4 (1964), and 24, no. 1 (1965).

16. Tim McDaniel, *The Agony of the Russian Idea* (Princeton: Princeton University Press, 1996), 35, 42.

17. St. Petersburg had been renamed Petrograd during the war, and

would be rechristened again, as Leningrad, after the leader's death in 1924.

18. "Kratkaia biografiia," 1. However, a search of military archives in 1936 showed him ordered to Vitebsk in early June 1916: Order of the Dvinsk Military District, 3 June 1916, RGASPI, f. 671, op. 1, d. 270, l. 31.

19. His "Kratkaia biografiia" does not mention radical activity during the war, although Yezhov noted years later on a questionnaire that he had been "repressed" in this period by the tsarist government and "exiled" from St. Petersburg in 1914: Personal questionnaire for delegates to the 14th Congress of the RKP(Bolsheviks), RGASPI, f. 54, op. 1, d. 126, l. 22. As we shall see, other sources written twenty years later at the height of Yezhov's power went further and claimed that he had been branded politically "unreliable" early on by the government and sent from St. Petersburg to a "punitive detachment" in the rear.

20. Leopold Haimson, "The Problem of Social Identities in Early Twentieth Century Russia" (with discussion), *Slavic Review* 47, no. 1 (1988).

21. M. D. Steinberg, *Voices of Revolution, 1917* (New Haven: Yale University Press, 2001), 17–19.

22. Haimson, "Problem of Social Identities."

23. Steinberg, *Voices of Revolution*, 21.

24. Among Marxists, the Mensheviks believed that the overthrow of the tsar in early 1917 represented the "bourgeois revolution" predicted by Marx and thought that the next, "proletarian" revolution was to be expected only after a long process of liberal democracy. Bolsheviks, on the other hand, wanted to compress the time between the two revolutions and under Lenin's leadership sought to bring out the proletarian, socialist revolution immediately. Bundists represented a separate Jewish workers' party, usually associated with the Mensheviks. Other parties (Trudoviks, Legal Marxists) also championed workers' interests, with various views on how to achieve them. Socialist Revolutionaries promoted a revolution of peasants rather than workers. Kadets resembled European liberals and advocated parliamentary government along English lines.

25. Overlaying this political chaos was the nationality question. Especially in multinational places like Vitebsk, which had substantial populations of Latvians, Poles, Jews, and others, it was not uncommon for members of these non-Russian populations to have their own party groups, either within the well-known parties or separately.

26. "Transcript of Comrade Drizul's memoir," RGASPI, f. 671, op. 1, d. 270, ll. 3, 12, 33; see also Yezhov's questionnaire and party card, d. 266, ll. 78, 82.

27. B. B. Briukhanov and E. N. Shoshkov, *Opravdaniiu ne podlezhit. Ezhov i Ezhovshchina, 1936–1938* (St. Petersburg: Petrovskii Fond, 1998), 9–12, doubt Yezhov's proletarian credentials, early radicalism, and devotion to the 1917 revolution in general. Without footnotes or other documentation, their account seems to be based on unspecified interviews and archival materials other than the Yezhov personal archive. Some of its points can be verified; others cannot.

28. "Transcript of Comrade Drizul's memoir," RGASPI, f. 671, op. 1, d. 270, l. 10. With the help of party editors, Drizul's characterization of a tedious orator who rarely spoke had to be edited and euphemized into a man with "fewer words, more deeds," one "for whom word never differs from deed." The latter was too pretentious for Yezhov, who crossed it off the text. See ibid., ll. 44, 57.

29. Ibid., RGASPI, f. 671, op. 1, d. 270, ll. 14, 18.

30. "Transcript of Comrade Drizul's memoir," RGASPI, f. 671, op. 1, d. 270, ll. 1, 3–4; Briukhanov and Shoshkov, *Opravdaniiu ne podlezhit,* 10.

31. "Transcript of Comrade Drizul's memoir," RGASPI, f. 671, op. 1, d. 270, l. 9.

32. Political commissars were appointed by the Bolshevik government and attached to various institutions to serve as watchdogs over the nominal chief. First used during the Civil War, political commissars constituted an answer to the distrust with which the Bolsheviks viewed nonparty holdover administrators from the old regime.

33. "Transcript of Comrade Drizul's memoir," RGASPI, f. 671, op. 1, d. 270, ll. 8–11.

34. "Kratkaia biografiia," 2.

35. Ibid.

36. "Questionnaire," RGASPI, f. 671, op. 1, d. 266, l. 78.

37. Briukhanov and Shoshkov, *Opravdaniiu ne podlezhit,* 13–15.

38. Steinberg, *Voices of Revolution,* 11, 13.

39. Nathalie Babel, ed., *The Complete Works of Isaac Babel* (New York: Norton, 2002), 231, 258.

40. Ibid., 359–61.

41. On the Civil War generally, see William G. Rosenberg, Diane P. Koenker, and Ronald G. Suny, eds., *Party, State, and Society in the Russian Civil War: Explorations in Social History* (Bloomington: Indiana University Press, 1989); V. Brovkin, *Behind the Front Lines of the Civil War* (Princeton: Princeton University Press, 1994); I. Babel, *The Red Cavalry and Other Stories* (London: Penguin, 2005); William Chamberlin, *The Russian Revolution, 1917–1921* (New York: Macmillan, 1935); Orlando Figes, *Peasant Russia, Civil War: The Volga Countryside in Revolution, 1917–1921* (London: Phoenix, 2001); Peter Kenez, *Civil War in South Russia, 1919–1920: The Defeat of the Whites* (Berkeley: University of California Press, 1971); Lars T. Lih, *Bread and Authority in Russia, 1914–1921* (Berkeley: University of California Press, 1990); Oliver H. Radkey, *The Sickle Under the Hammer: The Russian Socialist Revolutionaries in the Early Months of the Soviet Rule* (New York: Columbia University Press, 1963). On the psychological and social effects of the Civil War, see J. Arch Getty, "The Politics of Stalinism," in *The Stalin Phenomenon,* ed. Alec Nove (London: Weidenfelt and Nicolson, 1993).

42. We have Antonina Titova's "Registration blank for a member of the KPSS" and a short autobiography she wrote in 1933: RGASPI, f. 17, op. 100, 107. After completing her education in the famous Timiriazev Agricultural Academy, she worked for years in various agricultural research institutes until her death in 1988.

43. See miscellaneous biographical materials in RGASPI, f. 671, op. 1, d. 266, l. 89.

44. In 1919 the party had created three subcommittees of the Central Committee. The Politburo was to handle pressing political and strategic questions. The Orgburo was to deal with organizational matters, which

quickly came to mean personnel assignment. A Secretariat was to coordinate work between the other two committees and deal with correspondence and communication in the party. It proved significant for his rise to power that Joseph Stalin was the only person sitting on all three bodies.

45. *"Provedeniia klassovoi linii."* Yezhov to Petr Ivanov, 24 October 1922, RGASPI, f. 671, op. 1, d. 267, ll. 8–11.

46. E. Sudnitsyn to N. I. Yezhov, 10 February 1935, RGASPI, f. 671, op. 1, d. 268, ll. 6, 6 ob.

47. Steinberg, *Voices of Revolution*, 82, 96.

## 3. In the Provinces

1. V. I. Lenin, *Polnoe sobranie sochinenii* (Moscow: Gosizdat Politlitury, 1962), xlv, 95.

2. See Graeme Gill, *The Origins of the Stalinist Political System* (Cambridge: Cambridge University Press, 1990), chapter 1, for an analysis of this situation.

3. Entitled "On Party Discipline," the measure was a response to the appearance of several dissident groups within the party during the Civil War. *Desiatyi s"ezd RKP(b), mart 1921 goda. Stenograficheskii otchet* (Moscow: Gosizdat Politlitury, 1963), 571–73.

4. Gill, *Origins of the Stalinist Political System*, 114. See also Daniel Thorniley, *The Rise and Fall of the Soviet Rural Communist Party, 1927–39* (New York: St. Martin's, 1988).

5. T. H. Rigby, *Communist Party Membership in the USSR, 1917–1967* (Princeton: Princeton University Press, 1968), 52–53.

6. *Deviatyi s"ezd RKP(b), mart-aprel' 1920 goda. Stenograficheskii otchet* (Moscow: Gosizdat Politlitury, 1960), 36. On purges generally, see J. Arch Getty, *Origins of the Great Purges: The Soviet Communist Party Reconsidered, 1933–1938* (Cambridge: Cambridge University Press, 1985).

7. *Odinnadtsatyi s"ezd RKP(b), mart-aprel' 1922 goda. Stenograficheskii otchet* (Moscow: Gosizdat Politlitury, 1961).

8. Ibid., 555, 659; *Dvenadtsatyi s"ezd RKP(b), 17–25 aprelia 1923 goda. Stenograficheskii otchet* (Moscow: Gosizdat Politlitury, 1960), 790.

9. Protocol of the Orgburo of the CC, 10 February 1922, RGASPI, f. 17, op. 112, d. 287, ll. 2, 22–24.

10. Protocol of the Secretariat of the CC, 15 February 1922, RGASPI, f. 17, op. 112, d. 289, ll. 2, 6. At this time, the senior party leader of a territorial organization was designated "secretary" or "responsible secretary." Nearly always, party appointments were proposed by staff and ratified or rejected by the Orgburo or Secretariat. Although form dictated that the CC "recommend" a candidate to a district, in nearly all cases this amounted to appointment from above, rather than election by the committee as the party's rules required.

11. The best discussion of this centralization is Robert Service, *The Bolshevik Party in Revolution: A Study in Organizational Change, 1917–1923* (London: Macmillan, 1979).

12. A. N. Sakharov et al., eds., *"Top Secret": From the Lubianka to Stalin on the Situation in the Country, 1932–1934* (Moscow: Russian Academy of Sciences, 2002–6), 1: 117.

13. Party report Secretary Lure to CC, 1922 (n.d.), RGASPI, f. 17, op. 67, d. 118, l. 59.

14. Sakharov et al., *"Top Secret,"* 1: 144, 82, 304.

15. Materials for the 12th Party Congress, RGASPI, f. 17, op. 112, d. 440, l. 54.

16. *Odinnadtsatyi s"ezd,* 156.

17. For squabbles in nationality areas, see Terry Martin, *The Affirmative Action Empire: Nations and Nationalism in the Soviet Union, 1923–1939* (Ithaca: Cornell University Press, 2001).

18. *Vosmoi s"ezd RKP(b), mart 1919 goda. Protokoly* (Moscow: Gosizdat Politlitury, 1959), 184–85, 496; *Vosmaia konferentsiia RKP(b), dekabr' 1919 goda. Protokoly* (Moscow: Gosizdat Politlitury, 1961), 28, 215.

19. These categories had been prescribed in November 1918 but were not always observed by local report writers. See the CC's report to the 8th Party Congress: *Vosmoi s"ezd,* 496.

20. Compare, for example, Yezhov information letter, 1 September 1922 (RGASPI, f. 17, op. 67, d. 118, ll. 147–59), with the ungrammatical

and misspelled text of his personal letters of the same period (Yezhov to Berzina, 21 September 1922, RGASPI, f. 82, op. 2, d. 178, l. 28).

21. Yezhov Informational Letter to the CC for August 1922, RGASPI, f. 17, op. 67, d. 118, l. 146.

22. Ibid., ll. 147–50.

23. Yezhov to Petr Ivanov, 1 November 1922, RGASPI, f. 671, op. 1, d. 267, l. 12. Narkomprod was the agency responsible for collection and distribution of the food tax-in-kind.

24. The Democratic Centralists (1919–20) had argued for more collegial decision making at the top of the party and against the tendency of Lenin and a few key leaders to make decisions without consultation. The Workers' Opposition (1920–21) wanted more proletarian members in the party and favored giving the trade unions a significant role in government. See Robert Vincent Daniels, *The Conscience of the Revolution: Communist Opposition in Soviet Russia* (Boulder, Colo.: Westview, 1988).

25. See T. H. Rigby, "Early Provincial Cliques and the Rise of Stalin," *Soviet Studies* 33, no. 1 (1981), for an analysis of such squabbles.

26. Ibid. Gill, *Origins of the Stalinist Political System*, has convincingly shown how the weakness of institutionalization led to a strongly "personalized politics" in the Stalin period.

27. "Russian chauvinism" refers to the tendency of Russians to denigrate local traditions, marginalize native leaders, and/or "russify" local culture. Petrov to unknown comrades, 19 February 1923, RGASPI, f. 82, op. 2, d. 153, l. 11; Mari Obl. KK Secretary Volkov report to Moscow TsKK, 5 April 1923, RGASPI, f. 82, op. 2, d. 153, l. 14; Protocol of the Mari OblKK, 1 March 1923, RGASPI, f. 82, op. 2, d. 153, l. 6.

28. "On the Petrov Affair," RGASPI, f. 82, op. 2, d. 153, ll. 3–4. Although unsigned, this seems to be an internal report of the TsKK.

29. Yezhov report to the CC, June 1922, RGASPI, f. 17, op. 67, d. 118, l. 146.

30. Yezhov report to the CC, August 1922, RGASPI f. 17, op. 67, d. 118, ll. 147, 151.

31. Petrov to unknown comrades, ll. 10–11.

32. "On the Petrov Affair," l. 3.

33. Petrov to unknown comrades, l. 10.

34. "On the Petrov Affair," l. 3.

35. Protocols of the Mari OblKK, 1 March and 27 April 1923, RGASPI, f. 82, op. 2, d. 153, ll. 5–7.

36. Yezhov to Petr Ivanov, 9 March 1923, RGASPI, f. 671, op. 1, d. 267, l. 17.

37. On this see Martin, *Affirmative Action Empire.*

38. "On the Petrov Affair," l. 3.

39. Yezhov to Berzina, 21 September 1922, RGASPI, f. 82, op. 2, d. 178, l. 28; expletive deleted by Yezhov. This letter was found in Molotov's archive. It contained a reference to Aleksandr Shliapnikov, leader of the Workers' Opposition in the party. Police censors no doubt found this suspicious and sent the letter to Molotov, who was Yezhov's boss. Although Berzina was implicated in leftist opposition movements, it is not clear whether Yezhov was involved.

40. Yezhov to Petr Ivanov, n.d., RGASPI, f. 671, op. 1, d. 267, l. 3.

41. B. B. Briukhanov and E. N. Shoshkov, *Opravdaniiu ne podlezhit. Ezhov i Ezhovshchina, 1936–1938* (St. Petersburg: Petrovskii Fond, 1998), are mistaken in arguing that Yezhov was first removed, followed by Petrov for the sake of balance. The opposite was true: Petrov was forced out by January, while Yezhov was simply put on extended vacation and was technically on the Mari roster until March 1923, at a time when the TsKK was considering Petrov's expulsion from the party.

42. Orgburo protocol, 10 November 1922, RGASPI, f. 17, op. 112, d. 385, l. 146. In January 1923 a Mari report listed a Comrade Lur'e as party secretary: RGASPI, f. 17, op. 67, d. 118, l. 42. In that report, Lur'e complained of Petrov's "criminal behavior" even though Petrov was long gone from Mari.

43. Yezhov to Petr Ivanov, 1 November 1922, RGASPI, f. 671, op. 1, d. 267, l. 12.

44. See Rigby, "Early Provincial Cliques." Rigby seems to exaggerate the ability of outsiders to win control (10, 13).

45. Zinoviev's report for the Central Committee, *Vosmoi s"ezd,* 287.

46. Krestinsky's reports for the Central Committee, *Vosmaia Konferentsiia,* 29–30; *Deviatyi s"ezd,* 43; *Desiatyi s"ezd,* 45–46.

47. Central Committee memos, RGASPI, f. 17, op. 34, d. 114, ll. 10, 12, 80.

48. Rigby, "Early Provincial Cliques," 30; RGASPI, f. 17, op. 112, d. 312, l. 4; d. 288, ll. 2–3; d. 317, ll. 2–5.

49. Quoted in Rigby, "Early Provincial Cliques," 22. See also Martin, *Affirmative Action Empire,* on *skloki* centering around nationality issues.

50. Molotov's reports for the Central Committee, *Odinnadtsatyi s"ezd,* 54–55, 155, 654–56; *Dvenadtsatyi s"ezd,* 792–98.

51. "On the Petrov Affair," RGASPI, ll. 3–4.

52. See RGASPI, f. 17, op. 67, d. 118, ll. 21–25, 49.

53. Yezhov to Petr Ivanov, 24 October 1922, RGASPI, f. 671, op. 1, d. 267, ll. 8–11.

54. Kharakteristika na Sekretaria Marobkoma tov. Yezhova N. I., RGANI, f. 5, op. 98, d. 148732, l. 17.

55. Kharakteristika na chlena RKP(b) tov. Yezhova N. I., RGANI, f. 5, op. 98, d. 148732, ll. 18–19.

56. Sakharov, *"Top Secret,"* 1: 405.

57. Yezhov to Petr Ivanov, 1 November 1922, RGASPI, f. 671, op. 1, d. 267, l. 12.

58. Yezhov to Petr Ivanov, 24 October 1922, RGASPI, f. 671, op. 1, d. 267, ll. 8–11.

59. Yezhov to Petr Ivanov, 1 November 1922, 9 March 1923, RGASPI, f. 671, op. 1, d. 267, ll. 12–14, 17–19.

60. Orgburo protocol, 1 March 1923, RGASPI, f. 17, op. 112, d. 415, ll. 87, 275. The city of Semipalatinsk was at that time in Kirgizia but later became part of Kazakhstan.

61. Materials for the 12th Party Congress, RGASPI, f. 17, op. 112, d. 440, ll. 52–53.

62. Yezhov to Petr Ivanov, 15 April 1923, RGASPI, f. 671, op. 1, d. 267, ll. 20, 20 ob.

63. Semipalatinsk's population in early 1923 was 566,823 Kirgiz,

449,269 Russian, and 33,045 "other." Materials for the 12th Party Congress, l. 52.

64. *Dvenadtsatyi s"ezd*, 800–802.

65. *Odinnadtsatyi s"ezd*, 656. At this congress, the Central Committee berated Communists working in such areas for insufficient care, tact, and attention to the local population.

66. Sakharov, *"Top Secret,"* 1: 883; 2: 34, 186, 246, 16, 61, 124, 144–45; 3: 660.

67. Ibid., 1: 635, 673, 760, 821, 895–96, 913–14; 2: 43–44. One secret police report in December 1924, made the unsurprising observation that lowering taxes resulted in less peasant discontent! Ibid., 2: 260.

68. Report of Semipalatinsk Gubkom to the Central Committee, 10 February 1923, RGASPI, f. 17, op. 67, d. 87, ll. 256–60; Sakharov, *"Top Secret,"* 1: 673, 760; 2: 44, 131.

69. Report of Semipalatinsk Gubkom to the Central Committee, 10 February 1923.

70. "Guerilla aberrations and methods": *"partizanskie uklony."*

71. Materials for the 12th Party Congress, ll. 52–53. The Socialist Revolutionary (SR) Party had been the largest Russian political party in 1917, standing for a form of agrarian socialism. Its various wings had since come out against the Bolsheviks and had been outlawed by the Soviet government.

72. Sakharov, *"Top Secret,"* 1: 821, 895–96; 3: 722. A pud is a bit more than thirty-six pounds.

73. Antonina Titova, "Registration blank for a member of the KPSS," and autobiography, RGASPI, f. 17, op. 100, 107.

74. Uchraspred to Marobkom, March 1923, RGASPI, f. 17, op. 34, d. 558, l. 12; Spisok proshedshchikh cherez Uchraspred, 16 March 1923. RGASPI, f. 17, op. 34, d. 216, l. 27.

75. Yezhov closed letter to the Central Committee, 29 June 1923, RGASPI, f. 17, op. 67, d. 87, ll. 243–51.

76. Alexander Fadeev, "Nikolai Ivanovich Yezhov: Syn nuzhdy i bor'by" [Nikolai Ivanovich Yezhov: Son of necessity and struggle], RGASPI, f. 671, op. 1, d. 270, ll. 69–86.

77. "Yezhov Nikolai Ivanovich," in *Kto rukovodil NKVD, 1934–1941: Spravochnik,* ed. N. V. Petrov and K. V. Skorkin (Moscow: Zven'ia, 1999), 185.

78. For example, it was often the territorial party secretaries themselves who at party congresses demanded more help and direction from Moscow. See, for example, speeches by P. K. Kaganovich (Kursk) and P. Volin (Kostroma) at the 9th Congress: *Deviatyi s"ezd,* 62, 64. Even oppositionist critics of the CC majority reluctantly admitted that the CC had the responsibility to assign cadres centrally to make best use of scarce talent. See Trotsky speech at the 9th Congress: *Deviatyi s"ezd,* 76–77, and Preobrazhensky's at the 12th Congress: *Dvenadtsatyi s"ezd,* 146. By the mid-1920s, nobody disputed the CC's need to do this.

79. Yezhov to Akmolinsk Gubkom, 28 December 1924, RGASPI, f. 17, op. 67, d. 87, ll. 52–53.

80. Sakharov, *"Top Secret,"* 1: 913–14; 2: 122, 134, 179, 186, 246, 249, 289; 3: 584, 634.

81. Beys were members of traditional elites, roughly comparable to European nobles.

82. Sakharov, *"Top Secret,"* 2: 105, 111, 123; 3: 635–36, 700–701.

83. The Alash-Orda movement had been a generally liberal group favoring Kirgiz-Kazakh sovereignty in Turkestan. It had stood at the head of a short-lived state after the Russian Revolution (December 1917–May 1919). Alash-Orda had fought on both sides during the Civil War but sided with the Reds in the end. During the period of Yezhov's tenure in Central Asia, Alash-Orda was allied with the Bolsheviks, but increasing conflicts with the Bolsheviks led to its liquidation in 1927–28 as "anti-Soviet."

84. Naneishvili to Central Committee, 1924 (n.d.), RGASPI, f. 17, op. 67, d. 208, ll. 13–17.

85. Dzhangil'din to Stalin, 24 April 1925, RGASPI, f. 17, op. 67, d. 82, ll. 218–22.

86. Service, *Bolshevik Party in Revolution,* 175.

87. See, for example, CC letter, 22 December 1924, published in *Izvestiia TsK,* no. 12 (17), 1924, 4.

88. Khodzhanov to Stalin and Kuibyshev, 6 April 1925, RGASPI, f. 17, op. 67, d. 82, ll. 205–11.

89. Protocol of meeting of Kirgiz kraikom, 27 March 1925, f. 17, op. 67, d. 82, ll. 217, 217 ob.

90. Khodzhanov to Stalin and Kuibyshev, 6 April 1925, RGASPI, f. 17, op. 67, d. 82, l. 211.

## 4. The Party Personnel System

1. See Robert V. Daniels, "The Secretariat and the Local Organizations in the Russian Communist Party, 1921–1923," *American Slavic and East European Review* 16, no. 1 (1967); Graeme Gill, *The Origins of the Stalinist Political System* (Cambridge: Cambridge University Press, 1990), 131.

2. The classic work on Trotsky is still Isaac Deutscher, *The Prophet,* 3 vols. (New York: Oxford University Press, 1954–63).

3. See Robert Vincent Daniels, *The Conscience of the Revolution: Communist Opposition in Soviet Russia* (Boulder, Colo.: Westview, 1988).

4. Robert H. McNeal, *Stalin: Man and Ruler* (Oxford: Oxford University Press, 1988).

5. It is worth noting that the head of the personnel appointment staff (*Orgraspred*) for the second half of the decade was Ivan Moskvin, who sided with the Stalinist majority but who was never a Stalin intimate.

6. See T. H. Rigby, "Early Provincial Cliques and the Rise of Stalin," *Soviet Studies* 33, no. 1 (1981).

7. Ossinsky, Sapronov, and Zinoviev speeches to the 8th Congress, *Vosmoi s"ezd RKP(b), mart 1919 goda. Protokoly* (Moscow: Gosizdat Politlitury, 1959), 165–66, 169–71, 184–85, respectively.

8. Trotsky speech to the 9th Party Congress, *Deviatyi s"ezd RKP(b), mart-aprel' 1920 goda. Stenograficheskii otchet* (Moscow: Gosizdat Politlitury, 1960), 76–77.

9. When Preobrazhensky issued his warning in April 1923, only 30 percent of provincial party secretaries were being "recommended" rather than elected: Preobrazhensky speech to the 12th Party Congress, *Dvenadtsatyi s"ezd RKP(b), 17–25 aprelia 1923 goda. Stenograficheskii otchet* (Moscow: Gosizdat Politlitury, 1960), 146.

10. Zinoviev's coreport of the Central Committee to the 14th Party Congress, *XIV s"ezd Vsesoiuznoi Kommunisticheskoi Partii (b), 18–31 dekabria 1925 g. Stenograficheskii otchet* (Moscow: Gosizdat, 1926), 127.

11. See Molotov and Rumiantsev speeches to the 14th Party Congress, ibid., 484–85, 595.

12. Riutin speech to the 12th Party Congress, *Dvenadtsatyi s"ezd*, 181.

13. Gill, *Origins of the Stalinist Political System*, 94, 173; Rigby, "Early Provincial Cliques," 17.

14. Gill, *Origins of the Stalinist Political System*, 6.

15. RGASPI, f. 17, op. 113, d. 362. See also Molotov's scathing attack on the Leningraders' undemocratic delegate selection: *XIV s"ezd*, 482–83.

16. See the speeches by Molotov, Shkiriatov, and Rumiantsev: *XIV s"ezd*, 484–85, 568–71, 595.

17. Robert Service, *The Bolshevik Party in Revolution: A Study in Organizational Change, 1917–1923* (London: Macmillan, 1979), 128.

18. Molotov's organizational report to the 11th Party Congress, *Odinnadtsatyi s"ezd RKP(b), mart-aprel' 1922 goda. Stenograficheskii otchet* (Moscow: Gosizdat Politlitury, 1961), 54.

19. See Gill, *Origins of the Stalinist Political System*, 132–34.

20. Stalin noted this at the 12th Party Congress and observed that if oppositionists declined to accept new positions, there was little the CC could do about it. *Dvenadtsatyi s"ezd*, 198.

21. Unfortunately, the protocols of Orgburo and Secretariat meetings do not include the text of Orgraspred presentations and recommendations.

22. Stalin's organizational report to the 13th Party Congress, *Trinadtsatyi s"ezd RKP(b), Mai 1924 goda. Stenograficheskii otchet* (Moscow: Gosizdat, 1963), 118.

23. Gill, *Origins of the Stalinist Political System*, 114–19.

24. Ossinsky speech to the 8th Party Congress, *Vosmoi s"ezd*, 165.

25. Resolution of the 8th Party Congress, *Vosmoi s"ezd*, 426.

26. For a useful outline of these developments, see T. H. Rigby, "USSR Incorporated: The Origins of the Nomenklatura System," *Soviet Studies* 40, no. 4 (1988).

27. See *Vosmaia konferentsiia RKP(b), dekabr' 1919 goda. Protokoly* (Moscow: Gosizdat Politlitury, 1961), 30; *Desiatyi s"ezd RKP(b), mart 1921 goda. Stenograficheskii otchet* (Moscow: Gosizdat Politlitury, 1963), 56, 111; *Odinnadtsatyi s"ezd*, 56, 65.

28. Molotov's report to the 11th Party Congress, *Odinnadtsatyi s"ezd*, 53, 56.

29. D. Kursky's report to the 13th Party Congress, 131; Boris Bazhanov, *Vospominaniia byvshego sekretaria Stalina* (Paris: Frantsiia: Tretiia Volna, 1980), 36.

30. D. Kursky's report to the 14th Party Congress, *XIV s"ezd*, 87–89.

31. Nogin's report of the Accounting Department to the 11th Party Congress, *Odinnadtsatyi s"ezd*, 64–65. For examples of the constant complaints see *Vosmoi s"ezd*, 184–86 (Zinoviev), 181 (Kaganovich); *Vosmaia konferentsiia*, 28 (Krestinsky); *Desiatyi s"ezd*, 49 (Krestinsky); *Odinnadtsatyi s"ezd*, 63 (Nogin), 152 (Molotov); *Dvenadtsatyi s"ezd*, 803–4 (TsK Otchet).

32. Smolensk Archive file 116/154e, 88. Yezhov wrote the same thing to Stalin in August 1935: RGASPI, f. 558, op. 11, d. 1085, l. 12.

33. CC Draft Resolution, *Dvenadtsatyi s"ezd*, 804.

34. *Vosmaia konferentsiia*, 221; *XIV s"ezd*, 89.

35. See Nogin's and Molotov's reports to the 11th Party Congress, *Odinnadtsatyi s"ezd*, 81, 56, respectively. By mid-1924, the Secretariat faced three hundred to four hundred agenda items at each meeting.

36. Gill, *Origins of the Stalinist Political System*, 163; *Dvenadtsatyi s"ezd*, 804.

37. Gill, *Origins of the Stalinist Political System*, 164–65; Rigby, "USSR Incorporated," 532.

38. Before the Revolution, all regional party leadership positions were filled by appointment or by co-opting available talent.

39. D. Kursky's Accounting Dept. report to the 13th Party Congress, *Trinadtsatyi s"ezd*, 133.

40. Rigby, "USSR Incorporated," 533.

41. Politburo protocols are in RGASPI, f. 17, op. 3. Those of the Orgburo and the Secretariat are RGASPI, f. 17, op. 112, 113.

42. *Deviatyi s"ezd*, 13, 86; *Odinnadtsatyi s"ezd*, 143–44.

43. D. Kursky's Accounting Dept. report to the 13th Party Congress, *Trinadtsatyi s"ezd*, 130.

44. V. P. Nogin's report to the 12th Party Congress, *Dvenadtsatyi s"ezd*, 81. Gill rightly observes that the various high "councils of organizational notables" largely ratified staff proposals: Gill, *Origins of the Stalinist Political System*, 158–59.

45. See *Dvenadtsatyi s"ezd*, 702, for the appeals rule.

46. D. Kursky's Accounting Dept. report to the 13th Party Congress, *Trinadtsatyi s"ezd*, 133.

47. D. Kursky's Accounting Dept. report to the 14th Party Congress, *XIV s"ezd*, 88, 92.

48. Rigby, "USSR Incorporated," 531.

49. "Spisok zamov i pomov Orgraspreda i otvetstven. instruktorov TsK," n.d. (1928?), RGASPI, f. 17, op. 69, d. 547, ll. 56–59.

50. Ibid.; "Shtat orgraspreda Tsentral'nogo Komiteta VKP(b) na 15 noiabria 1928 g.," RGASPI, f. 17, op. 69, d. 547, ll. 25–30.

51. "Shtat orgraspreda Tsentral'nogo Komiteta," ll. 28–30.

52. N. I. Yezhov, "Ob"iasnitel'naia zapiska," 28 April 1928, RGASPI, f. 17, op. 113, d. 614, l. 185.

53. For such actions, among hundreds of examples see "Protokol no. 45 zasedaniia Sekretariata TsK VKP(b) to 22 iuniia 1928 g.," items 22, 23, 27, 28, 35. In the latter case, a personal transfer request from Dzerzhinskaia (widow of Lenin's friend and recently deceased secret police chief Feliks Dzerzhinsky) was declined; RGASPI, f. 17, op. 113, d. 634, ll. 1–13.

54. Based on a scan of the rosters and conference transcripts in RGASPI, f. 17, op. 69, d. 13.


## 5. Sorting Out the Comrades

1. See Kursk delegate P. K. Kaganovich's remarks to the 9th Party Congress in 1920, *Deviatyi s"ezd RKP(b), mart-aprel' 1920 goda. Stenograficheskii otchet* (Moscow: Gosizdat Politlitury, 1960), 62.

2. Antonina Titova, "Registration blank for a member of the KPSS," and autobiography, RGASPI, f. 17, op. 100, 107.

3. Frontiers: *"okraina."*

4. Yezhov to Molotov, 25 February 1924, RGASPI, f. 17, op. 67, d. 87, l. 233.

5. Political questions: *kharakteristika.* RGANI, f. 5, op. 98, d. 148732, l. 27.

6. Orgburo protocol, 4 January 1926, RGASPI, f. 17, op. 113, d. 158, l. 5. Several of Yezhov's performance reports had recommended that he enhance his natural proletarian instincts with formal Marxist education. See, for example, RGANI, f. 5, op. 98, d. 148732, ll. 16, 17, 18, 27.

7. Orgburo protocol, 8 February 1926, RGASPI, f. 17, op. 113, d. 166, ll. 9, 13, 51.

8. Secretariat protocol, 15 March 1926, RGASPI, f. 17, op. 113, d. 178, l. 189.

9. The phrase was Molotov's, who decades later so remembered Yezhov. Feliks Ivanovich Chuev, *Molotov: Poluderzhavnyi vlastelin* (Moscow: Olma-Press, 1999), 472. (This is an updated and corrected version of Vyacheslav Mikhaylovich Molotov and Feliks Ivanovich Chuev, *Sto sorok besed s Molotovym: iz dnevnika F. Chueva* [Moscow: "Terra," 1991].)

10. As the party's First General Secretary in overall charge of personnel, this had also been one of Stalin's paths to power.

11. Yezhov appears on a list of 127 people taking Marxism courses at the Communist Academy in a list of the CC Secretariat marked "conspiratorial," a secret designation for CC documents. RGASPI, f. 17, op. 113, d. 178, l. 189.

12. A. Fadeev, "Nikolai Ivanovich Yezhov," unpublished manuscript, RGASPI, f. 671, op. 1, d. 270, ll. 77–78.

13. Kurskom report to Communist Academy, RGASPI, f. 671, op. 1, d. 234, ll. 155, 159–60, 164. Yezhov's 225 rubles per month was not meager; no student was paid more, and even Central Committee department heads received the same salary. See RGASPI, f. 17, op. 69, d. 547, l. 28.

14. B. B. Briukhanov and E. N. Shoshkov, *Opravdaniiu ne podlezhit.*

*Ezhov i Ezhovshchina, 1936–1938* (St. Petersburg: Petrovskii Fond, 1998), 27–28, believe that Yezhov met Moskvin at the 14th Party Congress in December 1925. This seems unlikely. At the congress, Moskvin was a prominent Bolshevik leader at the center of the current Stalinist struggle with the Zinoviev Leningrad opposition. Yezhov, on the other hand, was a minor delegate from Kazakhstan who did not even have voting privileges at the meeting.

15. "O rabote t. Yezhova N. I.," Secretariat protocol, 14 July 1927, RGASPI, f. 17, op. 113, d. 310, ll. 9, 138.

16. V. P. Nogin's report to the 12th Party Congress, *Dvenadtsatyi s"ezd RKP(b), 17–25 aprelia 1923 goda. Stenograficheskii otchet* (Moscow: Gosizdat Politlitury, 1960), 81; D. Kursky's report to the 13th Party Congress, *Trinadtsatyi s"ezd RKP(b), Mai 1924 goda. Stenograficheskii otchet* (Moscow: Gosizdat Politlitury, 1963), 131; Kursky's report to the 14th Party Congress, *XIV s"ezd Vsesoiuznoi Kommunisticheskoi Partii (b), 18–31 dekabria 1925 g. Stenograficheskii otchet* (Moscow: Gosizdat Politlitury, 1926), 88–92. Gill calls these higher bodies "councils of organizational notables which rested upon a hierarchy of bureaucrats in the secretarial machinery." Graeme Gill, *The Origins of the Stalinist Political System* (Cambridge: Cambridge University Press, 1990), 158–59.

17. "Shtat orgraspreda Tsentral'nogo Komiteta VKP(b) na 15 noiabria 1928 g.," RGASPI, f. 17, op. 69, d. 547, ll. 28–30. Moskvin's formal title was *zaveduiushchii,* chief or head. The total of forty-four responsible workers under him does not include clerical secretaries, file clerks, archivists, and other technical personnel. The entire staff of Orgraspred was seventy-eight persons.

18. Ibid., ll. 56–59.

19. Yezhov to Orgburo, 25 August 1927, RGASPI, f. 17, op. 113, d. 203, ll. 141–42.

20. Voronezh Province Party Committee to Yezhov, 22 September 1927, RGASPI, f. 17, op. 120, d. 15, l. 128.

21. Confirmation of the date of Yezhov's promotion has not been located in the archives, but by early December he was listed as a deputy chief of Orgraspred on the roster of delegates to the 15th Party Congress.

*Piatnadtsatyi s"ezd VKP(b), dekabr' 1927 goda. Stenograficheskii otchet.* (Moscow: Gosizdat, 1962), 2: 1522.

22. Lev Emmanuilovich Razgon, *Nepridumannoe: povest' v rasskazakh* (Moscow: "Kniga," 1989), 13–14. Razgon writes that Moskvin had spotted Yezhov in the provinces and brought him to Moscow, giving him the position of Orgraspred instructor in 1927 (12). Briukhanov and Shoshkov repeat the story, taking it from Razgon; Briukhanov and Shoshkov, *Opravdaniiu ne podlezhit,* 30–31. We have found no record that Yezhov ever served as an instructor in Orgraspred, or that Moskvin had anything to do with Yezhov's arrival in Moscow, which, as we have seen, seems to have been engineered by Yezhov himself.

23. Briukhanov and Shoshkov, *Opravdaniiu ne podlezhit,* 32.

24. N. I. Yezhov, "Ob"iasnitel'naia zapiska," n.d., RGASPI, f. 17, op. 113, d. 614, l. 142.

25. "Spisok zamov i pomov Orgraspreda i otvetstven. instruktorov TsK," RGASPI, f. 17, op. 69, d. 547, l. 56.

26. See his various letters, notes, and remarks at Orgraspred conferences in RGASPI, f. 17, op. 69, d. 496, l. 223; op. 113, d. 203, ll. 141–42; d. 610, l. 101; d. 614, ll. 142, 185; d. 616, l. 134.

27. Although other Orgraspred responsible workers did so as well, Yezhov seems to have done rather more than his share. RGASPI, f. 17, op. 113, d. 614, ll. 142, 185; d. 616, l. 119; d. 628, l. 236; d. 634, l. 6.

28. Quoted in Razgon, *Nepridumannoe* 14.

29. "Zasedanie komissii O.B. TsK po voprosy o proverke sostava i merakh po ukrepleniiu rabotnikov sel'skogo khoziaistva to 23/XII–29," RGASPI, f. 17, op. 74, d. 2, ll. 1–2.

30. Orgraspred conference, c. January 1928, RGASPI, f. 17, op. 69, d. 496, ll. 161–62. Yezhov's speech was always terribly ungrammatical and elliptical, requiring numerous insertions in translation.

31. Ibid., ll. 27–28.

32. Ibid., l. 29.

33. Ibid., ll. 29–30.

34. Orgraspred conference, 14 August 1928, RGASPI, f. 17, op. 69, d. 510, ll. 2, 3, 16.

35. Voronezh Gubkom memo to Orgraspred CC, 7 September 1927, RGASPI, f. 17, op. 120, d. 15, l. 128.

36. Yezhov's name does not appear on Stalin's office calendar until his appointment as Orgraspred chief in November 1930. Stalin rarely attended meetings of the Orgburo or the Secretariat, and a search of the protocols of those organizations has located very few meetings at which both were present.

37. R. W. Davies, *The Soviet Economy in Turmoil, 1929–1930* (Cambridge: Harvard University Press, 1989), 240–41.

38. Politburo protocol, 15 December 1929, RGASPI, f. 17, op. 3, d. 768, l. 4.

39. Ibid.

## 6. Yezhov on the Job

"Kadry reshayut vse" — Cadres decide everything — was the title of a highly publicized Stalin speech in 1935, and it became a widely promulgated slogan in the 1930s. It does not mean that party cadres decided policy questions; a more accurate, if less pithy, interpretation would be "personnel allocation is the most important factor."

1. On collectivization generally see Moshe Lewin, *Russian Peasants and Soviet Power: A Study of Collectivization* (New York: Norton, 1975); R. W. Davies, *The Socialist Offensive: The Collectivization of Soviet Agriculture, 1929–1930* (London: Macmillan, 1980); and Lynne Viola, *Peasant Rebels Under Stalin: Collectivization and the Culture of Peasant Resistance* (New York: Oxford University Press, 1996).

2. Prikazy Narkomzem SSSR, *Rossiiskii gosudarstvennyi arkhiv ekonomiki* (hereafter RGAE), f. 7486, op. 1, d. 11, ll. 32, 77, 85, 90.

3. For examples of these routine appointments, see RGAE, f. 7486, op. 1, d. 13.

4. Yezhov to Yenukidze, 30 November 1930, RGAE, f. 7486, op. 39, d. 17, l. 67.

5. See Yezhov to the Council of Labor and Defense, 10 October 1930, RGAE, f. 7486, op. 19, d. 52, ll. 161–62.

6. For examples of his reports to the Collegium of Narkomzem, see RGAE, f. 7486, op. 19, d. 9, l. 189.

7. RGAE, f. 7486, op. 1, d. 2, l. 126. At about this time, the Yezhovs separated. Antonina continued her career in agricultural research and lived until 1988. Around 1930 Yezhov married Yevgenya Gladuna, a typist at the newspaper *Krest'ianskaia gazeta*. She later edited the popular journal *USSR Under Construction* and ran a literary salon in their apartment that attracted such leading writers as Isaac Babel and Mikhail Kol'tsov. She came under suspicion in 1938 (at the same time as Yezhov) for talking too much about politics with her guests. She committed suicide on 23 November 1938, after writing to Stalin protesting her innocence. Virtually all her literary guests and friends were arrested and were executed, along with Yezhov, in early 1940. See Marc Jansen and Nikita Petrov, *Stalin's Loyal Executioner: People's Commissar Nikolai Ezhov, 1895–1940* (Stanford: Hoover Institution Press, 2002), 16–17, 120, 68–69, 90–91.

8. Yezhov to Petr Ivanov, 1 November 1922. RGASPI, f. 671, op. 1, d. 267, l. 14.

9. Jansen and Petrov, *Stalin's Loyal Executioner*, 13–14. On the cultural revolution of the period, see Sheila Fitzpatrick, *Cultural Revolution in Russia, 1928–1931* (Bloomington: Indiana University Press, 1984).

10. Yezhov to V. M. Molotov, 16 February 1930, RGAE, f. 7486, op. 39, d. 10, l. 59.

11. Quotation marks in original. Yezhov used the word *prorabotka*, which indeed means study but which in Stalinist documents sometimes carries the connotation of endless or inconclusive examination of a question: working it to death. Yezhov's intercession with Molotov may have succeeded. The first Higher Courses for leading workers in Narkomzem USSR opened on 20 June 1930, with an enrollment of 152 students. "Prikaz Narkomzema," 15 June 1930, RGAE, f. 7486, op. 1, d. 12, ll. 58–59.

12. See his order in RGAE, f. 7486, op. 1, d. 11, l. 68.

13. RGAE, f. 7486, op. 19, d. 9, ll. 214–15.

14. Yezhov to CC, 12 April 1930, RGAE, f. 17, op. 39, d. 10, l. 118.

15. Yezhov to Moscow Party Committee (copied to Orgraspred), 14 June 1930, RGAE, f. 17, op. 39, d. 10, l. 120.

16. See, for example, his letters to the Orgburo and Secretariat, 4, 16, and 30 October, RGAE, f. 17, op. 39, d. 10, ll. 195, 201, 213.

17. Yezhov order, 26 March 1930, RGAE, f. 7486, op. 1, d. 11, l. 85.

18. See the blank form in RGAE, f. 7486, op. 1, d. 10, l. 51.

19. Stenogram of Yezhov conference with peasants, RGAE, f. 7486, op. 79, d. 24, l. 9.

20. Politburo protocol, 14 November 1930, RGASPI, f. 17, op. 3, d. 804, l. 14.

21. Jansen and Petrov, *Stalin's Loyal Executioner,* 13.

22. Ibid., 15–21. *Chistka* literally means a sweeping or cleaning.

23. Politburo protocols, RGASPI, f. 17, op. 3, d. 808, l. 2; d. 1994, l. 4; d. 2068, l. 3; d. 2059, l. 8.

24. Ibid., f. 17, op. 3, d. 808, l. 2; d. 807, l. 12; d. 1928, l. 5; d. 1929, l. 5; d. 1932, l. 4; d. 857, l. 45; d. 856, l. 2; d. 1975, l. 4; d. 1994, l. 6; d. 2057, l. 2; d. 2068, l. 1; op. 162, d. 9, ll. 161, 165; d. 10, l. 45; d. 11, ll. 48, 63; d. 15, ll. 95, 168, 2; d. 14, l. 96; op. 120, d. 104, l. 1.

25. Ibid., op. 3, d. 1977, ll. 2, 4; op. 162, d. 11, l. 122; d. 12, ll. 39–40; d. 14, l. 44; d. 15, ll. 80, 113.

26. Ibid., op. 3, d. 1928, l. 9; d. 1988, l. 6; d. 2001, l. 6; d. 2002, l. 9; d. 2021, ll. 12, 13.

27. Ibid., d. 2037, l. 13; d. 2043, l. 17; op. 162, d. 9, l. 124; d. 15, l. 2.

28. Ibid., op. 120, d. 52, ll. 188–200. My thanks to Lynne Viola for this reference.

29. Ibid., op. 3, d. 942, l. 2, and discussion in J. Arch Getty and Oleg V. Naumov, *The Road to Terror: Stalin and the Self-Destruction of the Bolsheviks, 1932–1939* (New Haven: Yale University Press, 1999), 159.

30. For examples of his reports to the Orgburo and Secretariat, see RGASPI, f. 17, op. 114, d. 299, l. 18.

31. Yezhov speech to Raspredotdel workers, January 1933: RGASPI, f. 671, op. 1, d. 2, ll. 1–10.

32. Yezhov speech to conference of ORPO workers, 16 August 1935, RGASPI, f. 671, op. 1, d. 9, ll. 6–8, 24.

33. See J. Arch Getty, *Origins of the Great Purges: The Soviet Communist Party Reconsidered, 1933–1938* (Cambridge: Cambridge University Press, 1985), chapter 2, for a description of party purges. See also T. H. Rigby, *Communist Party Membership in the USSR, 1917–1967* (Princeton: Princeton University Press, 1968), 204, for a discussion of these nonpolitical targets.

34. Politburo protocols, RGASPI, f. 17, op. 3, d. 922, ll. 50–55.

35. P. N. Pospelov et al., *Istoriia Kommunisticheskoi Partii Sovetskogo Soiuza* (Moscow: Gosizdat Politlitury, 1971), 283.

36. See Getty and Naumov, *Road to Terror,* for further discussion.

37. RGASPI, f. 671, op. 1, dd. 100, 101. Yezhov spoke generally on the screening to a Raspredotdel conference; RGASPI, f. 671, op. 1, d. 2.

38. RGASPI, f. 17, op. 120, dd. 98, 99. For detailed examination of the suspicion of foreign Communists, see William Chase, *Enemies Within the Gates? The Comintern and the Stalinist Repression, 1934–1939* (New Haven: Yale University Press, 2001), chapters 3–4; Terry Martin, "The Origins of Soviet Ethnic Cleansing," *Journal of Modern History* 70, no. 4 (1998).

39. Yezhov to Stalin, Molotov, Kaganovich, 19 April 1934, RGASPI, f. 17, op. 82, d. 905, l. 19.

40. Politburo protocols, RGASPI, f. 17, op. 3, d. 2030, l. 6; d. 2044, l. 5; d. 2056, l. 8.

41. See, for example, RGASPI, f. 17, op. 3, d. 2024, l. 1; d. 2044, ll. 6, 26; f. 671, op. 1, d. 44, ll. 1–5.

42. RGASPI, f. 671, op. 1, dd. 20, 44.

43. B. B. Briukhanov and E. N. Shoshkov, *Opravdaniiu ne podlezhit. Ezhov i Ezhovshchina, 1936–1938* (St. Petersburg: Petrovskii Fond, 1998), 160.

44. Orgburo protocols, RGASPI, f. 17, op. 163, d. 924, l. 20.

45. Yezhov to Kaganovich, April 1934, RGASPI, f. 671, op. 1, d. 52, ll. 1–5; Shkiryatov to Yezhov, ibid., d. 268, l. 109.

46. For examples see RGASPI, f. 17, op. 120, d. 114, l. 17 (Zimin to Kaganovich to Yezhov); f. 671, op. 1, d. 18, l. 10 (Amosov to Stalin to Yezhov); d. 52, ll. 48–52 (Krupskaia to Stalin to Yezhov).

47. Beria to Yezhov, 16 February 1934, RGASPI, f. 671, op. 1, d. 18, ll. 4–8.

48. See RGASPI, f. 671, op. 1, d. 22, ll. 30, 83–86, 165–71.

49. Litvinov to Yezhov, 9, September 1935, RGASPI, f. 671, op. 1, d. 18, ll. 99–100.

50. Akulov to Yezhov, 28 April 1935, RGASPI, f. 671, op. 1, d. 57, l. 11.

51. Sudnitsin to Yezhov, 10 February 1935, RGASPI, f. 671, op. 1, d. 268, ll. 4–5.

52. For examples, see RGASPI, f. 268, op. 1, ll. 1–17, 35–36, 93–94.

53. See, for example, the requests in RGASPI, f. 671, op. 1, dd. 22, 52.

54. Krupskaia to Stalin to Yezhov on schools and museums, RGASPI, f. 671, op. 1, d. 52, ll. 48–52; Angarov to Yezhov on dispute with Bubnov on schools, ibid., ll. 87–89.

55. I analyze the rise and fall of these plenipotentiaries in J. Arch Getty, *Pragmatists and Puritans: The Rise and Fall of the Party Control Commission* (Pittsburgh: Center for Russian and East European Studies, University of Pittsburgh, 1997).

56. Sheboldaev to Yezhov, 6 February 1936, RGASPI, f. 671, op. 1, d. 89, ll. 3–5; Undated Yezhov notes on conversations with Kaganovich, ibid., d. 52, ll. 14–20.

57. Frenkel' to Stalin and Yezhov, 22 May 1937, RGASPI, f. 671, op. 1, d. 89, ll. 127–30.

58. Yezhov notes, RGASPI, f. 671, op. 1, d. 89, ll. 221–58.

59. Yezhov to Stalin, 26 March 1935, RGASPI, f. 671, op. 1, d. 18, ll. 18–19. Sometimes Stalin asked a question or two. When in March 1934 Yezhov approved Ammosov's request for more party workers for the railroads, Stalin jotted to Yezhov, "What's this about?" Yezhov explained and Stalin approved.

60. Yezhov to Stalin, n.d., RGASPI, f. 671, op. 1, d. 18, l. 97.

61. We have found no cases in the archival sources in which Stalin disapproved one of Yezhov's personnel recommendations.

62. See J. Arch Getty, "Afraid of Their Shadows: The Bolshevik Recourse to Terror, 1932–1938," in *Stalinismus vor dem Zweiten Weltkrieg. Neue Wege der Forschung,* ed. Manfred Hildermeier and Elisabeth

Mueller-Luckner (Munich: Oldenbourg, 1998); Gabor T. Rittersporn, "The Omnipresent Conspiracy: On Soviet Imagery of Politics and Social Relations in the 1930s," in *Stalinism: Its Nature and Aftermath — Essays in Honour of Moshe Lewin,* ed. Nicholas Lampert and Gabor T. Rittersporn (London: Macmillan, 1992).

63. Politburo protocols, 3 December 1934, RGASPI, f. 17, op. 162, d. 17, l. 87. The "Law of 1 December 1934" recalled a similar emergency procedure that followed the assassination of Soviet ambassador to Poland Vorovsky in 1927, when measures were implemented to execute suspects without prosecution, defense, or appeal. See V. N. Khaustov, "Deiatel'nost' organov gosudarstvennoi bezopasnosti NKVD SSSR (1934–1942)," Ph.D. diss., Akademiia FSB, 1997, 95.

## 7. Yezhov and the Kirov Assassination

1. "Vokrug ubistva Kirova," *Pravda,* 4 November 1991; A. Yakovlev, "O dekabr'skoi tragedii 1934 goda," *Pravda,* 28 January 1991.

2. In 1956 Khrushchev had formed a commission chaired by N. Shvernik to investigate the Kirov murder. It "found nothing against Stalin. . . . Khrushchev refused to publish it — it was of no use to him." F. Chuev, *Sto sorok besed s Molotovym* (Moscow: "Terra," 1991), 353.

3. J. Arch Getty and Oleg V. Naumov, *The Road to Terror: Stalin and the Self-Destruction of the Bolsheviks, 1932–1939* (New Haven: Yale University Press, 1999), 140–57; Adam Ulam, *Stalin: The Man and His Era* (New York: Viking, 1973), 375–88; Robert Conquest, *Stalin and the Kirov Murder* (New York: Oxford University Press, 1989); J. Arch Getty, *Origins of the Great Purges: The Soviet Communist Party Reconsidered, 1933–1938* (Cambridge: Cambridge University Press, 1985), appendix; J. Arch Getty, "The Politics of Repression Revisited," in *Stalinist Terror: New Perspectives,* ed. J. Arch Getty and Roberta T. Manning (Cambridge: Cambridge University Press, 1993), 40–62; S. V. Kulashov, O. V. Volobuev, E. I. Pivovar, et al., *Nashe otechestvo. chast' II.* (Moscow: Mysl', 1991); Iu. N. Zhukov, "Sledstvie i sudebnye protsessy po delu ob ubiistve Kirova," *Voprosy istorii,* no. 2 (2000); Boris Starkov, "Ar'ergard-nye boi staroi partiinoi gvardii," in *Oni ne molchali,* ed. A. V. Afanas'ev

(Moscow: Politizdat, 1991), 215; O. V. Khlevniuk, *1937-i: Stalin, NKVD i sovetskoe obshchestvo* (Moscow: Izd-vo "Respublika," 1992), 46; Anna Kirilina, *Rikoshet, ili skol'ko chelovek bylo ubito vystrelom v Smol'nom* (St. Petersburg: Obshchestvo "Znanie," 1993). The best and most recent summary of the evidence pro and con is M. Lenoe, "Did Stalin Kill Kirov and Does It Matter?" *Journal of Modern History* 74, no. 2 (2002).

4. Of course, if Stalin had engineered the assassination through the Leningrad NKVD, the best way to organize a cover-up inquiry would have been to leave them in charge.

5. The fear was *vedomstvo*, institutional loyalty and the inclination of chiefs to protect their subordinates and the reputation of their organization.

6. See Leonid Naumov, *Bor'ba v rukovodstve NKVD v 1936–38 gg.* (Moscow: self-published, 2003).

7. Yezhov's notebook, RGASPI, f. 671, op. 1, d. 271, ll. 560, 560 ob.

8. See *Leningradskaia pravda*, 6, 8, 11, 12, 18 December 1934 for reports. Such retaliations repeated the spasmodic executions of 1927, when Soviet ambassador to Poland Vorovsky had been assassinated. See V. N. Khaustov, "Deiatel'nost organov gosudarstvennoi bezopasnosti NKVD SSSR (1934–1942)," Ph.D. diss., Akademiia FSB, 1997, 95.

9. *Leningradskaia pravda*, 20 March 1935.

10. Yagoda to Stalin, 26 February 1935, *Arkhiv Prezidenta Rossisskoi Federatsii* (hereafter APRF), f. 3, d. 58, l. 174/41; Yezhov to Stalin, n.d., RGASPI, f. 671, op. 1, d. 147, ll. 52–53.

11. Yezhov had approvingly summarized Zakovsky's report of 16 February in a memo to Stalin, RGASPI, f. 671, op. 1, d. 147, ll. 49–53.

12. Prokofev and Zakovsky to Yezhov, January–March, 1935, RGASPI, f. 671, op. 1, d. 129, ll. 10–30, 36–44, 92, 145–61.

13. *Izvestiia TsK KPSS*, no. 7 (1989).

14. Agranov to Stalin, 4 December 1934, RGASPI, f. 671, op. 1, d. 114, ll. 8–10. Leningrad had been G. E. Zinoviev's power base for his struggle against Stalin in the late 1920s, and these three had worked then in the Leningrad party apparatus.

15. At the top of the written statement, the time is given as "con-

ducted at 16:45," an impossibly early fifteen minutes after the shooting, because we know from another document (RGASPI, f. 671, op. 1, d. 113, l. 1) that the order for her arrest was not even given until 18:20. At the bottom of the interrogation record, the time is given as 19:10, which is probably correct. Interrogations of Draule, RGASPI, f. 671, op. 1, d. 114, ll. 1–5. Draule was subsequently executed for complicity in the assassination.

16. Yezhov's notebooks, RGASPI, f. 671, op. 1, d. 271, l. 541. For his close supervision of the interrogations in general, see ibid., ll. 529–52.

17. The following account is taken from records of Nikolaev's interrogations on 5, 7, 8, 9, 14, 15, 18 December 1934 in Yezhov's files, RGASPI, f. 671, op. 1, d. 114, ll. 8–10, 11, 16, 54, 58, 65, 68, 76–94, 180, 214.

18. See their interrogations in Yezhov's files, RGASPI, f. 671, op. 1, dd. 114, 120–21, 126–28, 134, 136.

19. This was the case with Shatsky, Rumiantsev, and another accused conspirator named Yuskin. In addition to their interrogations in the previous note, see the transcript of their closed trial in RGASPI, f. 617, op. 1, d. 128.

20. Interrogation of Zinoviev, RGASPI, f. 617, op. 1, d. 134, ll. 164–65.

21. Kotolynov's testimony in RGASPI, f. 617, op. 1, d. 128, ll. 62–72.

22. *Pravda,* 23 December 1934, 16 January 1935; *Izvestiia TsK KPSS,* no. 7 (1989), 70; I. V. Kurilov, N. N. Mikhailov, and V. P. Naumov, eds., *Reabilitatsiia: Politicheskie protsessy 30–50-x godov* (Moscow: Politizdat, 1991), 166.

23. Yezhov to Stalin, 20 February 1935, RGASPI, f. 671, op. 1, d. 148, ll. 18–21.

24. RGASPI, f. 671, op. 1, dd. 135, 137, 140–41, 144–49.

25. Ibid., dd. 150–60.

26. Yezhov to Stalin, December 1934, RGASPI, f. 671, op. 1, d. 52, l. 21.

27. Volkova file in Yezhov notes, RGASPI, f. 671, op. 1, d. 116, ll. 2–35.

28. Agranov report on Borisov autopsy, RGASPI, f. 617, op. 1, d. 114, l. 13. For the report of the autopsy on Borisov, see ibid., ll. 48–51.

29. According to a Politburo document, the Leningrad NKVD had "put their weapons aside and [fallen] asleep." A. Yakovlev et al., *Lublianka. Salin i VChK-GPU-OGPU-NKVD, Yanvar' 1922-Dekabr' 1936* (Moscow: ROSSPEN, 2003), 592–93. My thanks to Igal Halfin for this reference.

30. *Pravda,* 23 January 1935. N. V. Petrov and K. V. Skorkin, eds., *Kto rukovodil NKVD, 1934–1941: Spravochnik* (Moscow: Zven'ia, 1999), 296.

31. Khaustov, "Deiatel'nost organov," 131.

32. Ibid., 38.

33. Yezhov to Stalin, 23 January 1935, RGASPI, f. 617, op. 1, d. 118, l. 25. Typically, reports and memos written to Stalin in response to his request or order contain phrases like "in response to your order," wording that is absent in Yezhov's letter.

34. Ibid., ll. 6, 29.

35. Ibid., l. 32.

36. Ibid., l. 34.

37. The meeting's transcript is RGASPI, f. 671, op. 1, d. 5.

38. Yezhov to Stalin, 23 January 1935, RGASPI, f. 671, op. 2, d. 118, l. 1. Yezhov's speech to the NKVD chiefs is in d. 5. See also Khaustov, "Deiatel'nost organov," 340.

39. RGASPI, f. 17, op. 162, d. 9, l. 54.

40. RGASPI, f. 558, op. 11, d. 174, ll. 137–38.

41. See Zakovsky speech to the February 1937 CC Plenum, RGASPI, f. 17, op, 2, d. 598, ll. 2–4, 12–18. For Agranov's recollections, see ibid., ll. 23–26, 29–35, 41–42. See also Kurilov, Mikhailov, and Naumov, *Reabilitatsiia,* 153–54, 84, and Yezhov's statement at his own trial in *Moskovskie novosti,* no. 5 (1994). At his trial in 1938, Yagoda's bureaucratic defense in 1935 would be interpreted not as guarding his authority but as a treasonous attempt to protect the terrorists Yezhov was trying to uncover.

42. *Izvestiia TsK KPSS,* no. 7 (1989), 85.

43. *Izvestiia TsK KPSS,* no. 8 (1989), 95–115.

44. RGASPI, f. 671, op. 1, d. 273, ll. 1–65, cited from the first 1935 draft. In later drafts of the book in 1937, this section was rewritten to

make Zinoviev and Kamenev not only the direct organizers of the Kirov murder but spies and wreckers as well. Obviously, this interpretation had not been foreseen in 1935.

45. The party purge had been planned in late 1934 before Kirov's assassination, but the killing served to put it higher on the agenda. Because Yezhov was not involved in the political education campaign, it will not be treated here. See Getty, *Origins of the Great Purges,* for a discussion of that effort, in which A. A. Zhdanov played a prominent role.

## 8. Enemies Large and Small

1. Orgburo protocol, RGASPI, f. 17, op. 3, d. 961, l. 16.

2. Yezhov speeches, 1935–36, RGASPI, f. 671, op. 1, d. 3, ll. 67–129.

3. See RGASPI, f. 17, op. 120, d. 198, ll. 1–3; d. 211, ll. 20–23; f. 671, op. 1, dd. 47, 56.

4. *Izvestiia TsK KPSS,* no. 7 (1989), 65–93.

5. Tsybulnik to Yezhov, 22 March 1935, RGASPI, f. 671, op. 1, d. 103, ll. 1–5.

6. Yezhov notation to secretaries, 22 March 1935, RGASPI, f. 671, op. 1, d. 103, l. 1.

7. The group consisted of Yezhov, Shkiryatov, and Belenky. Their report to Stalin is dated 29 March, RGASPI, f. 671, op. 1, d. 103, ll. 1–5.

8. Closed Letter of Central Committee, 19 July 1935, RGASPI, f. 671, op. 1, d. 106, l. 28.

9. See RGASPI, f. 671, op. 1, dd. 108–11.

10. In the draft outline of his speech, Yezhov listed seventeen points he wanted to make. The Yenukidze matter was number fourteen. RGASPI, f. 671, op. 1, d. 8, ll. 42–47.

11. Kamenev's real name was Rozenfeld. Kamenev was his revolutionary alias.

12. Interrogation of Zinoviev, 19 March 1935, RGASPI, f. 671, op. 1, d. 109, l. 34.

13. Interrogation of Kamenev, 11 April 1935, RGASPI, f. 671, op. 1, d. 111, l. 19.

14. Interrogations of Zinoviev, 19 March 1935, and Kamenev, 11 April

1935, RGASPI, f. 671, op. 1, d. 111, ll. 19–26; d. 109, ll. 35–59.

15. Interrogation of Kamenev, 11 April 1935, RGASPI, f. 671, op. 1, d. 111, l. 26.

16. Yezhov speech to Central Committee Plenum, 6 June 1935, RGASPI, f. 17, op. 2, d. 542, ll. 55–86.

17. See, for example, the December 1936 plenum at which Yezhov directly accused Bukharin of treason. Faced with Bukharin's denial, Stalin sent Yezhov back to the drawing board to get more "evidence." J. Arch Getty and Oleg V. Naumov, *The Road to Terror: Stalin and the Self-Destruction of the Bolsheviks, 1932–1939* (New Haven: Yale University Press, 1999), 303–26.

18. Yagoda speech to Central Committee Plenum, 6 June 1935, RGASPI, f. 17, op. 2, d. 542, ll. 175–78.

19. Yenukidze to Yezhov, 29 June 1935, RGASPI, f. 671, op. 1, d. 105, ll. 127–34. Yezhov neither quoted nor mentioned the letter in his speech.

20. Yenukidze speech to Central Committee Plenum, 6 June 1935, RGASPI, f. 17, op. 2, d. 542, ll. 125–41.

21. Kaganovich speech to Central Committee Plenum, 6 June 1935, RGASPI, f. 17, op. 2, d. 542, ll. 158–59.

22. RGASPI, f. 671, op. 1. d. 106, ll. 1–26.

23. Uncorrected stenogram, Central Committee Plenum, 6 June 1935, RGASPI, f. 17, op. 2, d. 547, ll. 69–70.

24. Printed stenographic report, Central Committee Plenum, 6 June 1935, RGASPI, f. 17, op. 2, d. 544, l. 22.

25. Stalin to Kaganovich, September 1935, RGASPI, f. 81, op. 3, d. 100, ll. 92–93.

26. Stalin comments to Central Committee Plenum, 3 June 1936, RGASPI, f. 17, op. 2, d. 572, ll. 73–75. Readmitting Yenukidze then (June 1936) was a curious irony. For it was at that plenum that the Politburo announced the upcoming capital trial of Zinoviev and Kamenev for the assassination of Kirov, the theory Yezhov had unsuccessfully put forward at the plenum that expelled Yenukidze.

27. Yezhov manuscript "From Fractionalism to Open Counterrevo-

lution (on the Zinovievist Counterrevolutionary Organization," RGASPI, f. 671, op, 1, d. 273, ll. 36–37, 40.

28. Already in late 1933 the Orgburo had discussed an operation whereby members would exchange old party cards for new ones that would be properly and exactly registered: RGASPI, f. 671, op. 1, d. 12, ll. 5–7. Nothing was done then, and the matter was proposed again in November 1934 before the Kirov assassination. See J. Arch Getty, *Origins of the Great Purges: The Soviet Communist Party Reconsidered, 1933–1938* (Cambridge: Cambridge University Press, 1985), chapters 2 and 3, for a discussion of the disarray in party files and lack of control over membership cards in the early 1930s.

29. Orgburo protocols, 7 December 1933, RGASPI, f. 671, op. 1, d. 12, l. 27. Shkiriatov represented the Control Commission, Malenkov the cadres office, and Koserev the Komsomol.

30. See RGASPI, f. 17, op. 3, d. 2077, l. 3. For Yezhov's draft of the order see RGASPI, f. 671, op. 1, d. 28, ll. 62–94. See also Smolensk Archive file 499, ll. 308–9.

31. One regional secretary said that Yezhov or his staff called almost every day for progress reports, RGASPI, f. 17, op. 2, d. 561, l. 164.

32. For the reports to Stalin, see RGASPI, f. 671, op. 1, d. 28, ll. 141–73, 186–211, 234–38.

33. Stenogram of Conference, 25 September 1935, RGASPI, f. 17, op. 120, d. 179, ll. 34–77.

34. RGASPI, f. 17, op. 120, d. 184, ll. 64–65; d. 181, ll. 153–55.

35. For examples see his orders on Smolensk, 23 June 1935, RGASPI, f. 671, op. 1, d. 32, ll. 1–6; and on Azov–Black Sea territory, 31 July 1935, RGASPI, f. 17, op. 114, d. 590, l. 2.

36. Previous screenings had been conducted either by the control commissions (before 1933) or by special ad hoc purge commissions (1933).

37. Yezhov frequently noted, in 1935 but not later, that allowing party committees to purge themselves was a good idea. See, for example, RGASPI, f. 17, op. 120, d. 77, l. 4.

38. By the beginning of 1937, Yezhov was interpreting regional secretaries' protection of their own people as treason: "protecting enemies of

the people." At that time, two very prominent regional party leaders in the Ukraine (P. P. Postyshev) and Azov–Black Sea (B. P. Sheboldaev) were demonstrably fired for this. See Getty and Naumov, *Road to Terror,* chapter 9.

39. The famous Aleksei Stakhanov, the shock worker who gave his name to the Stakhanovist movement, was one of those who had lost his party card. On 17 June 1936 NKVD department head Molchanov wrote to Yezhov that Stakhanov was always fighting with his wife and "could not exclude" the possibility that his wife had sold it. His party secretary suggested a divorce, but Stakhanov refused. Molchanov to Yezhov, RGASPI, f. 671, op. 1, d. 253, ll. 122–23.

40. Yezhov memo, 8 February 1936, RGASPI, f. 671, op. 1, d. 39, ll. 111, 179.

41. See, for example, Yezhov to Stalin, July–October 1935, RGASPI, f. 671, op. 1, d. 28, ll. 181, 235.

42. Yezhov speech to Central Committee Plenum, 8 December 1935, RGASPI, f. 17, op. 120, d. 177, ll. 20–22. This number is almost certainly incomplete. A subsequent internal Central Committee memo of February 1937 inexplicably gave a figure of 263,885 proverka expulsions; RGASPI, f. 17, op. 120, d. 278, l. 2. It was not uncommon in this period for the same agencies to give wildly varying figures for party membership.

43. These new data on NKVD participation in the proverka revise the earlier conclusions in Getty, *Origins of the Great Purges,* where it was argued on the basis of other archives that the police played little role in the operation. See Getty and Naumov, *Road to Terror,* chapter 5.

44. See, for example, the reports on the proverka from Ivanovo and Ukraine: RGASPI, f. 17, op. 120, d. 184, ll. 60–66.

45. Stenogram of conference, 25 September 1935, RGASPI, f. 17, op. 120, d. 179, ll. 34–77, 253–68.

46. Ibid.

47. See Yezhov's and Stalin's remarks to the June 1936 plenum of the Central Committee, RGASPI, f. 17, op. 2, d. 572, ll. 67–75.

48. Central Committee memo, RGASPI, f. 17, op. 120, d. 278, l. 7.

49. Khlevniuk has written that eventually more than two hundred thousand expelled party members were placed under NKVD surveillance. O. V. Khlevniuk, *1937-i: Stalin, NKVD i sovetskoe obshchestvo* (Moscow: Izd-vo "Respublika," 1992), 57. It is difficult to imagine how this was possible. For Yezhov's monitoring of the appeals see RGASPI, f. 671, op. 1, dd. 29, 40, 92.

50. *Pravda*, 5 June 1936. Apparently for security reasons, it was customary for *Pravda* to announce Central Committee plena only after they had been completed.

51. See, for example, *Pravda*, 7–10 June 1936. Although no CC resolution was passed, there was a "closed letter" sent to party organizations with the new line. Yezhov wrote it. RGASPI, f. 671, op. 1, d. 29, ll. 99–110.

52. Yezhov speech to Central Committee Plenum, 3 June 1936, RGASPI, f. 17, op. 2, d. 568, ll. 135–36.

53. Yezhov speech to Central Committee Plenum, 3 June 1936, RGASPI, f. 17, op. 2, d. 572, l. 67. On the importance of variant texts see Getty and Naumov, *Road to Terror,* esp. chapters 5 and 10.

54. Yezhov Conference on Proverka, 4 March 1936, RGASPI, f. 671, op. 1, d. 39, ll. 263–64.

55. For Stalin's speech, see RGASPI, f. 17, op. 2, d. 572, ll. 73–75.

56. Yezhov speech to Central Committee Plenum, 3 June 1936, RGASPI, f. 17, op. 2, d. 568, ll. 13, 141, 154–55.

57. In the Exchange of Party Documents in 1936 Yezhov got more of what he wanted: expulsions of oppositionists. If in the Proverka only 2.8 percent of those expelled were "Trotskyist/Zinovievist," in the Exchange the number rose to 8.8 percent. RGASPI, f. 17, op. 120, d. 278, ll. 2–3.

## 9. Angling for the Job

1. This chapter is limited to Yezhov's role in the events leading up to the full-blown terror of 1937–38. For broader treatments, see O. V. Khlevniuk, *Politbiuro: mekhanizmy politicheskoi vlasti v 1930-e gody* (Moscow: Rosspen, 1996), and J. Arch Getty and Oleg V. Naumov, *The*

*Road to Terror: Stalin and the Self-Destruction of the Bolsheviks, 1932–1939* (New Haven: Yale University Press, 1999).

2. Yezhov file "Unusual Events," RGASPI, f. 671, op. 1, d. 244.

3. On this point see J. Arch Getty, "Afraid of Their Shadows: The Bolshevik Recourse to Terror, 1932–1938," in *Stalinismus vor dem Zweiten Weltkrieg: Neue Wege der Forschung,* ed. Manfred Hildermeier and Elisabeth Mueller-Luckner (Munich: Oldenbourg, 1998).

4. Baulim to A. Ya. Yakovlev, 4 April 1937, RGASPI, f. 17, op. 123, d. 1, ll. 34–35.

5. Politburo resolution, 23 April 1937, RGASPI, f. 17, op. 162, d. 21, l. 30.

6. Kharitonov to Yezhov, n.d., RGASPI, f. 671, op. 1, d. 262, ll. 7–8.

7. See RGASPI, f. 671, op. 1, d. 234; d. 57, ll. 86–89; f. 17, op. 120, d. 264, ll. 1–5; d. 270, ll. 2–3.

8. RGASPI, f. 671, op. 1, d. 66.

9. Memo, Industrial Department to Yezhov, RGASPI, f. 17, op. 120, d. 195, ll. 88–89. See RGASPI, f. 671, op. 1, d. 18, for other instances of Yezhov's high-level personnel refereeing in 1936.

10. Rumiantsev to Yezhov, 27 August 1936, RGASPI, f. 671, op. 1, d. 18, l. 88. For other examples of Yezhov's high-level refereeing between top party and state leaders, see RGASPI, f. 671, op. 1, d. 91.

11. RGASPI, f. 671, op. 1, d. 48, ll. 8–9. In his letter, Bukharin addressed Yezhov as "*tezka.*" In Russian this means someone with identical first name and patronymic: both Bukharin and Yezhov were Nikolai Ivanovich. This file contains numerous requests from various persons for Yezhov's permission to travel abroad.

12. French Comintern delegates to Yezhov, 9 July 1935, RGASPI, f. 17, op. 120, d. 204, ll. 27, 29–30.

13. Yezhov worked through several drafts of his letter to Stalin and apologized for not having had time to interview each participant individually. RGASPI, f. 671, op. 1, d. 254, ll. 13–15; d. 63, ll. 47–66.

14. Ironically, Yezhov himself would become victim to the xenophobia he had abetted. These approved vacations eventually contributed to Yezhov's undoing. When he himself was arrested and interrogated, he

was forced to admit that he had been recruited by foreign intelligence services while on vacation abroad. See Yezhov's interrogation in APRF, f. 3, op. 24, d. 375, ll. 122–64.

15. Yezhov conference stenograms, February, May 1936, RGASPI, f. 671, op. 1, d. 63, ll. 67–75, 99–108.

16. For examples, see RGASPI, f. 671, op. 1, d. 20, ll. 17–21, 44–45, 56–71, 86–98.

17. Troianovsky to Yezhov, 25 January 1936, RGASPI, f. 671, op. 1, d. 87, ll. 38–41.

18. RGASPI, f. 17, op. 120, dd. 98, 99; op. 162, d. 19, ll. 4, 98–100.

19. Manuilsky to Yezhov, 4 January 1936, RGASPI, f. 671, op. 1, d. 73, ll. 1–3. The same week, Yezhov organized a commission to send first 250, then 300 experienced party workers to "strengthen" NKVD border security in the Far East against former White Guards, Trotskyists, Koreans, and others suspected of spying for the Japanese. The commission was also to examine suspicious backgrounds of workers from the Far Eastern Railroad. RGASPI, f. 17, op. 162, d. 19, ll. 25, 34.

20. NKVD memo to Yezhov, February 1936, RGASPI, f. 671, op. 1, d. 73, ll. 4–26.

21. RGASPI, f. 671, op. 1, d. 70, ll. 62–77.

22. Yezhov to Stalin, 20 February 1936, RGASPI, f. 671, op. 1, d. 73, ll. 31–37. There are several drafts of Yezhov's letter to Stalin in his archive. It was in the final draft that Yezhov took his swipe at the NKVD.

23. Frinovsky was to become one of Yezhov's chief intimates and deputies at NKVD in 1936–38.

24. CC draft resolution, RGASPI, f. 671, op. 1, d. 73, ll. 53–57.

25. Terry Martin, "The Origins of Soviet Ethnic Cleansing," *Journal of Modern History* 70, no. 4 (1998); A. E. Gur'ianov, ed., *Repressii protiv poliakov i pol'skikh grazhdan* (Moscow: Zveniia, 1997), 33; I. L. Shcherbakova, ed., *Nakazannyi narod: repressii protiv rossiiskikh nemtsev* (Moscow: Zven'ia, 1999), 44.

26. Yezhov commission report, RGASPI, f. 671, op. 1, d. 73, l. 96.

27. RGASPI, f. 671, op. 1, d. 78, passim. Ostensible accusations in-

cluded suspicion of being a provocateur, connections with suspicious people, suspicion of being a Polish agent, having been expelled from the Polish CP. In June 1936 the Politburo and NKVD forbade any connections between Soviet citizens and German representatives in the USSR.

28. Dmitrov and Manuilsky to Yezhov, 8 June 1936, RGASPI, f. 17, op. 120, d. 266, l. 73. Delo 266 contains other memos criticizing MOPR and Stasova's leadership.

29. *Izvestiia TsK KPSS,* no. 8 (1989), 84; no. 9 (1989), 36; RGASPI, f. 558, op. 11, d. 174, ll. 137–38.

30. Sometimes Agranov even reported directly to Stalin, bypassing his chief, Yagoda. See, for example, his memo to Stalin of 25 April 1935, RGASPI, f. 558, op. 11, d. 174, l. 33. At the end of December 1938, Agranov was named chief of the Administration of State Security (GUGB) within Yezhov's NKVD, RGASPI, f. 17, op. 3, d. 983, l. 2.

31. See Yagoda's interrogation, RGASPI, f. 558, op. 11, d. 176, ll. 59–76.

32. This was the story Yezhov and his friends in the NKVD told at the February–March 1937 plenum of the Central Committee. See Yezhov speech in *Voprosy istorii,* no. 10 (1994), 13–27.

33. *Izvestiia TsK KPSS,* no. 8 (1989), 85. This may have been the time that Stalin forced Yagoda to comply by threatening to "punch him in the nose." Ibid., 69.

34. RGASPI, f. 671, op. 1, dd. 146, 245.

35. RGASPI, f. 671, op. 1, d. 177.

36. *Izvestiia TsK KPSS,* no. 8 (1989), 82–83. It is not hard to see how V. P. Olberg attracted attention. He was a German citizen with a Honduran passport and permanent residency in the USSR. RGASPI, f. 671, op. 1, d. 164, l. 268.

37. Yagoda to Stalin, before 8 April 1936, RGASPI, f. 671, op. 1, d. 163, l. 2.

38. *Izvestiia TsK KPSS,* no. 8 (1989), 82–83.

39. G. E. Prokof'ev to Stalin, 23 February 1936, RGASPI, f. 671, op. 1, d. 162, ll. 1–7. For the transfer of Trotskyist archives and documents to Yezhov, see Politburo resolution, RGASPI, f. 17, op. 162, d. 19, l. 78.

40. *Izvestiia TsK KPSS,* no. 8 (1989), 83.

41. RGASPI, f. 671, op. 1, d. 193, l. 2.

42. *Izvestiia TsK KPSS,* no. 8 (1989), 85–86.

43. Interrogation of Kamenev, 23–24 July 1936; interrogation of Zinoviev, 26 July 1936, RGASPI, f. 671, op. 1, d. 170, ll. 125–39, 153–54.

44. "Zaslizhennyi prigovor," forwarded by Molchanov to Yezhov, 4 August 1936, RGASPI, f. 671, op. 1, d. 172, ll. 497, 525.

45. Politburo protocols, 19 August 1936, RGASPI, f. 17, op. 162, d. 20, l. 52. See also RGASPI, f. 558, op. 11, d. 93, l. 21, for Stalin's approval. See RGASPI, f. 671, op. 1, dd. 189–99, for Yezhov's files on the trial.

46. Stalin to Kaganovich and Molotov, 6 September 1936, RGASPI, f. 558, op. 11, d. 94, l. 31.

47. Ivo Banac, ed., *The Diary of Georgi Dimitrov, 1933–1949* (New Haven: Yale University Press, 2003), 51, Dmitrov's diary entry for 11 February 1937. Stalin also reviewed in advance the verdicts to be handed down by the court. An early draft of the verdict included the phrase "the sentence is final and no appeal is possible." Stalin noted that this would create a bad impression abroad, even though it was true, RGASPI, f. 558, op. 11, d. 93, l. 61.

48. *Izvestiia TsK KPSS,* no. 8 (1989), 100–115.

49. The left and right oppositionists had in fact formed a secret "bloc" in 1932, but there is no evidence that terror was part of its program then. See J. Arch Getty, "Trotsky in Exile: The Founding of the Fourth Internationale," *Soviet Studies* 38, no. 1 (1986). It is not clear when Yagoda's NKVD learned about it, although his agents surely suspected it.

50. Memo on Kotsiubinsky, RGASPI, f. 671, op. 1, d. 240, ll. 1–28.

51. Piatakov's name had come up more or less innocently in the testimony of some of the defendants at the August 1936 trial.

52. Balitsky to Yezhov, February–August 1936, RGASPI, f. 671, op. 1, d. 239, ll. 1–59. The series of investigations and interrogations that eventually framed and condemned Piatakov included securing the testimony of several of his friends, coworkers, and secretaries. See RGASPI, f. 671, op. 1, d. 175.

53. Balitsky to Yezhov, 10 September 1936, RGASPI, f. 671, op. 1, d.

239, l. 185. Balitsky used the familiar second-person "ty" with Yezhov from this point.

54. For background on these and other events in 1936, see Getty and Naumov, *Road to Terror,* chapter 7; Marc Jansen and Nikita Petrov, *Stalin's Loyal Executioner: People's Commissar Nikolai Ezhov, 1895–1940* (Stanford: Hoover Institution Press, 2002), chapter 2; Khlevniuk, *Politbiuro,* chapter 5.

55. Balitsky to Yezhov, 30 December 1934, RGASPI, f. 671, op. 1, d. 240, l. 30.

56. Since the spring of 1936 Yezhov had been "verifying" the staff of the government newspaper *Izvestiia,* which the former rightist Bukharin edited. After weeding out numerous former supporters of Zinoviev and Trotsky, Yezhov ominously concluded that Bukharin bore responsibility for the oppositionist "clutter" and general lack of vigilance. See RGASPI, f. 671, op. 1, d. 49.

57. The effort to accuse and arrest Bukharin and Rykov broke down. At a confrontation between the arrested Sokol'nikov and Bukharin, the former refused to testify that he personally knew of Bukharin and Rykov's participation in the conspiracy. Tomsky, the other supposed middleman, was dead. Procurator Vyshinsky therefore concluded, "Therefore it can be established that the basic source to confirm Zinoviev, Kamenev, [I. I.] Reingold, and Sokolnikov on the membership of Bukharin and Rykov in the Trotskyist-Zinovievist bloc is Tomsky, the questioning of whom is impossible because of his death. . . . The investigation is closed." RGASPI, f. 671, op. 1, d. 176, ll. 69–70. Yezhov's moves against Bukharin and Rykov would receive another setback at the December 1936 Central Committee plenum, when Stalin rejected Yezhov's evidence against the two rightists and postponed a decision. See Getty and Naumov, *Road to Terror,* 303–30.

58. The final version of Yezhov's letter is found in Stalin's personal archive: RGASPI, f. 558, op. 11, d. 729, ll. 81–84.

59. Yezhov's rough draft is in his archive: RGASPI, f. 671, op. 1, d. 52, ll. 190–94. O. V. Khlevniuk, *Stalinskoe Politbiuro v 30-e gody: sbornik dokumentov* (Moscow: Airo—XX, 1995), 205–6, and Jansen

and Petrov, *Stalin's Loyal Executioner,* 51, correctly note that Yezhov never sent this letter to Stalin but did not find the version in Stalin's archive that Yezhov actually sent. Here and below, sections of Yezhov's first draft that he removed before sending the letter to Stalin are in italics.

60. By accident or as the result of his investigations, Yezhov was close to the truth here in his assessment of the 1932 situation. Getty, "Trotsky in Exile." Testimony on the 1932 bloc was also provided by Sokol'nikov, Uglanov, and others. See RGASPI, f. 671, op. 1, d. 175, ll. 216–30; d. 176, l. 2.

61. Yezhov was right. See the story of Stalin's contradictory and hesitant moves against Bukharin in Getty and Naumov, *Road to Terror,* 303–30, 364–419.

62. Even so, Yezhov's recommendations in the final letter went beyond what Stalin was willing to approve at the time. Although mass shootings without trial and according to "simplified procedure" would take place, the victims would be kulaks, common criminals, and ordinary citizens, and Stalin would not order this until July 1937. See J. Arch Getty, "'Excesses Are Not Permitted': Mass Terror and Stalinist Governance in the Late 1930s," *Russian Review* 61, no. 1 (2002). Yezhov's categories were approved by the Politburo only a month later, and at that time Stalin removed Yezhov's first category recommendation for summary executions. See the discussion in Getty and Naumov, *Road to Terror,* 273.

63. Particularly harsh repressive policies were always presented as originating somewhere else. The bloody mass operations of 1937 and the shooting of the Polish officers at Katyn in 1940 were posed as "proposals" of the NKVD, not of Stalin. Even dekulakization and collectivization in 1929–30 were said to have resulted from a spontaneous upsurge from below, and when disaster forced Stalin to beat a retreat with his "Dizzyness with Success" article in 1930, it was therefore possible to blame excesses on others.

64. Feliks Ivanovich Chuev, Vyacheslav Mikhaylovich Molotov, and Albert Resis, *Molotov Remembers: Inside Kremlin Politics, Conversations with Felix Chuev* (Chicago: I. R. Dee, 1993), 257.

65. The 1936 testimony of Dreitser incriminating himself and other Trotskyists was one of the papers on which Yagoda had written "nonsense" and "impossible." Yezhov's implication then and later was that Yagoda was protecting Dreitser to avoid expanding Yezhov's inquiries.

66. Dukelsky to Yagoda and Yezhov, 9 March 1935–13 September 1936, RGASPI, f. 671, op. 1, d. 27, ll. 1–26.

67. As a Yezhov client, Dukelsky might have been expected to fall with his sponsor in late 1938. But he was lucky, after a fashion. In the summer of 1937 he was involved in an automobile accident that required long recuperation. When he recovered, in March 1938, he became chairman of the Cinema Committee of the USSR. During the war he was a plenipotentiary of the State Defense Committee, and later deputy RSFSR minister of justice. He retired in 1953 and died peacefully in his bed in 1960. See N. V. Petrov and K. V. Skorkin, eds., *Kto rukovodil NKVD, 1934–1941: Spravochnik* (Moscow: Zven'ia, 1999), 179–80.

68. Interrogation of Molchanov, RGASPI, f. 558, op. 11, d. 174, ll. 134–37.

69. Stalin, Zhdanov telegram to Politburo, 25 September 1936, RGASPI, f. 558, op. 11, d. 94, l. 123. The appointment was confirmed by the Politburo officially on 11 October 1936, when Stalin returned from vacation. Politburo protocols, 11 October 1936, RGASPI, f. 17, op. 36, d. 981, l. 50.

70. RGASPI, f. 85, op. 27, d. 93, ll. 12–13.

71. Stalin to Yagoda, 26 September 1936, RGASPI, f. 558, op. 11, d. 94, l. 131.

72. Jansen and Petrov, *Stalin's Loyal Executioner,* 56.

73. See, for example, Politburo protocols, RGASPI, f. 17, op. 3, d. 2101, l. 3.

74. Mikhail Shreider, *NKVD iznutri: Zapiski chekista* (Moscow: Vozvrashchenie, 1995), 35.

75. A. M. Larina, *Nezabyvaemoe* (Moscow: APN, 1989), 269–70.

76. Kaganovich to Ordzhonikidze, 30 September 1936, RGASPI, f. 85, op. 27, d. 93, ll. 12–13.

## Conclusion

1. Marc Jansen and Nikita Petrov, *Stalin's Loyal Executioner: People's Commissar Nikolai Ezhov, 1895–1940* (Stanford: Hoover Institution Press, 2002), 203–11, who write that "In the present state of our knowledge this is indeed the most plausible explanation."

2. Catherine Merridale, *Night of Stone: Death and Memory in Russia* (London: Granta, 2000).

3. Jansen and Petrov, *Stalin's Loyal Executioner*, 203, 208.

4. On resistance see Lynne Viola, *Contending with Stalinism: Soviet Power and Popular Resistance in the 1930s* (Ithaca: Cornell University Press, 2002), and Jeffrey J. Rossman, *Worker Resistance Under Stalin: Class and Revolution on the Shop Floor* (Cambridge: Harvard University Press, 2005). For accommodation see Sheila Fitzpatrick, *Everyday Stalinism: Ordinary Life in Extraordinary Times, Soviet Russia in the 1930s* (New York: Oxford University Press, 1999). On subjectivity and belief, see Igal Halfin, *Terror in My Soul: Communist Autobiographies on Trial* (Cambridge: Harvard University Press, 2003), and Jochen Hellbeck, *Revolution on My Mind: Writing a Diary Under Stalin* (Cambridge: Harvard University Press, 2006).

5. Kees Boterbloem, *The Life and Times of Andrei Zhdanov, 1896–1948* (Montreal: McGill-Queen's University Press, 2004); Derek Watson, *Molotov: A Biography* (Basingstoke, Hampshire: Palgrave Macmillan, 2005).

6. Khlevniuk reminds us that each Politburo member had groups of followers in the provinces and in the *vedomstvy* he controlled. O. V. Khlevniuk, *Politbiuro: mekhanizmy politicheskoi vlasti v 1930-e gody* (Moscow: Rosspen, 1996), 262–63. Stalin frequently acted as referee among them and their empires.

7. For a discussion of decision making among Stalin and his lieutenants, see J. Arch Getty, "Stalin as Prime Minister: Power and the Politburo," in *Stalin: A New History*, ed. Sarah Davies and James Harris (New York: Cambridge University Press, 2005), 83–107.

8. RGASPI, f. 558, op. 11, d. 779, ll. 23, 29–31, 33. See also O. V. Khlev-

niuk et al., eds., *Stalin i Kaganovich: perepiska. 1931–1936 gg.* (Moscow: Rosspen, 2001), 21; Khlevniuk, *Politbiuro,* 85.

9. See Khlevniuk, *Politbiuro,* chapter 2. Khlevniuk quotes Moshe Lewin's remark about Stalin converting his lieutenants into "slaves" (245).

10. Jansen and Petrov, *Stalin's Loyal Executioner,* 209.

11. Yezhov to Stalin, n.d., RGASPI, f. 671, op. 1, d. 265, ll. 29–41. At the Politburo session that attacked him for stalling certain investigations and protecting people, Yezhov took notes: RGASPI, f. 671, op. 1, d. 271, ll. 1–79. See also V. N. Khaustov, "Deiatel'nost organov gosudarstvennoi bezopasnosti NKVD SSSR (1934–1942)," Ph.D. diss., Akademiia FSB, 1997.

12. Jansen and Petrov, *Stalin's Loyal Executioner,* 203.

13. This argument is developed in J. Arch Getty and Oleg V. Naumov, *The Road to Terror: Stalin and the Self-Destruction of the Bolsheviks, 1932–1939* (New Haven: Yale University Press, 1999), J. Arch Getty and Roberta Thompson Manning, eds., *Stalinist Terror: New Perspectives* (Cambridge: Cambridge University Press, 1993), and a great many other works on other aspects of Stalinist policy making.

14. N. I. Yezhov, "From Fractionalism to Open Counterrevolution (on the Zinovievist Counterrevolutionary Organization)," RGASPI, f. 671, op. 1, dd. 273–86. Compare, for example, d. 273, ll. 59–65, with ll. 597–699. As Stalin gradually decided that the conspiracy went beyond Zinoviev, the manuscript's title was changed to "From Fractionalism to Fascism."

15. Politburo resolution "On Comrade Yezhov," RGASPI, d. 17, op. 3, d. 951, l. 1. See also Jansen and Petrov, *Stalin's Loyal Executioner,* 124.

16. Boterbloem, *Life and Times.*

17. For Yezhov's correspondence with these people, see RGASPI, f. 671, op. 1, d. 270.

18. For some of Mints's notes, see RGASPI, f. 671, op. 1, d. 270, ll. 1–39.

19. Fadeev's unpublished manuscript, "Nikolai Ivanovich Yezhov: Syn nuzhdy i bor'by" [Nikolai Ivanovich Yezhov: Son of necessity and struggle], is in RGASPI, f. 671, op. 1, d. 270, ll. 69–86.

20. *Pravda,* 3 December 1937.

21. Compare the drafts in RGASPI, f. 671, op. 1, d. 270, ll. 40–41.

22. V. K. Vinogradov et al., eds., *Genrikh Yagoda. Narkom vnutrennix del SSSR, Generalnyi komissar godsudarstvennoi bezopasnosti. Sbornik dokumentov* (Kazan: Karachaev-Cherkesskaia Otdeleniia Rossiiskoi Inzhenernoi Akademii, 2000), 440–41.

23. Ibid., 89–93.

24. B. B. Briukhanov and E. N. Shoshkov, *Opravdaniiu ne podlezhit. Ezhov i Ezhovshchina, 1936–1938* (St. Petersburg: Petrovskii Fond, 1998), 133–34.

25. Jansen and Petrov, *Stalin's Loyal Executioner,* 195, 197–98.

26. For examples see RGASPI, f. 17, op. 120, d. 114, l. 17 (Zimin to Kaganovich to Yezhov); RGASPI, f. 671, op. 1, d. 18, l. 10 (Amosov to Stalin to Yezhov); RGASPI, f. 671, op. 1, d. 52, ll. 48–52 (Krupskaia to Stalin to Yezhov).

27. Stalin to Yezhov, 11 July 1935, RGASPI, f. 671, op. 1, d. 52, l. 30.

28. Jansen and Petrov, *Stalin's Loyal Executioner,* 196.

29. Stalin to Yezhov, 19 September 1935. Stalin's personal concern was noted in a Politburo resolution: RGASPI, f. 17, op. 163, d. 1079, l. 63.

30. Stalin asked for periodic reports on Yezhov's health and treatments. See, for example, RGASPI, f. 558, op. 11, d. 84, l. 14.

31. Graeme Gill, *The Origins of the Stalinist Political System* (Cambridge: Cambridge University Press, 1990).

32. See Moshe Lewin's discussion of the contradiction between statism and arbitrariness as "two models in one." Moshe Lewin, *The Making of the Soviet System: Essays in the Social History of Interwar Russia* (New York: New Press, 1994), 280–85.

33. Stenogram of Yezhov conference, RGAE, f. 7486, op. 79, d. 24, l. 9.

34. Ibid., l. 24.

35. Of course, such an understanding and personalized practice was based on patronage, patrons, and clients—familiar features of the Soviet (and post-Soviet) systems. Stalin was the supreme patron of the system; his clients were themselves patrons of those below them, and

so forth. To a considerable extent, the ubiquity of patronage and personal favoritism mitigated against the selection of personnel strictly according to qualifications.

36. Yezhov speech to conference of ORPO workers, 16 August 1935, RGASPI, f. 671, op. 1, d. 9, ll. 6–8.

37. These include M. I. Litvin, V. E. Tsesarsky, S. B. Zhukovsky, and I. I. Shapiro, all of whom Yezhov made NKVD department heads.

38. Jansen and Petrov, *Stalin's Loyal Executioner,* 199, 202–3.

39. Nor does it imply an impersonal modern and modernizing bureaucratic machine that carried out holocausts and massacres in order to excise "evil weeds" or transform humanity (Zygmunt Bauman, *Modernity and the Holocaust* [Cambridge: Polity Press, 1989]). All bureaucracies are led by political people, decision makers who launch terrors for their own reasons, which, explicitly at least, seem to have nothing to do with modernity. Moreover, the prewar Soviet bureaucracy was hardly modern. It was a ramshackle collection of inefficient, overlapping personal fiefdoms inherently incapable of developing a single strategy or even outlook.

40. Hannah Arendt, *Eichmann in Jerusalem: A Report on the Banality of Evil,* rev. and enl. ed. (New York: Penguin, 1994).

41. On the ubiquity of belief in conspiracies in the Stalin years, see Gabor T. Rittersporn, "The Omnipresent Conspiracy: On Soviet Imagery of Politics and Social Relations in the 1930s," in *Stalinism: Its Nature and Aftermath — Essays in Honour of Moshe Lewin,* ed. Nicholas Lampert and Gabor T. Rittersporn (London: Macmillan, 1992).

42. M. D. Steinberg, *Voices of Revolution, 1917* (New Haven: Yale University Press, 2001), 13, 16, 17, 19.

43. Yezhov to Petr Ivanov, 24 October 1922, RGASPI, f. 671, op. 1, d. 267, ll. 8–11.

44. Tim McDaniel, *The Agony of the Russian Idea* (Princeton: Princeton University Press, 1996), 35.

45. Steinberg, *Voices of Revolution,* 82, 96.

46. McDaniel, *Agony of the Russian Idea,* 42.

# Index

Afghanis, 9
Agranov, Yakov, 138, 140, 141, 143, 145, 146, 152, 158, 159, 180, 187–88, 194, 264n30
agriculture, xix, 27, 30, 43, 69–70, 74, 77, 97, 106, 107, 113–20, 131, 217; collectivization of, xxv, 113–20, 121, 222; Kirgiz, 59; Mari, 51; Yezhov as Deputy Commissar of Agriculture, 113–14, 115–20, 121, 217, 218
aircraft industry, 126
Akmolinsk Provincial Party Committee, 61–63, 78
Akulov, Ivan, 128
Alash-Orda intelligentsia, 64–65, 240n83
"although" style, 46
anarchists, 21
Andreev, A. A., 156
anti-Semitism, 15
Arendt, Hannah, xxi, 221
Arkhangelsk, 54
Ashurov, Second Secretary, 132

"assignment" task, 84
Astrakhan, 54, 57, 87
Azoz–Black Sea region, 180, 260n38

Babel, Isaac, 28–29, 249n7
Babushkin, Ivan, 17
Balitsky, V. A., 194
Baltsevich, 146
Belorussia, 138
Beria, Lavrenty, xviii, 1, 11, 127, 225n2, 229n34
blame shifting, 186–87, 201, 202
Bolsheviks, xx, 19, 20, 21, 22, 33, 82, 213, 231n24, 232n32, 240n83; attitudes toward institutions, 217; "ban on factions," 39; beliefs of, 220–24; bureaucracy, 71–95, 217–19, 272n39; Civil War, 26–31, 34–35; contenders for Lenin's succession, 70–75; early regime, 24–35; factionalism, 47–55, 58, 64–65, 67, 77, 80; 14th Party Congress, 73, 79–81; Kirgiz, 57–67, 95, 99–100;

Bolsheviks (continued)
Mari, 41–57, 100; 1917 Revolution,
21–26, 32, 35, 41, 82, 214; 1920s
administrative rule in provinces,
36–67, 77; 1933 purge, 121, 124–25;
October coup, 24; party membership, 40, 78, 83, 124–25, 166–73;
personnel system, 68–95, 219–20;
proverka (1935), 166–78, 189;
report writing, 44–46; 17th Party
Congress, 126, 131; squabbles, 47–
49, 51, 53–55, 77; 10th Party Congress, 35, 70; territorial party secretaries, 36–67; 12th Party Congress,
242n20; Yezhov joins, 22. See also
Communist Party
Borisov, 140, 141
Briansk, 54, 87
Brotherhood of Avvakum, 140
Bukharin, Nikolai, xviii, 2, 3, 4–5, 10,
69, 71, 74, 128, 179, 182, 194, 196,
197, 205, 216, 227n9, 258n17, 262n11,
266nn56–57; trial of, 10
Bulgarians, 9
Bundists, 21, 231n24

cadres, xx, 44, 123, 219, 240n78, 248.
See also personnel system
cannibalism, 28
Caucasus, 43, 107
Central Asia, 37, 43, 57–63, 96–99,
116, 240n83
Central Committee (CC), xvii, xxiv,
4, 5, 6, 10, 31, 41, 45–57, 59, 60, 62,
65, 83, 84–95, 102, 109–112, 235n10,
239n65, 240n78, 242n20, 261n50;
bureaucracy, 71–95; Kirov assassination and, 135–55; proverka and,
173–78, 189; secretarial apparatus,
71–95; subcommittees, 71; Yezhov
as secretary of, 156, 158–65, 176, 181,
183–88, 204

Central Executive Committee of
Soviets (TsIK), 116, 157; 1935 investigation of, 157–65
chauvinism, Russian, 47–49, 50, 65,
66–67, 236n27
CHEKA, 4, 27, 28, 34–35, 138; origi-
nation of, 28
Chemical Workers' Union, 31
China, 76
Chirkov, 61–63
Chou En-lai, 1
citizenship, 217
Civil War (1918–21), xix, 26–35, 36,
37, 38, 39, 44, 69, 70, 82, 85, 101,
129, 139, 214–15, 223, 232n32,
234n3, 240n83; end of, 31–34;
legacy of, 29–30
clans: Kirgiz, 61, 64–66; Mari,
43–44, 50–52
collectivization, xxv, 15, 113–20, 121,
222, 267n63
Comintern, 6, 125, 184, 192
Commissariat of Agriculture, Yezhov
as, 113–14, 115–20, 121, 217, 218
Communist Academy, 40, 100–102,
245n11
Communist Party, xxii, 38, 82, 83,
103, 136; corruption, 59–60, 166;
membership, 40, 78, 83, 124–25,
166–73; 1920s administrative rule
in provinces, 36–67, 77; 1933 purge,
121, 124–25; obedience, 207–11;
personnel system, 68–95, 219–20;
proverka (1935), 166–78, 189;
squabbles, 47–50, 51, 53, 55, 77;
See also Bolsheviks; government;
politics
"Concerning the Terroristic Activity
of the Trotskyist-Zinovievist
Counterrevolutionary Bloc"
(letter), 3
conferences, Orgraspred, 105–12

Index

Constituent Assembly, 26
counterrevolutionary organizations, 140, 142, 160, 189, 223
Credentials Commission, 126
Czech Legion, 37

Dagestan, 87
Dalstroi mining trust, 121–22
death rates, 15
death sentences, 134; "Kirov Law," 133–34
democratic centralism, 69–70, 83
Democratic Centralists, 76, 236n24
Department of Leading Party Organs. See ORPO
disease, 27, 30, 42, 58
dissidents, anti-Stalin. See oppositionists
Dmitrov, Georgi, 186, 192, 265n47
Draul, Mil'de, 140, 141, 255n15
Dreitser, 203, 268n65
Dukelsky, S. S., 203–204, 268n67
Dzerzhinskaia, 244n53
Dzerzhinsky, Feliks, 204, 244n53
Dzhambul, xviii, 214, 215
Dzhangildin, 64–66

economy, 18, 33, 36, 69–71, 116–17, 126, 217; collectivization of agriculture, 113–20; New Economic Policy, 34, 61, 69–71, 74, 116; post-Civil War, 34, 74
education, 30, 116–17, 217
Eichmann, Adolf, xxi, 1, 221
elite, 7, 8, 10, 31–32, 88, 91; purging of, 6–8, 10
Esperanto, 7
Estonian Communists, 184, 186
Estonians, 9
ethnic politics, 15, 42, 44, 101; Kirgiz, 58–67; Mari, 42–44, 50–52
evil, 221, 224

Exchange of Party Cards (1936), 169, 173–74, 177, 261n57
expulsion, 167; appeals and complaints, 172–78; proverka, 166–78, 260nn42–43, 261nn49–57; reasons for, 167, 168

factories, 14–19, 26, 32, 34, 35, 181–82; accidents, 16–17; class consciousness, 16–17; Mari, 42
Fadeev, Alexander, 19, 61, 96, 101, 214
famine, 27–28, 30, 34, 42, 58, 115, 122
Far Eastern Railroad, 263n19
Fascism, 125, 182, 222
Finn Communists, 184, 186
Finns, 9, 15
Fomin, 146
food industry, 105
foreigners: foreign Communists in USSR, 6, 125–26, 182, 184–86, 264n27; "green corridor," 184; 1930s threat of, 182–86; 1937–38 "mass operations" against, 6, 182–86
French Communists, 182–83
Frinovsky, M., 185, 263n23

Gai, M. I., 185
Georgia, 11, 181
German Communists, 185, 186, 264n27
"German Operation," 9
Germans, 6, 9, 125
Germany, 6, 76
Giliarovsky, V. A., 17
Gladuna, Yevgenya, 12, 249n7
gold, 121, 122
Golubenko, N. V., 194
Gombard, V. V., 184
Gorbachev, Mikhail, xviii, 136
government, xx; Bolshevik coup, 24; bureaucracy, 71–95, 217–19, 272n39; contenders for Lenin's succession, 70–75; early Bolshevik

275

government (continued)
regime, 24–35; Kirgiz, 57–67; Kirov assassination, 135–55, 158–64, 177–78, 187–204; Mari, 41–57; of 1917, 21–26, 41, 82, 214; 1920s provincial, 36–67, 77; obedience, 207–211; parallel, 38–39; personnel system, 68–95, 219–20; report writing, 44–46; territorial party secretaries, 36–67; "us" vs. "them" conflict, 19–21, 28, 35, 139, 156, 223–24
Great Britain, 116, 183
Greeks, 9
"green corridor," 184
Grozny, 87
*gubkoms,* 40–41, 83
guilt, 222
Gulag camps, 103, 147, 221

Heavy Industry administration, 181–82, 194
Hitler, Adolf, 1, 182
housing, 15

industry, xix, 14–19, 26, 34, 35, 69–70, 74, 107, 117, 121–22, 126, 131, 181–82, 194, 217; Mari, 42; post-Civil War, 34
infant mortality, 15
influenza epidemic (1918), 27
intelligentsia, 16, 64, 106–107, 140; Alash-Orda, 64–65
Inturist, 125
Irkutsk, 87
Ivanov, I. I., 55
Ivanov, Petr, 50, 56, 116
Ivanovo, 87
*Izvestiia,* 5, 53, 192, 216, 266n56

Japan, 6–7, 11, 263n19
Jews, 15, 232n25

Kabakov, I., 130
Kaganovich, L. M., 1, 31, 95, 99, 106,
107, 112, 113, 127, 130, 133, 157, 163–64, 180, 202, 204, 205, 214
Kalinin, 133
Kamenev, Lev, 2, 4, 7, 69, 70–71, 73, 76, 78–80, 142–43, 148, 153–54, 157, 158, 166, 191, 192, 193, 212, 257n44, 266n57; trial of, 160, 258n26; Yezhov's interrogations of, 158–64, 165, 177, 191
Kandelaki, David, 128
Katyn, 267n63
Kazakhstan, 51, 63, 102, 130, 238n60
Kazakhstan Territorial Party Committee, 61
Kazan, 27–28, 30, 31, 33, 34, 39, 54, 56, 57, 223
Kerensky, A. F., 25
KGB, 136
Kharbin, 87
Khataevich, M., 104
Khodzhanov, Kitgiz, 65–67
Khrushchev, Nikita, xviii, 1, 6, 107, 136, 209, 212, 253n2
Kirgizia, 57–67, 74, 79, 84, 238n60, 240n83; corruption, 59–60; ethnic politics, 58–67; society, 58–67; tax collection, 59, 60, 64; Yezhov's appointment in, 57–67, 95, 99–100
Kirgiz Obkom, 61–62
Kirov, Serge, 11, 31, 127, 133, 135. *See also* Kirov assassination
Kirov assassination, 11, 133, 135–55, 158–64, 166, 212, 253n2, 254n4, 255nn15–19, 257nn44–45, 258n26; investigation, 137–55, 156, 158–64, 177–78, 187–204; Stalin's possible involvement in, 136–37, 146, 152, 254n4
"Kirov Law," 133–34, 253n63
Kol'tsov, Mikhail, 249n7
Koreans, 9
Kork, S. I., 7
Kosarev, A. V., 127, 166, 259n29

Kosior, S. V., 104, 106
Kostroma, 54
Kotolynov, 141, 142
Kotsiubinsky, 193–94
KPK, 10, 11, 126, 130–32, 144, 203; plenipotentiaries and party first secretaries, 130–32; Yezhov leadership, 157, 176, 181, 220
Krasnokokshaisk, 41, 51–52
"Kremlin affair," 157
Krestinsky, N., 53, 54, 85
Krupskaya, Nadezhda Konstantinovna, 80
Kubiak, N. A., 41, 42
Kuibyshev, 123, 130–31
Kuibyshev Commission, 123
kulak operation, 8–9
Kursky, D., 86

labor, 15–19, 105, 106; factory, 14–19, 23, 26, 32; Lena massacre, 19; movement, 18; unions, 16, 105, 236n24; unrest, 15–19
Land and Liberty, 140
Latvia, 180
Latvian Communists, 184, 186
Latvians, 9, 15, 232n25
"Law of 1 December 1934," 133–34, 253n63
Lena massacre, 19
Lenin, Vladimir Ilich, xxi, 4, 21, 24, 32–33, 36–38, 55, 71, 80, 83–84, 89, 231n24, 236n24, 244n53; "ban on factions," 39; death of, 38, 70, 83, 97; democratic centralism and, 69–70, 83; succession struggle, 70–75, 83–84
Leningrad, 7, 79–81, 231n17, 254n14; "former people" expelled from, 139–40; Kirov assassination, 133, 135–55; purge of NKVD ranks, 147; Yezhov's investigation of NKVD, 137–55

Lewin, Moshe, 270n9
Lithuania, 19
Lithuanians, 15
Litvin, M. I., 95, 272n37
Litvinov, Maxim, 128, 182
Liushkov, G., 11, 12, 229n37

Maisky, Ivan, 183
Malenkov, G. M., 92, 95, 166, 167, 168, 181, 212, 259n29
Manchuria, 11
Manuilsky, Dmitri, 184, 185, 186
Mao Zedong, 1
Mari, 32, 41–57, 58, 67, 84, 94, 237nn41–42; ethnic conflicts, 42–44, 50–52; tax collection, 46–48, 51; Yezhov's appointment in, 32, 41–57, 100
Mar'iasin, Lev, 7–8
Mari Control Commission, 49
Mari Soviet Executive Committee, 47–49
Marx, Karl, 33, 101, 182, 231n24
Marxism, 15, 19, 22, 48, 207, 245n11
mass operations (1937–38), 6, 221–24, 267n63; origin of, 182–86; responsibility for, 206–207
Medved, Filip, 138, 146
Meerzon, Zh. I., 91, 95
Mekhlis, L. D., 107
membership, party, 40, 78, 83, 124–25, 166–73; verification operation, 166–78, 189
Mensheviks, 19, 21, 22, 60, 231n24
Merridale, Catherine, 207
Mezhlauk, V., 95
Mikoian, A. I., 53, 133
military, 6–7, 122; Civil War, 26–31, 34; NKVD crackdown of, 6–7
Mints, I. I., 214
Molchanov, 151–52, 188, 204, 260n39
Molotov, V. M., xxiii, 41, 43, 54, 71, 73, 81, 85, 88–89, 95, 106, 107, 112,

Molotov, V. M. (continued)
117, 127, 133, 137, 190, 202, 210, 211,
237n39, 245n9; Yezhov and, 97–99,
117–18, 249n11
MOPR, 125, 126, 184–86
Moscow, 26, 31, 40, 41, 44, 49, 61,
81, 95, 180, 240n78, 247n22;
"Kremlin affair," 157; Yezhov
requests transfer to, 96–100;
Yezhov's early work in, 100–114
Moscow show trials, 2–6, 10, 142;
first, 2–5; second, 5–6; third, 5–6, 10
Moskvin, Ivan, 92, 93, 96, 102–104,
108, 111, 120, 127, 241n5, 246n14,
247n22

Naneishvili, First Secretary, 65, 66
Narkomzem SSSR, 115–20, 121,
249n11
National Committee to Struggle for
Peace, 181
"national operations," 9–10
National Socialism, 125
Naumov-Lekakh, D. B., 194
New Economic Policy (NEP), 34, 61,
69–71, 74, 116
New York, 183
Nicholas II, Tsar, 16; overthrow of,
20–21, 24, 231n24
Nikolaev, Leonid, 133, 134; Kirov
assassinated by, 133, 135–36,
140–45; trial of, 143
NKVD, xvii, xix, 1, 4, 122, 260n43,
263nn19–23, 272n37; agents and
informers, 149, 150; anti-Yagoda
movement, 148–52, 161–66, 169,
177, 179–81, 185, 187–205, 213;
Kirov assassination and, 135–55,
158–64, 187–204; kulak operation,
8–9; Leningrad, 137–55, 254n4,
256n29; "national operations,"
9–10; order no. 447, 8; proverka
and, 169–73; purges, 2–10, 147;

xenophobic terror operations,
184–86; Yezhov as chief of, xix,
xxii, 1–13, 148, 178, 179, 204–5,
213, 220; Yezhov's decline in, 10–13
Nogin, V. P., 86, 88
nomenklatura system, 87–91, 104
Novgorod, 87
Novgorod, Nizhnyi, 53

obedience, Soviet, 207–11
October Revolution (1917), xix,
21–26, 32, 35, 41, 82, 214, 223
Odessa, 87
OGPU, 10, 104–5, 113, 122, 123, 125,
126, 138
Olberg, V. P., 190, 264n36
Omsk, 54
"On Party Discipline," 234n3
opium, 60
oppositionists, 68–82, 112, 124, 133,
152, 261n57, 265n49, 266nn56–57;
Kirov assassination and, 135–55,
158–64, 177–78, 187–204;
Leningrad, 138–55; of 1920s,
68–82; proverka and, 166–78, 189;
Trotskyist, 76, 152, 167, 168, 177,
178, 179, 189–204, 266n57;
Yezhov's cases against, 152–54,
158–64, 187–204; Zinovievist,
70–81, 138–45, 152–55, 168, 177, 178,
179, 189–204, 266n57
Ordzhonikidze, G. K., 31, 106, 107,
112, 120, 181–82, 194, 204, 205
"organizational" task, 84
Orgburo, xvii, xxiv, 32, 41, 49–50, 57,
71, 85–95, 100, 102, 103, 118, 157,
183, 233n44, 235n10, 242n21,
259n28; creation and function of,
85; Yezhov's membership in,
126–34, 148, 156, 176, 181
Orgotdel, 120
Orgraspred, 82, 85–95, 102–13,
120, 242n21, 246n17; conferences,

105–12; Yezhov's assignment at, 102–13, 118, 129, 218, 220, 246n21, 247nn 22–27, 248n36

ORPO, 61 157; Yezhov as head of, 157, 181

Ossinsky, V. V., 73, 84

Outer Mongolia, 9–10

overseas travel, 183–84, 262nn11–14

parallel government, 38–39

Paris, 182, 183

Party Control Commission. See KPK

party documents, 1935 proverka of, 166–78, 189

patronage, 68, 72–73, 75, 80, 81, 98, 128–29, 202, 271n35, 272n35. See also personnel system

Pauker, 180

peasantry, 15, 21, 34, 37, 38, 69–70, 82–83, 120, 223, 231n24, 239n67; Civil War, 28–35; collectivization of agriculture, 113–20, 121; Kirgiz, 58–67; kulak operation, 8–9; Mari, 42; "us" vs. "them" conflict, 19–21, 28, 35, 139, 156, 223–24

Penza, 57

personnel system, xix, xx, 68–95, 104–105, 113, 123–24, 127–29, 132–33, 181, 219–20, 243n38, 271n35; file system, 86–87; nomenklatura system, 87–91, 104; oppositionists and, 68–82; patronage and, 68, 72–73, 75, 80, 81, 98, 128–29, 202, 271n35, 272n35; systemization of, 87–91; transfers, 94–95, 96–100

Peterhof, 20

Peterson, Karl, 158

Petrograd, 20, 21, 24, 25, 26, 230n17; Bolshevik coup, 24

Petrosian, L., 95

Petrov, I. P., 47–49, 237nn 41–42; squabble with Yezhov, 47–50, 51, 53, 55, 67, 77

Piatakov, G. L., 5, 194, 198, 265n52

plenipotentiaries, KPK, 130–32

Poland, 9, 19, 34, 184

Poles, 9, 15, 125, 232n25

police. See CHEKA; NKVD; specific organizations

Polish Communists, 9, 184, 186, 264n27

Polish Legionnaires, 25

"Polish Operation," 9

Politburo, xvii, xxiv, 11, 31, 39, 70, 71, 79, 83, 85–95, 102, 113, 120, 122, 157, 164, 177, 184, 207, 233n44, 258n26, 267n62, 268n69, 269n6, 270n11; creation and function of, 85; Kirov assassination and, 135–55; "Kirov Law," 133–34

political émigrés, 184–86

politics, xx, 29; blame shifting, 186–87, 201, 202; bureaucracy, 71–95, 217–19, 272n39; Kirov assassination, 135–55, 158–64, 177–78, 187–204; of 1917, 21–26, 41, 82, 214; 1920s provincial, 36–67, 77; obedience, 207–211; "us" vs. "them" conflict, 19–21, 28, 35, 139, 156, 223–24

Postyshev, P. P., 131, 260n38

Pravda, 69, 174, 192, 215, 261n50

Prelovsky Necktie Factory, 19

Preobrazhensky, Ye., 73, 241n9

prison camps, 8, 9, 10, 103, 147, 221

Procuracy, 170

Prokofev, G. E., 190

propaganda, 25, 43

proverka (1935), 166–78, 189, 260nn 42–43, 261nn49–57; NKVD and, 169–73; problems with, 166, 169, 173–78

provinces, 36–67, 77, 83, 89, 95, 99–100, 216, 269n6; Kirgizia, 57–67, 95, 99–100; Mari, 41–57, 100; 1920s government, 36–67, 77; NKVD agents and informers, 150. See also specific provinces

Provisional Government, 21, 22, 25, 37; overthrow of, 24
Pskov, 57
purges (1930s), xviii, 2–10, 113, 121, 124, 221–24, 259nn37–38; Leningrad NKVD, 147; 1933 party leadership, 121, 124–25; of *1937–38*, 6, 182–86, 221–24, 267n63; proverka (1935), 166–78, 189, 260nn42–43, 261nn49–57; responsibility for, 206–207; Yezhov's role in, 2–10
Putilov Plant, 16–19, 23, 32

Radek, K., 5, 194, 198
radicalism, 19, 20–22, 26, 223, 231n19, 232n27
railroads, 107
Raspredotdel, 120, 157; Yezhov as chief of, 120–26, 127, 129, 132
Razgon, Lev, 7, 103–104, 108
Red Army, 6–7, 24, 25, 26–31, 54, 70, 101, 129, 140, 216
"registration" function, 84
religion, 19–20, 60
report writing, 44–46; "although" style, 46
responsibility, for 1930s purges, 206–207
Revolution (1905), 16, 19
Revolution (1917). *See* October Revolution
Riabinin, First Secretary, 181–82
Riutin, Martymian, 73–74
Roshal', 95
Rostov, 130
Rozenfeld, B. N., 159
Rumiantsev, I. P., 73, 141, 142, 182, 255n19
Russian Empire, 14, 15
Russian Imperial Army, 20, 23, 25
Russian Orthodox traditions, 19–20
Russian Party of Fascists, 140
Russian Republic (RSFSR), 113

Russian Social Democratic Labor Party (RSDRP), 19, 22; Internationalists, 22
Rykov, Aleksei, 4, 5, 69, 194–95, 196, 197, 204, 227n9, 266n57

St. Petersburg, 14–17, 230n17, 231n19
Samara, 81
sanitation, 15
Sapronov, Timofei, 73
Saratov, 27, 54
2nd Radiotelegraph Base, 27
Secretariat, xvii, xxiv, 41, 71, 85–95, 102, 103, 118, 234n44, 235n10, 242n21, 243n35, 248n36; creation and function of, 85
Semipalatinsk, 57–63, 99, 238nn60–63
Shablygin, 181–82
Shadunts, First Secretary, 132
Shapiro, I. I., 272n37
Shatsky, 141, 142, 255n19
Shcherbakov, A. S., 107
Sheboldaev, B., 95, 130, 260n38
Shepilov, Dmitri, 216
Shkiriatov, M. F., 106, 166, 203, 259n29
Shliapnikov, Alexander, 128, 237n39
Shmidt, V. V., 196
Shvernik, N. M., 107, 253n2
Siberia, 20, 37, 87
Smolensk, 182
soap, 122
Socialist Realism, 19, 101
Social Revolutionaries, 21, 59, 60, 231n24, 239n71
society, 14–16, 32–33, 223; Civil War and, 28–35; class consciousness, 15–16, 19–21, 33; Kirgiz, 58–67; labor unrest, 15–19; Mari, 42–44, 50–52; "us" vs. "them" conflict, 19–21, 28, 35, 139, 156, 223–24
Society of Old Bolsheviks, 157
Sokolnikov, G., 195, 266n57

Special Designation Battalion, 26–27
squabbles, 47–49, 51, 53–55, 67, 77
Stakhanov, Aleksei, 260n39
Stakhanovist movement, 260n39
Stalin, Joseph, xvii, xviii, xix, xx, 1, 4,
    11, 20, 22–23, 54, 65, 113, 127, 160,
    229n34, 234n44, 236n26, 242n20,
    245n10, 256n35, 265n47, 270nn9–14;
    character of, 22, 72–73, 79, 207,
    215; flip-flops, 74; inner circle of,
    133–34; Kirov assassination and,
    135–55, 158–64, 177–78, 187–204,
    254n4; leadership style, 79, 107,
    201, 208–211; NKVD operations
    and, 187–89; obedience to, 207–
    211; oppositionist critiques of,
    68–82, 158–64, 179, 187–204;
    personnel policy, 68–95, 132–33,
    219–20, 271n35; proverka and,
    166–78, 189; responsibility for ter-
    ror, 206–207, 212; rise to power,
    68–82; Yagoda removed by, 204;
    Yezhov and, 11–12, 72, 112, 127,
    132–34, 151, 165, 185, 192, 195–202,
    207, 211–20, 248n36, 252nn59–61,
    262n13, 271n30; Yezhov's letter to,
    195–202, 267nn59–62
Stalinism, origins of, xix, 30
Stasova, Elena, 186–87
State Bank, 109, 110
Sudnitsin, L. F., 129
Sudnitsyn, Yevgeny, 33–34
sugar, 122
Supreme Council of National Econ-
    omy (VSNKh), 120
Supreme Court, 10
Sverdlov, Yakov, 30, 84
Sverdlovsk, 169
Sweden, 183

Tajikistan, 132
Tashkent, 116
Tatar, 30–31, 39, 104

Tatar Party Committee, 27
tax collection, 18, 43, 46047, 69, 77,
    239n67; Kirgizia, 59, 60, 64; Mari,
    46–48, 51
telephone communication, 116
timber industry, 42, 122, 127
Timriazev Agricultural Academy, 97,
    116, 233n42
Titova, Antonina Alekseevna, 30–31,
    44, 96–97, 102, 233n42; agricul-
    tural research career, 97, 233n42,
    249n7; marriage to Yezhov, 31,
    249n7; Semipalatinsk appoint-
    ment, 60
Tomsky, Mikhail, 4, 69, 195–96,
    266n57; suicide of, 195
Trans-Siberian Railroad, 37
travel abroad, Soviet, 183–84,
    262nn11–14
Troianovsky, Ambassador, 184
Trotsky, L. D., xviii, 3, 4, 64, 69,
    70–71, 73, 74, 76, 78, 80, 152, 158,
    179, 190, 217, 266n56; marginaliza-
    tion of, 70, 71
Trotskyists, 76, 152, 167, 168, 177, 178,
    179, 263n19, 266n57, 268n65; Kirov
    assassination investigation and,
    178, 179, 189–204
Trudoviks, 21, 231n24
tsarism, 7, 16, 21, 37, 217, 231n19; over-
    throw, 20–21, 24, 231n24
Tsesarsky, V. E., 272n37
Tsybul'nik, 157
Tukhachevsky, M. N., 7
Tula, 87
Turkestan, 240n83
Tver, 87
typhus, 27, 30

Uborevich, I. P., 7
Uchraspred, 85, 86, 87, 90, 108
Uglanov, N. A., 227n9
Uglov, A. T., 7, 27

Ukraine, 80, 81, 194, 260n38
United Opposition, 71
United States, 183, 184
Urals, 80, 87, 122
*USSR Under Construction,* 249n7
"us" vs. "them" conflict, 19–21, 28, 35, 139, 156, 223–24

Vareikis, I., 95
Viatsk, 105
Vitebsk, 20, 21, 22–25, 214, 231n18, 232n25; railroad blockades, 25; Red Guards, 24–25
Vladimir, 87
Volga River, 27, 28
Volkova, 145–46
Volovich, 180–81
Voronezh, 54, 112, 181, 203–204
Vorovsky, Ambassador, 253n63
Vyshinsky, A. Ya., 2, 190, 195, 266n57
Vysshy Volochek, 26

Water Transport, 10; Yezhov as Commissar of, 10–11
Webb, Sydney, 183
wheat, 122
White Army, 59, 60, 133, 214, 215, 263n19
women's rights, 43
Workers' Opposition, 76, 236n24, 237n39
working class, 14–19, 21, 32, 223; Civil War, 28–35; "us" vs. "them" conflict, 19–21, 28, 35, 139, 156, 223–24
World War I, 9, 19, 20, 24
World War II, 31

xenophobia, 182–86, 262n14

Yagoda, Genrikh, 1–2, 5, 11, 129, 138–40, 148–52, 158, 215, 264n30, 265n49, 268n65; transfer to Commissariat of Communications,

204; trial of, 256n41; Yezhov's campaign against, 148–52, 161–66, 169, 177, 179–81, 185, 187–205, 213, 264n33
Yakir, I. E., 7
Yakovlev, Ya. A., 7, 113, 115, 120, 136
Yakovlev commission, 136
Yekaterinburg, 87
Yenukidze, Avel, 156, 157–65, 188, 192, 258n26; arrest and execution of, 165; Yezhov's initiative against, 157–65
Yezhov, Nikolai Ivanovich, xvii-xxiii; as Agriculture Deputy Commissar, 113–14, 115–20, 121, 217, 218; archive, xxiii-xxiv, 211, 216, 226n9; army service, 20, 26–31, 214–15; arrest of, 12, 225n2, 262n14; autobiography, 230n13; beliefs of, 220–24; campaign against Yagoda, 148–52, 161–66, 169, 177, 179–81, 185, 187–205, 213, 264n33; cases against oppositionists, 152–54, 158–64, 187–204; as CC secretary, 156, 158–65, 176, 181, 183–88, 204; character of, xxi, 1, 23, 33–34, 51, 104, 107–108, 112, 214, 215–16, 222–24; chauvinism, 47–49, 50, 65, 66–67; Civil War and, 26–35, 214–15; Communist Academy studies, 100–102, 245n11; cruelty of, 7–8, 121, 221–24; debut in role of hatchet man against "enemies," 156–65; decline in status of, 10–13; drinking of, 11, 12; early life, 18–19; early work in Moscow, 100–114; education, 18, 32, 100–102, 245nn6 –13; execution of, 13, 225n2; factory work, 16–19, 23, 26, 32; "From Factionalism to Open Counterrevolution (On the Zinovievist Counterrevolutionary Organization)," 154, 165, 212, 270n14; health problems, 216; investigation of

Leningrad NKVD, 137–55; joins Bolshevik Party, 22; Kirgiz experience, 57–67, 95, 99–100; Kirov assassination investigation, 137–55, 156, 158–64, 177–78, 187–204; KPK leadership, 157, 176, 181, 220; kulak operation, 8–9; letter to Stalin, 195–202, 267nn59–62; making of a Bolshevik, 14–35; Mari appointment, 32, 41–57, 100; marriage to Antonina Titova, 31, 249n7; marriage to Yevgenya Gladuna, 249n7; Molotov and, 97–99, 117–18, 249n11; Moscow show trials, 5–6, 10; "national operations," 9–10; as NKVD chief, xix, xxii, 1–13, 148, 178, 179, 204–205, 213, 220; as obedient tool of Stalin, 207–211; Order of Lenin awarded to, 7; Orgburo membership, 126–34, 148, 156, 176, 181; Orgraspred assignment, 102–13, 118, 129, 218, 220, 246n21, 247n22–27, 248n36; origins of later police job in early career, 121–23; as ORPO head, 157, 181; party career begins, 31–35; Petrov squabble, 47–50, 51, 53, 55, 67, 77; physical appearance, xxi, 23, 104, 216; in prison, 12; proverka (1935), 166–78, 189; purge of Leningrad NKVD, 147; radicalism of, 19, 20, 22, 26, 223, 231n19, 232n27; as Raspredotdel chief, 120–26, 127, 129, 132; report writing, 44–46; rise in Stalinist administration, 156–57, 211–20; role in purges, 2–10; Semipalatinsk assignment, 57–63, 99; Stalin and, 11–12, 72, 112, 127, 132–34, 151, 165, 185, 192, 195–202, 207, 211–20, 248n36, 252nn59–61, 262n13, 271n30; style of work, 98–99, 105–108, 112–13, 119–20, 123, 181, 213–14; transfer request to Moscow, 96–100; trial of, 12–13, 225n2; TsIK investigation, 157–65; "unusual events" file of, 180–81; Water Transport appointment, 10–11; xenophobic terror operations, 182–86, 262n14; Yenukidze affair, 157–65

Zafran, 203, 204
Zakovsky, Leonid, 138, 139–40
Zhdanov, A. A., 1, 127, 210, 212, 214
Zhukovsky, S. B., 272n37
Zimin, N., 92
Zinoviev, Grigory, 2, 3, 4, 39–40, 53, 69, 70–71, 73–81, 142–43, 148, 152–54, 158, 166, 179, 193, 212, 246n14, 254n14, 257n44, 266n56, 270n14; confession of, 191–92; trial of, 160, 192, 258n26; Yezhov's interrogations of, 158–64, 165, 177, 191–92
Zinovievists, 70–81, 138, 168, 177, 178, 179, 266n57; Kirov assassination investigation and, 138–45, 152–55, 178, 179, 189–204
Zubtsov, 26–27